Massacre at Oradour, France, 1944

Massacre at Oradour
France, 1944

Coming to Grips with Terror

Jean-Jacques Fouché

Translated by
David Sices and
James B. Atkinson

Introduction by
Jay Winter

NORTHERN ILLINOIS UNIVERSITY PRESS / DEKALB

Published by the Northern Illinois University Press, DeKalb, Illinois 60115

Design by Julia Fauci

"Ouvrage publié avec le concours du ministère français chargé de la culture." [This work has been published with the assistance of the French Ministry of Culture–Centre National du Livre.]

Publication of this book is supported in part by a grant from Dartmouth College.

Library of Congress Cataloging-in-Publication Data
Fouché, Jean-Jacques, 1940-
[Oradour. English]
Massacre at Oradour, France, 1944 : coming to grips with terror / Jean-Jacques Fouché ; translated by David Sices and James B. Atkinson ; introduction by Jay Winter.
p. cm.
Includes bibliographical references and index.
ISBN 0-87580-601-5 (alk. paper)
1. Oradour-sur-Glane Massacre, 1944. 2. World War, 1939-1945—France—Oradour-sur-Glane. I. Title.
D804.G3F6813 2005
940.54'05'0944662—dc22
2004016971

Contents

Introduction
ORADOUR-SUR-GLANE AND THE DEGENERATION OF WAR
by Jay Winter vii

Translators' Note
by David Sices and James B. Atkinson xiv

Maps xvi

1—WHAT IS KNOWN ABOUT THE MASSACRE? 3
Can Ruins Speak? [3] "Oradour Is a Complicated Business..." [5] Seven Publications... and a Few Others [10] The Archives Are Opened [12]

2—THE WAR CULTURE OF THE WAFFEN SS 16
Berlin, 1933 [16] Bavaria: Joining the SS [17] The "Brutal" War in the East [23] The War in the East for the Das Reich Division [28]

3—THE SS DAS REICH DIVISION IN FRANCE 33
Preparing for the "Invasion" [33] Drafting Frenchmen from Annexed Alsace [35] "Segregating" the Resistance: The "Bands" [38]

4—A HOT SPOT: THE MASSIF CENTRAL 42
The Situation Deteriorates [42] The Attack on the Town of Tulle [48] The Waffen SS in Limoges [50] Harassment and Repression [53] Preparations for a "Brutal Operation" [58] The Waffen SS Butchers Leave for Oradour [64]

5—WAS ORADOUR JUST AN ORDINARY VILLAGE? 67
"It Is a Verdant Hollow by a Murmuring Stream" [67] Economy and Politics in the Village [72] The Refugees [78] Interventions by Vichy [83] Food Supplies, the "Gray Market," and the Black Market [91] Changing Opinions and Behavior [94] There Were No Maquis [96] Just an Ordinary Village [99] The Population of Oradour in June 1944 [100]

6—ACCOUNT OF THE MASSACRE 102

Surprise Attack [102] Surrounding the Village [104] A Roundup without Exceptions [107] Waiting on the Fairgrounds: The Demand for Hostages [113] Separation [115] The Men Are Kept Waiting in the Square [117] Execution of the Men in Enclosed Areas [119] Pillaging, Arson, and Butchery in the Streets [123] The Massacre in the Church [127] The Survivors' Flight [133] The Horrifying Discovery of the Town on Fire [134] Some of the Troops Leave [137] Night in the Devastated Town [139] Searching for the Missing [140] Corpses Desecrated [144] Silence Concerning Acts of Sexual Violence [145] The Waffen SS Troops after the Massacre [147]

7—THE VICTIMS 150

Counting the Dead [150] The Escapees [153] Burying the Dead [155] The Process of Memorialization [158] Commemorating [173]

8—CONFLICTING ACCOUNTS 179

The Accounts Given by the Perpetrators [179] The Instrumentalization of Oradour [184] The Inaudible Account of Justice [188] Amnesty, the Memory of the Forced Draftees [194] Oradour's Own Account, a Collective Memory? [196] Why? [199]

9—SOUVIENS-TOI—REMEMBER 204

Afterword—ORADOUR-SUR-GLANE, JULY 16, 1999—
Opening Ceremony 207

Glossary of Abbreviations and Foreign Terms 213

Notes 217

Bibliography 253

Index 260

The Author 270

Introduction

ORADOUR-SUR-GLANE AND THE DEGENERATION OF WAR

Jay Winter

The Face of Radical Evil

This book tells the story of a war crime. Two days after the Allied invasion of Normandy on June 6, 1944, elements of the second armored Waffen SS Das Reich division based in Montauban, in the center of France, moved north toward the Allied beachhead. Orders were to terrify and intimidate the local population en route, so the local people would turn their backs on the scattered resistance groups operating sporadically in the countryside. This SS unit was made up of several thousand soldiers who had survived combat on the Eastern front, together with other, less experienced conscripts from Romania, Hungary, and Alsace, then annexed to Germany. When a detachment of this force reached the small village of Oradour-sur-Glane, on June 10, they gathered the inhabitants in the market square and separated the men from the women and children. The men were divided into smaller groups and summarily shot in village barns. The women and children were herded into the local church. Then the SS turned their guns on these defenseless people and set the church and other buildings on fire. In this act of destruction, 642 local inhabitants were murdered. Why?

This book is an investigation of that question. It complements an earlier study of the incident by Sarah Farmer. Her book provides an insightful account of the commemorative impulses that have unfolded in the half-century since the crime was committed.[1] What Jean-Jacques Fouché offers is an analysis of this event on the basis of new archival material and within the framework of a new approach to the cultural history of warfare in the twentieth century.

Among the scholars who have developed this school of thought, Stéphane Audoin-Rouzeau and Annette Becker are particularly prominent. They are among a group of scholars, based in the Historial de la Grande Guerre, a museum of the 1914–1918 war in Péronne in the north of France, who have approached the history of warfare in terms of what they call "war culture." This phrase encompasses the signifying practices, norms of behavior, and attitudes toward violence that emerge in the course of industrialized military conflict. Drawing from much anthropological research, and from the work of the late George Mosse, these historians focus on the multiple ways in which war "brutalizes" the language and comportment of both soldiers and civilians. Men become brutal; societies are brutalized.[2]

This interpretation has been contested, and it is at the center of a growing debate about the ways in which brutality becomes "normalized" during wartime. Some scholars are unpersuaded by this line of argument; others bridle at the unity of the term *war culture* and prefer *war cultures*, modulated by gender, class, and race. Others doubt that soldiers who see brutality must necessarily become brutal; some do, and some do not. Some scholars argue that the process of brutalizing a society is limited by prewar cultural forms and traditions that offer antibodies, as it were, against criminal norms or criminal acts. Other scholars go part of the way and see the seeds of brutalization in the blurring of the distinction between military adversaries and civilian noncombatants, starting from the very first days of World War I and continuing throughout the twentieth century.[3]

Fouché's study of Oradour is a study in the brutalization of warfare, and it provides much evidence in support of the arguments advanced by Audoin-Rouzeau and Becker. But the interest of this book goes beyond this particular issue. One important facet of Fouché's historiographical turn is that, more and more, the two world wars are analyzed together. Whether in terms of a second "thirty years' war" or as part of the ideological struggle unleashed by the Russian Revolution of 1917, the two wars have been placed in a context of violence made possible by the industrialization of warfare. It is not that atrocity was born in 1914—on the contrary. Anyone looking at Goya's drawings of the French wars in early nineteenth-century Spain will conclude otherwise. It is that, since 1914, atrocity has become industrialized: the killing machines are more effective, the constraints on using them less effective, the propaganda machines grinding out hatred more ubiquitous, and as a consequence, the boundaries that separate war from murder have been blurred almost to vanishing point. There is abundant evidence that war crimes have become part and parcel of the fabric of the internal civil wars that inevitably accompanied the international conflicts spreading across the globe both in 1914–1918 and in 1939–1945.[4] In a sense, we have seen the worst of both worlds in warfare: an increase in mass killing through high technology as well as an expansion of the space for what Joanna Bourke terms "intimate" or face-to-face killing.[5] Together, there is overwhelming evidence that there has been a degradation of war in the twentieth century, in such a way as to make it inevitable that atrocities of staggering proportions are built into the very structure of armed conflict.

Oradour-sur-Glane is one instance of this broader deformation of the institutions and practices of war. It was therefore not an isolated incident. Rather, the massacre there was a symptom of something terrifying that occurred in many different parts of the world between 1914 and 1945 and beyond.

War crimes never come out of thin air. As Fouché shows, the behavior of the Waffen SS soldiers who massacred the inhabitants of this sleepy Limousin town cannot be separated from their prior military history. Many of the men in this unit, and its officers in particular, had served on the Eastern front. There the notion of waging war against civilians was at the heart of their mission. From the very first day of the Nazi invasion of the Soviet Union in June 1941, Jews and Communists were systematically massacred. The killings were so widespread behind the rapidly advancing German lines that even suppressed nationalities, brutally persecuted by the Soviet regime, rallied to the defense of the regime. Only war as systematic mass murder could have restored the coherence of the Soviet Union and its army, whose military power had been eviscerated by Stalin himself in a series of military purges just three years before his front lines were smashed by Nazi armored columns. In a matter of weeks, most of European Russia was in Nazi hands, and so was the population of ideological or racial enemies they were determined to exterminate. Here is the setting of the Holocaust, and of many crimes committed by the German army during World War II.

Consider the position of a Waffen SS unit transferred from the Eastern front to occupied France in 1944. Their view of partisan warfare born in the Pripet marshes or in the Ukranian forests fitted oddly into the farming country of the Limousin. But partisan warfare of a murderous kind is what they had known before, and it was precisely this kind of brutal warfare they would wage again. Here is the key to answering the question, Why Oradour? The massacre was not a rational response to where the Waffen SS were or what they saw; it grew out of the war they had fought before. They became criminals not because of something that happened to them in France. It was who they were and what they had become that accounts for their murderous acts.

There was no major Resistance activity in the vicinity of Oradour-sur-Glane; there was no stash of arms or cash for use by those attempting to harass or otherwise interfere with German troops or their local collaborators. There is no shred of evidence that the people in the village, when summoned by German troops to the center of the town, resisted in any way whatsoever. The face of what Immanuel Kant termed "radical evil" was visible in Oradour-sur-Glane on June 10, 1944. It was a transposition of the war of extermination in Eastern Europe into a totally different—and hardly threatening—environment.

Yet this account of the crime still leaves some unanswered questions. Many other units in the German army returned from the Eastern front to France, Italy, or the Low Countries without descending into such crimes. What stopped them from doing so? No one knows for sure; was it temperament, religious inclinations, pure accident?

To be diffident on this point is essential, for all we can say is that participation in one set of murderous military encounters may prepare the ground for their repetition, even without the slightest provocation. The unfortunate inhabitants of Oradour-sur-Glane were unlikely victims of the way the German army had waged war in the East, a thousand miles away. There were others.

The war the German army ultimately lost in Russia determined the outcome of World War II as a whole. The level of ferocity with which the war was waged is hard to convey. A mild metaphor for this kind of conflict is the term *total war*.[6] In fact, total war is a metaphor—for there is no instance in which all facets of social, political, economic, and cultural life are drawn into the waging of armed conflict. The best way to understand the force of the term is to see it as suggesting that industrial warfare is "totalizing," in that it draws into its vortex more and more of the elements that make daily life possible. In the process, the restraints against arbitrary violence are slowly but surely lifted; in extreme cases they cease to exist altogether. Russia between 1941 and 1945 was one such place; there were many other parts of Europe—Yugoslavia, for instance—in a similar state.

It is this "totalizing" context that enables us to link what happened in Oradour-sur-Glane to other war crimes of World War II, including the Holocaust. From their own point of view, what the German units in this Limousin town did was to execute 642 hostages, "pour encourager les autres." Here was an act of frightfulness, of "Shrecklichkeit," a way of letting it be known to all and sundry that even to look in the eyes of a German soldier was to court execution. Civilian hostages were executed by German units and their allies throughout France and indeed throughout Europe. This was the way "total war" was waged—against civilians who were either potential or (as in the case of Jews) racial enemies of the Reich. Killing infants, mothers, the elderly was simply part of the way these soldiers conducted war and occupation. Racial ideology reserved special treatment for Jews, but if one needed to see what extermination in the context of total war meant, one should come to Oradour-sur-Glane.

Witnessing and Remembrance

Of those responsible for hundreds of cases of atrocities committed by German soldiers during World War II, only a handful were ever brought to justice, despite the creation of mechanisms for the judgment of war crimes. Major Otto Diekmann, the commander of the unit responsible for the massacre, was never brought to trial. He was killed later in the year. The overall commander of the Das Reich division, General Hans Lammerding, lived out his years, untouched, in Germany. Twenty-one soldiers in this unit were tried for the crime in Bordeaux in 1953. Two men were sentenced to death but had their sentences commuted. Others received terms of imprisonment, but in an act of national reconciliation General de Gaulle, then in power, pardoned the Alsatians who had been convicted of participation in the atrocity. By 1958, five years after the trial, all those found guilty of the massacre had been freed.

Trials are only one facet of the remembrance of war. Witnesses appear to tell the story of wartime events long after they occurred. Since the 1970s, such witnesses have become part of what may be termed the contemporary "memory boom," an exponential increase in interest both inside and outside the academy in the subject of memory and the multiple ways in which it is expressed.

Commemoration is precisely that—a bonding together of people who bear the scars of war with those who see the traces and honor the victims, usually in very ordinary places. The ruins of Oradour have been preserved as a memorial site, where visitors learn of what happened on June 10, 1944. And with the aid of this book, among others, they can begin to fathom these events in the very landscape where they took place.

One of the merits of Jean-Jacques Fouché's book on Oradour is that he tells the story precisely from this provincial point of view. What Pierre Nora has termed "sites of memory" are mostly local in character.[7] Fouché's book is local history, parochial history, history in miniature, but all the more powerful for that. By looking at one place, at one terrible moment, he has captured an essential truth about World War II and about the degeneration of warfare in general in the twentieth century.

It is the evocative power of the place that turns a name like Oradour into a metaphor. But metaphors move beyond the events that trigger them. For this reason, historians continue to go over the ground again and tell the story with as much authority as they can muster from the documentation available to them. Commemoration entails both feeling and thinking; this book encourages both, and in ways that may not make us particularly comfortable. It is easy to condemn the criminals of Oradour, and to place them in a world remote from our own. Read alongside Sarah Farmer's study of the subject, Jean-Jacques Fouché's *Massacre at Oradour, France, 1944,* reveals to us much about the past but also much about the world in which we still live.

Armies of occupation are facts of contemporary life. They are never immune from the temptation to strike out at or to murder the people they control. Learning this lesson is a chastening matter in the twenty-first century, when new kinds of warfare frame older, yet very familiar, moral challenges. Brutalization is still a matter for deep concern, perhaps even more so now that war and terrorism have created a new continuum of cruelty and violence. This book is very much what the French term "l'histoire du temps présent," the history of today, and alas almost certainly of tomorrow.

Translators' Note

David Sices and James B. Atkinson

Our translation was initially inspired by a visit to the ruins of Oradour-sur-Glane, which have been preserved as a memorial site since 1944. Anyone who visits these ruins must feel deeply moved. It was only, however, after reading Jean-Jacques Fouché's study of the events leading up to, during, and following the terrible massacre there that we felt we had gained a real understanding of what happened. Among all the studies devoted to these events, this one, published in France under the title of *Oradour,* seemed remarkable because it maintained the best balance between deep personal feeling and scientific objectivity.

In translating Fouché's distinguished investigation into one of the most tragic events of the Nazis' World War II occupation of France, an event too little known in America or in England, we have sought to adhere as closely as possible to Fouché's original text, while making it as accessible to an English-language public as its devastating subject deserves to be.

Jean-Jacques Fouché was the founding director of the Centre de la Mémoire d'Oradour. One of the essential, original qualities of his scholarly study is its extensive research into French, German, American, and English archives, as well as English-, French-, and German-language articles and monographs. In dealing with his citations of these, we have quoted wherever possible from English-language versions of the texts; when that was impractical, we have indicated to readers where the English-language text can be found; we have noted original German-language volumes when no English translation exists. This information is supplied in the Bibliography.

The only other changes incorporated into our translation are explanatory notes, identified as translators' notes and set within square brackets, concerning aspects of French history, geography, or politics that non-French readers could not be expected to know; maps whose aim is to help these readers; and a more exhaustive bibliography and index. The selection of illustrations is different. In addition, the text of the current Afterword was originally published as the Prologue in the French edition, but we felt it made a more suitable, chronological ending.

The Afterword is the most personal section of Jean-Jacques Fouché's book. It clearly illustrates the tension between objectivity and personal involvement so typical of what he has achieved, not only in this study but in his work as founding director of the museum and visitors' center at Oradour. We cannot thank him enough for his generous aid in making our work of translation possible. The alterations to his text that we have felt necessary have been made in consultation with him.

We would also like to thank Jean-Pierre Juillard, Jacqueline Sices, and Gretchen Holm, as well as the editorial and production staff of the Northern Illinois University Press. Each knows the importance of the contribution made to our effort, but we alone bear the ultimate responsibility for it.

Occupied France, 1940–45

The Limousin Region and Neighboring Départments

Massacre at Oradour, France, 1944

I What Is Known about the Massacre?

The vision of horror offered by the ruins bonds our emotions with the victims' misfortunes. Might emotion and pity be the vectors of a lesson to be drawn from the ruins? People immediately "saw" them as both material and symbolic evidence, and preserved them, in order to keep them visible.

Can Ruins Speak?

Since I grew up in the neighboring département, the Charente, I visited the ruins of Oradour in the early 1950s like many of the region's schoolchildren. I was left with an impression of tall gaping façades, of openings that opened out onto the void. Daily life was gone, so the houses no longer had any "inside." "The Germans had passed through, not a single inhabitant had escaped the massacre. There was a war on . . ." Fate had struck—or chance, or both. The visit constituted an overwhelming ritual, dominated by the strange feeling of a disaster that we would not have escaped had we been there.

On an overcast, intermittently rainy afternoon in February 1994, I returned to Oradour. I wandered through the ruins of the martyred village without again experiencing my former feelings. The circumstances had changed, and the ruins, as well. As a historical monument, preserved thanks to regular maintenance, they had been through bad weather and restorations. Contrary to the familiar idea that ruins can speak, they are silent concerning the tragedy that took place there. How can we picture what happened in this "ideal village"? How can we imagine the worst? And yet, as in all massacres, the worst is within our grasp: it is passed down to us through the victims' stories.[1]

Ruins are a setting conducive to flights of the imagination; they render space transparent, eliminate visual limits, disturb us. They belong to the poetic and pictorial world of Romanticism. Oradour's ruins offer up the wounds of a tragedy but tell nothing about what happened.

I was making a visit with the eyes of a museum professional, noting down improper restorations: doors obstructed for security reasons by low, window-sill-high walls made of rubble from the site; layer on layer of signs from different periods, accumulating descriptions with no coherence among them. Intrusions such as these blur our reading of information and our understanding of spaces. School slates put there in the late 1980s point to vanished trades practiced by former occupants. The ruins seemed to be becoming an ecological museum of Limousin rural life.[2] The charred wreckage of an automobile displayed prominently on the fairgrounds had been restored; it was labeled by Ministry of Culture officials as "Doctor Desourteaux's car." The guides were recruited in Oradour, so they know the information is incorrect: it is a car that belonged to a wine salesman.[3] Why weight the story down with dubious anecdotes?

Right after the massacre, the regional préfet came to deliver a speech that was published in Resistance leaflets. As early as July 1944 [just one month after the massacre], the administration had thought of rebuilding the destroyed town outside the ruins, and entrusted the operation to an architect of the Bâtiments de France who was an inspector-general of the Monuments historiques.[4] With the support of church authorities, Vichy had undertaken to turn the village of Oradour into sacred ground, a holy place consecrated by both spiritual and temporal powers. A discussion had begun then about preserving the ruins—transfigured as the Rheims cathedral might have been if it had not finally been restored: "Our hatred will keep watch over this rubble. To bear witness to barbarism, we need sacred ruins."[5]

Did the memory of Rheims bear any weight in the decision to preserve Oradour? Once the principle had been agreed upon (rapidly), there remained the question of practical means. The director of works assigned by Vichy was reconfirmed by the new government in January 1945. The first preservation work was begun locally without awaiting the services of the Beaux-Arts, which was uncertain concerning technical aspects.[6] The message of the ruins had become a pawn to be absorbed into each movement or party's political ideas.

Preservation resulted from political decisions. As early as June 1944, the regional préfet formulated the idea of a pilgrimage to the massacre site. In October, a few weeks after the Liberation, a Committee of Remembrance undertook the first measures to preserve the site. On November 28, 1944, a ruling of the provisional government of the Republic (followed by a law in 1946) devoted specific attention to the ruins. They were to be preserved "in the condition they appeared in after the fire." The declaration of intent went on: "Oradour-sur-Glane will be made into a city of the dead over which decorum, austerity, respect, and silence shall reign."[7] A surrounding wall was constructed, with gates at the two ends of the village. It is impossible to preserve ruins just as they were when witnesses discovered them, and no preservation expert can justify the undertaking scientifically. More than physical remains, it is an "idea" that is being preserved.

Why do we visit the ruins of Oradour? To confirm our ingrained awareness of ritual crimes and the violence fundamental to societies? To see in them proof of human nature's fallibility and to console ourselves in advance for apparently unpredictable resurgences of barbarism? To be reassured as to our identity, so different from that of the perpetrators of the massacre? What is the reason for the ruins' renown, equivalent almost to that of the pilgrimage site in nearby Rocamadour?[8]

"Oradour Is a Complicated Business . . ."

The councillor-general of the rural township in which Oradour-sur-Glane is located leaves his sentence unfinished.[9] There is a moment's silence. It is March 1994; we are in the office of the mayor of Saint-Junien, the oldest Communist municipality in France. Roland Mazouin, a firsthand observer of local political life, is a Communist

Party activist and elected official. He sat in the National Assembly as Marcel Rigout's deputy when Rigout became a minister in the Union of the Left in 1981. The Communists of the département of Haute-Vienne subsequently distanced themselves from the national leadership of the PCF [Parti communiste français (French Communist Party)] and reorganized on their own. Roland Mazouin affirms he "remained faithful to the ideal of [his] youth." Devoted to an electorate he respects, he is reelected constantly in his township. His opinions count, but in this case he expressed a puzzle.[10]

Yet, dictionaries and encyclopedias summarize widely shared knowledge about Oradour, and they have some responsibility for its renown:

— The *Petit Larousse* (1980 edition): "Massacre of the entire population (642 inhabitants) by the Germans." And in the 2000 edition of the same dictionary, partially revised: "Massacre of all the inhabitants by the SS."

— The *Grand Dictionnaire encyclopédique Larousse* (1984 edition) states: "The village was burned down by SS troops of the 'Das Reich' division on June 10, 1944, after they savagely massacred 642 inhabitants."

— The *Grand Robert des noms propres* (1984 edition) notes: "History: on June 10, 1944, the Germans as a retaliatory measure massacred 643 persons, including 500 women and children who perished in the church, which was deliberately burned down. The ruins have been preserved and the village was reconstructed nearby. The name of Oradour lives on as one of the symbols of Nazi barbarism."

— *Dictionnaire encyclopédique Quillet* (1970): "This village was burned down by German troops on June 10, 1944; its inhabitants were shot or burned alive. Its ruins, near which the village has been rebuilt, have been preserved as testimony to Hitler's brutality and classified as a historical monument."

For collective memory furnished with this basic knowledge, Oradour signifies "massacre."[11] It is even an archetype.[12] This exceptional status can be explained by various aspects of the event. First of all is the scope, unequaled anywhere else in France: 642 legally acknowledged deaths, about one-third of them children under fourteen, and more than a third of them women. The next is the total destruction of the village by fire: the town hall, schools, post office, railroad station, houses, workshops, stores, cafés, hotels, covered market, barns, garages, stables, sheds; everything was looted and then burned down. The final aspect is the executioners' methods: their organization; their systematic bent, to which the escapees' stories bear witness; the mass deaths of women and children; the deliberate looting and burning; the absence of any moral—even humane—consideration for the victims. All these make all understanding impossible. For those who lived through it, who suffered from it and are still suffering from it, the event remains incomprehensible. Disaster struck, unforeseeable, pitiless, final. Why?

How may we answer this Why? except through recourse to the word *barbarism*? The violence and cruelty seem to be without cause or reason. Unless we think: even if its origins remain unknown, this does not mean it was unmotivated; there might be some hidden reason behind it.

Some among the witnesses believe there is: although Oradour is the site of a well-known and recognized tragedy, secrecy reigns over the causes: "They will never be known," as two escapees wrote in 1998.[13] And so people are caught between a desire to understand and an inability to formulate this knowledge. This paradoxical situation is exploited by the negationist far right, which accuses the Resistance and absolves the Waffen SS of their crime.[14]

Many rumors circulated immediately following the massacre; some of them persist. They constitute "possible" answers to the question of cause, unofficial answers inserted in the cracks within the authorities' official speeches, which did not explain everything. The rumors are part of a body of community knowledge that is based "on faith, not on proof."[15]

One rumor relates to the presence of Alsatians both among the 1939 refugees [see Chapter 3] *and* in the Waffen SS. In 1946, at the time of the first trial (of a forced draftee from annexed Alsace before the court of justice in Limoges), witnesses "positively" identified the accused man's features as those of an adolescent they had seen several years earlier.[16] He was allegedly among those evacuated from Alsace [before the Occupation]. Badly treated by the village inhabitants, he allegedly took revenge by acting as a guide for the SS.

A second rumor is built around the confusion of two localities whose name begins with Oradour. Here is a personal story, from September 1997: the scene is a street in the old section around the Limoges cathedral. Some young men are leaving a social services clubhouse just as I am taking a model of the city hall for the new town of Oradour back to its owner after a public showing. The model interests them, and one of them recounts the story to his friends. According to him, the massacre supposedly was the result of a mistake. The SS had confused two Oradours: Oradour-sur-Vayres, located southeast of Rochechouart, in the heart of an underground Resistance zone, and Oradour-sur-Glane, to the northeast, where there was no underground. This rumor started in Saint-Junien as early as the evening of June 10, 1944, and was repeated to an American investigator in October 1944 by Colonel Rousselier, who commanded the département's French forces.[17] Its persistence has been taken as proof of the innocence of the people of Oradour-sur-Glane, whereas the people of the other Oradour might have been guilty of helping the underground Resistance.

These rumors have become part of the stories of some of the witnesses. Unverifiable by their very nature, they are combinations of elements that sometimes are separately verifiable but that do not hold up under historical scrutiny. Nevertheless, the conviction of the people spreading them contributes to perpetuating the aura of mystery surrounding the massacre.

The National Association of Martyrs' Families, created in early 1945, exercises implicit supervision over the municipal government and over the historical monument of the martyred village's ruins, which is state property. The origins of this association, like its title, are not neutral. As the lawful guardian of local collective memory, the association seeks to play a national role, and this kind of representativity leads it to address the highest governmental authorities as a natural interlocutor: the procedures for the opening of the Centre de la Mémoire d'Oradour only confirm this position. Is everything concerning Oradour really a matter of state?

The association's origins, like the preservation of the ruins, fall into the province of local politics. In September 1944, an association for the defense of the victims was created at the same time as several memorial committees, and they started to compete with one another, particularly after Jean Chaintron, the département's préfet and a Communist, lent his support to one of them. The commissioner of the Republic, Pierre Boursicot, a Gaullist, required that the committees merge. An official Memorial Committee was then set up, to be presided over by the new sous-préfet of Rochechouart, Guy Pauchou, the chief secretary of the sous-préfecture at the Occupation's end. The official committee was composed exclusively of public figures. A new representative association was established: the National Association of the Martyrs' Families.

Aided by Doctor Masfrand, a physician from Rochechouart and the unpaid conservator of the sous-préfecture museum who was made conservator of the Oradour ruins in October 1944, the sous-préfet wrote a pamphlet for the Office of Enemy War Crimes. The two men subsequently wrote the "Official Work of the Memorial Committee and the National Association of Martyrs' Families," which was published in June 1945. Its royalties went to the association, thus creating a debt that "morally" prohibited their text from being modified. Fifty years after its first publication, this book is still distributed by the association; its illustrations are modified, but the text is unchanged. In Oradour it is treated as the "official book," presented to important visitors and sold for the benefit of the association. But can it really be considered to be the story of the massacre?[18]

After a few clashes between 1945 and 1953 when the village government was under Communist leadership, Jean Brouillaud, the president of the National Association of Martyrs' Families, became the mayor of the village. Cloaking themselves in the claim to be above politics, which in reality meant every political power except the Communists, the Socialists thus hoped to take over once again a town government they had controlled before the war. The president of the town council was still a Communist, however. Reacting to the 1953 trial verdict (in particular the amnesty benefiting the forced draftees), both the National Association of Martyrs' Families and the village government, presided over by the same man, rejected a monument erected by the state.[19] They set up a private monument, the Tomb of the Martyrs, as a center for commemorations.

Seven Publications ... and a Few Others

Apart from Sarah Farmer's academic study dealing with the creation of the memory of Oradour (not with the story of the massacre), there are no standard reference works. And yet much has been published about Oradour.

In the year following the massacre seven publications appeared, crowned with great success, covering the entire spectrum of public opinion at the time and combining texts with illustrations, to which we can add many pamphlets that were not illustrated. Along with clandestine publications—texts reproduced by several typists, tracts from Resistance organizations, articles in the underground press *(Cahiers du témoignage chrétien, Lettres françaises),* anonymous pamphlets, and radio broadcasts picked up in France (from Algiers, London, Switzerland)—these testify to the amazing, immediate renown of Oradour. During the period of the Liberation, the objective of these publications was mobilization. This was the case for certain FTP [Franc-tireurs et partisans (Snipers and Partisans)] resistance fighters, like Madeleine Riffaud ("Rainer"), who spent her vacations there at the end of the 1930s, with her parents who were schoolteachers in Saint-Junien.

All the publications of this time were similar, reflecting the prevailing image of the war that had emerged from World War I, particularly the idea of German barbarism. The war in progress was not in evidence, apart from a call for mobilization to end it. The war of extermination in the East—with its collective slaughters, massive hangings of hostages, genocide of Jews, concentration camps—went unnoticed. It would be noticed later on, but it had no effect on the building of Oradour's memory.

These publications took the literary form of fairy tales: "Once upon a time a peaceful village, happy in its tranquility, was brutally attacked by a barbarous horde."[20] The illustrations reinforce this thesis: old postcards conjure up rural happiness, and the photos from after the massacre display the scars of the tragedy. The description of the village corresponds fairly closely to that in *Le Bonheur de Barbezieux* by Jacques Chardonne, a Petainist writer who had family ties in Limoges, writing in 1938 about a county seat in Charente that exemplified the virtues of the soil later advocated by the Vichy regime.[21]

The publications of the 1944–1945 period shaped public opinion. They are no longer available in bookstores except for the "official book" [by Pauchou and Masfrand].

The second generation of publications came after the 1953 trial. Some of them presented general or anecdotal points of view, at times in the form of rumor-based fiction. Some works of a historical nature written for the general public give little indication of their sources.

To these is added a negationist publication, whose distribution is illegal. The negationist movement is interested in Oradour as if it were a lock that the movement would like to force, by spreading an ideology promoted to the level of methodology.[22]

An attempt at oral history by the makers of a documentary film shown on television in 1989, based on a collection of first-person accounts, was quickly abandoned.[23] The escapees told of their sufferings in a village attacked without reason: "There was no underground in Oradour, so why?" But the oral investigation was faced with one insurmountable legal problem in particular: the impossibility of questioning convicted people who had been granted amnesty. Thirteen Frenchmen tried in 1953 benefited from an amnesty because they had been drafted against their will. Contacting them on the subject was therefore ruled out. Interviewing the

German perpetrators was out of the question: some had died without being in any way troubled about their conviction in absentia in France; others were more or less in hiding (in 1995 the SS colonel commanding the Der Führer regiment at the time of the massacre was living in the province of Carinthia, in Austria). When reporters from German television interviewed former Waffen SS men for documentary films about "Hitler's soldiers" and the Waffen SS, their remarks were disappointingly conformist: they were obeying orders; they were never Nazis, in any case, but "professional soldiers"; they sometimes considered themselves to be victims of Nazism!

The only remaining recourse was to archives thought to be inaccessible and dispersed.

The Archives Are Opened

Fifty years after the event, various administrations sensitive to the needs of research granted the necessary legal dispensations for researchers to consult their archives. Archivists proved very helpful, the reception of researchers generally quite warm. Numerous records had never been consulted since they were put in the archives. This material was rich, the discoveries often surprising; gradually, the complexity of Oradour became clearer. The project director gradually changed into the author of the historical account, at the risk of seeing his own legitimacy to produce this account questioned at any moment.

Among the records consulted, thanks to authorization by the Ministry of Defense, was the dossier kept in the archives of military justice: records of the procedures leading up to the trial before the permanent military tribunal of Bordeaux in 1953.[24]

The département archives of the Haute-Vienne contain documents that enabled me to write a monograph about the village of Oradour from the turn of the century up to the 1990s. I also consulted the records of the Limoges prefecture and records of police activities under the Occupation, as well as the records of the court of justice that examined collaborators who went with the SS and Waffen SS.

The records of the Ministry of Justice in the National Archives allow us to follow the political aspects of the Oradour "affair" and the evolution of the penal doctrine concerning war crimes. The records in the Ministry of Reconstruction and Urban Planning show how the construction of the new Oradour turned into a political game. The archives of the German military command in France, supplemented by military archives published in Germany, permit us to understand how the occupation army assessed the situation in the Limousin.

The Army Historical Service in Vincennes has archives of the German units operating in France from 1940 onward, in particular those of the Das Reich division and its chain of command, as well as documents about the Resistance forces, and other documents coming most notably from Vichy's Ministry of State for Defense.

The Ministry of Culture's Media Library has archives at its disposal that relate to the classification procedures for Monuments historiques, the rebuilding of the church, and the monument projects for within the classified walled area.

Some of these sources, for the most part freely accessible, may have already been used in parts. But no one had ever consulted, analyzed, and cross-referenced them in their entirety.

Three specific dossiers and one film are representative of the finds, exemplary for the profound oblivion into which they had fallen. This oblivion can be explained by the fact that the finds could not be fitted into the Oradour community's way of reading[25] the events.

The Communist Party, which held the mayoralty in the village at the time, organized its own commemorations of the massacre during the cold war period, from 1948 to 1952. The June 12, 1949, celebration brought a considerable number of people together at the initiative of the Mouvement de la Paix [Movement for Peace], the Conseil national des écrivains [National Council of Writers], and *Lettres françaises* [French Letters]. Sarah Farmer found out about this event, held with the participation of Louis Aragon and Frédéric Joliot-Curie, who made a speech.[26] But when she was working in Oradour in the mid-1980s, nobody told her of the existence of a document presented to the village community on that occasion. Original statements by artists, writers, and intellectuals who were Communists or "fellow-travelers" had been gathered into a visitors' album[27] containing drawings by artists (such as Picasso, Léger, Gromaire, Fougeron, for example), autographed letters from writers, filmmakers, actors, and so on, and an original poem by Aragon. This remarkable album, which remained forgotten in the town hall, was a vestige of the past that had been repressed by the village. Its chance discovery was very moving. The dossier, together with the artwork by the artists who had contributed to it, was exhibited at Oradour-sur-Glane in 1995, after it was registered in the village inventory.[28]

The reactions of Wehrmacht General Gleiniger after the massacre are known from the reports of the regional prefect. The general's correspondence with his higher command was preserved by the Communist daily *L'Humanité*. These records had been recovered from the offices of the German forces upon the liberation of Limoges. *L'Humanité* used extracts from these records, particularly in 1953 at the time of the Bordeaux trials. The records contained the originals, known from some copies, including a letter from the bishop of Limoges to the German general, and an excerpt—certified—from the war diary of the Der Führer Battalion 1 giving the body count of "enemy dead" at Oradour on June 10.[29]

The Allied military high command (SHAEF) sent an investigator named Munn to Oradour-sur-Glane at the beginning of October 1944. His report in English, dated October 14, 1944, is sixteen pages long and is preceded by a two-page summary. It contains eyewitness accounts, authenticated by dated photographs of witnesses as well as photographs by the investigator, or collected by him.[30]

A film came to our attention during the first three months of 1999.[31] It was the report of a Jewish funeral. Part of the ceremony took place in the ruins of Oradour. It was announced by the local press and had been organized on September 21, 1944, in Limoges by the Union de résistance et d'entraide des Juifs de France [Union of the Jews of France for Resistance and Mutual Aid], a Communist organization usually known under the acronym UJRE.[32] No one in Oradour ever mentioned this ceremony, with the exception of the descendants of militant Communists.

The archives allow us to construct a historical account of the massacre by comparing the victims' testimony with the executioners' hearings. This new account assumes the risk of describing what none of the witnesses had the possibility of *seeing*.

"Why did the Waffen SS come to Oradour?" Seeking an answer to this painful question of the victims requires that we move away from Oradour and talk about the Waffen SS, their past, and how they conceived of their activity during the final days of the Occupation.

Could Oradour-sur-Glane have been outside of time?

The War Culture of the Waffen SS

The crime of Oradour-sur-Glane was committed by a Waffen [armored] SS unit of the Das Reich division. SS policemen stationed in Limoges participated in the preparations for this collective massacre. They were accompanied by the Milice of Maintien de l'ordre [Maintaining Order], the Vichy government's auxiliary police. Who were these SS policemen and Waffen SS? Where did they come from? How could they have imagined such an "action"? Why and under what circumstances did they arrive in Oradour on June 10, 1944? In order to try and answer these questions, to arrive at an understanding and an explanation, requires that we take a broader view and search through various plot levels that lead up to such a tragic denouement. We propose to unfold these various plots, both primary and secondary ones, and to show how they were motivated by a definite logic or rationale.

Berlin, 1933

"The air has become almost unbreathable," Walter Benjamin wrote in a letter. He was one of the first Jewish intellectuals to leave Nazi Germany. Robert Musil, who would also go into exile a few years later, observed in his *Journal:* "Disturbing impression. Late in the evening a police car with swastika flags and Schupos singing, speeding down the Kurfürstendamm." In March, when the Nazis had been in power for two months, he noted his anxiety once again: "Three days ago the Reichstag went up in flames. Yesterday the emergency regulations to eliminate the Communist Party and the Social Democrat Party appeared. The new men don't wear kid gloves."[1] For a number of years the Nazis systematically employed violence to achieve their ends. "Congenital violence," as Philippe Burrin stated: "Violence formed the heart of Nazism and defined its identity, prescribing its historical face."[2]

1933. "Hitler is Chancellor." Like so many others, Klaus Mann, the eldest son of Thomas and a nephew of Heinrich, could not believe it! The elections took place in a climate of violence, implemented by shock groups of the Nazi Party, the SA ("assault teams," with the main aim of protecting the Nazi Party demonstrations) and SS ("protection teams").[3] Immediately after the elections, the opposition—Communists and "Marxists," that is, Socialists—were locked up in makeshift camps, guarded not by civil police but by members of the party in power, usually members of the SA.

Legality yielded to arbitrary force, based on a racial argument exalting the purity of the "community of German people." Divergent opinions, or behavior termed "deviant," were no longer permitted. Based on doctrine, verbally impassioned, enflamed by a cult of manly heroism, "the affirmation of the right of the strongest, a discourse of salutary harshness, violence was not only a means, it constituted an end in itself, with the value of a law of nature."[4] Those who did not flee within the first week or were not interned in concentration camps—Musil compared them to prison galleys—found themselves shut up within their own country, under surveillance by the Nazi Party organizations and subjected to the arbitrary whims of police who were less and less controlled by constitutional mechanisms. Karl Jaspers, an academic philosopher, was to write later, in 1945, that Germany had "become a penitentiary."[5]

The Nazi regime suppressed every possibility of opposition. The people accepted this with "panic, loyalty, self-pity, and lies in a psychological mixture that made them morally blind to the excesses committed by the regime."[6]

Bavaria: Joining the SS

In the summer of 1933 a young middle-class man from Würzburg in Bavaria applied to join the SS. Like so many others, Otto Weidinger would later become a full-fledged member of the new elite and an officer in the Waffen SS. He would be on the staff of the Der Führer regiment, present in Limoges on the day of the massacre.

Weidinger, born in 1914, became a candidate for the Allgemeine [General] SS of his city in July 1933, then joined the Nazi Party (NSDAP) two months later. First under the authority of the local SS, he was then sent for training to Dachau—where the SS had opened the first concentration camp—to be trained as an "SS trooper." He became one in November 1934, with the serial number 114921. Promoted to corporal in March of the following year, he was sent for training to the SS cadet school in Braunschweig, where he studied military science and ideology.

Waffen SS recruitment methods appear to have been fairly complex. The principle of voluntary enlistment was a smokescreen, more an affirmation of ideology than a consistent reality.[7] The first Waffen SS came from the general SS, with a cadre of former officers and noncoms from the irregulars in the immediate post World War I period. At this stage recruitment was a matter of political selection with a thin racial veneer. Instructions for recruiting men for the Waffen SS, valid until 1939, specified of course a minimum height (1.74 meters)[8] and maximum age (twenty-three years), and required a certificate of "good conduct" (issued by the police—meaning a member of the SS), as well as medical and racial ones. Since the SS recognized five levels of "nordicity"—from "pure nordic" to a "suspicion of contamination by non-European blood"—the range of recruitment possibilities was wide open. The candidates' political conduct was given priority in examinations. Because "German blood" (being *Volksdeutsche,* that is, having German blood though without German citizenship) was considered "educable," none of its components was rejected. More importance was given to physical aptitude tests than to tests of knowledge or intelligence, the latter developed later from a perspective that was specifically SS, with appropriate pedagogy.

After the war began, voluntary enlistment was supplemented by a demand for recruitment quotas by the Wehrmacht high command (OKW), with which the SS found itself in competition. The success of these quotas varied according to the times. A second method of recruitment was the enlistment of volunteers without taking OKW quotas into account. In cases of multiple applications, enlistment in the Waffen SS was given priority. Finally, recruiting in occupied territories let the SS find men of "nordic blood" from within population sources not available to the Wehrmacht. These three recruiting methods were maintained until the end of the war, but they could not make up for the losses. The Waffen SS recruited foreigners with only a remote connection—marked in any case by an imaginary ideology—to "nordicity": prisoners who were Russian or of other USSR nationalities could become "volunteers." Numerous auxiliaries (known as Hiwis), transformed into combat troops for lack of personnel in the units, must also be included. By the end of the war, at most 40 percent of the Waffen SS recruits came from inside the Reich. By then voluntary enlistment had long since become merely an ideological principle maintained for propaganda purposes. "Forced volunteers" were the norm from 1943 onward. This mixture of recruiting methods ended up producing groups of diverse national origins and ill-assorted troops, including those in the Das Reich division.

The training of officers in the SS special schools did not mean they were destined exclusively for the Waffen SS troops. Avenues between different administrations were expressly provided for. SS Reichsführer Himmler's ambition was to militarize all sectors of the SS and the police. SS officers joined an "order," and their allegiance was strengthened by way of their careers. The syllabus of SS "cadet" training included not only an introduction to the command of sections and combat companies but specific SS items as well. In the syllabus, the "educational mission of the army according to Adolf Hitler's *Mein Kampf*" and "the SS officer as political educator of his men and his influence over the people's political orientation" were set forth.[9] "Study Directors" in the units played the same role as National-Socialist propaganda officers in the Wehrmacht: setting up lectures, libraries, and ceremonies and distributing party brochures and newspapers. According to its promoters, SS training ensured that troops would acquire firm ideological beliefs enabling them to stand fast when they might otherwise lose ground, and to outdo themselves under the most critical conditions. But more than ideology, it was the terror fostered by the officers that maintained discipline.

In addition to the privileges they enjoyed, particularly in respect to military equipment, the Waffen SS divisions achieved a surprising notoriety for the extent of their human losses, including a great number of SS officers. These losses played a part in creating a Waffen SS legend. At the end of 1943, the "historic" divisions established prior to 1939 had lost more officers than the other troops.[10] Between death, wounds, and transfers, company commanders and battalion chiefs seldom remained more than three or four months at the head of their units. These extensive losses, which we will note for the members of the Das Reich division, conjure up the image of an archaic fighting style, in which manly hand-to-hand combat contrasted with up-to-date equipment.

The average SS regimental commander was thirty-one or thirty-two years old; battalion commanders were thirty years old or less. The youth of the SS officers, who showed greater enthusiasm than ability, was an element of the archaic virtue of manliness. As a result it was not unusual for sections, at times even companies, to be commanded by noncommissioned officers. The lack of reserves among SS officers to fill out or rebuild units would have consequences for the command structure, for the training of new recruits, and for the functional capabilities of Waffen SS units.

Nevertheless, as a result of losses and the constraints of the war, some men managed to spend their careers exclusively in the Waffen SS. The case of Otto Weidinger seems a model of what SS education could produce, as well as of the failure of postwar denazification. The last commander of the fourth regiment of the Der Führer SS Panzer [tank] Grenadiers, this officer had his entire career in the Das Reich division.[11] In 1935 he was an "SS Cadet" (the SS ranks constituted in themselves an anomaly). He returned to Dachau as a sergeant, a platoon leader. His first assignment was with the SS Verfügungstruppe [Reserve Unit], from which the Das Reich division was drawn.

We intend not to write a history of the division whose main episodes are reflected in Weidinger's career, but rather to point up certain elements that shed light on its situation and the aims it had in carrying out the massacre at Oradour.[12]

The Nazis regarded this SS formation with the reverence due an "elite division": an opinion that some of those who fought against it, at least in Western Europe, seem to have shared. This reputation seems considerably exaggerated, unless we consider that spreading terror can be a source of prestige, or unless we set much store in the greatest number of Nazi decorations received (seventy-two Ritterkreuz medals). A study of the archives comparing these records with recent historiography allows the construction of a different vision, one that demolishes this myth of "the elite of the German army." The Waffen SS, political soldiers, were an elite in only their own eyes.[13]

The unit in Oradour belonged to the fourth regiment, Der Führer, of armored SS grenadiers. It was one of the earliest formations of Waffen SS, created as a standard-bearer regiment of "combat-ready troops" in Austria in July 1938, at the time of that country's annexation to Germany. The regiment grouped together SS units commanded by former officers of the Imperial army, members of the Nazi Party who had played a part among the irregular forces in setting up the regime. The troops and lower-echelon noncoms had been trained in SS cadet schools at Braunschweig and Dachau. The regiment, designated by its initials DF, was stationed in Austria (Vienna, Graz, and Klagenfurt) before being engaged successively in the annexation operations of the Sudetenland and then in Poland. It was at this time that the first oppression was carried out against civilian populations, particularly Polish Jews, who were manhandled, assassinated, at times burned alive in synagogues. In the West, little attention was paid to the brutality of the invasion and the violence of the Nazis against the Polish people.

His participation in the annexation of Austria earned Weidinger his first decoration and promotion to the rank first of master sergeant, then of SS adjutant. The occupation of the Sudetenland occasioned still another honor.

In the autumn of 1939, the formation of the motorized infantry division (SS division Verfügungstruppe), ordered by Hitler and Himmler after the Polish campaign, began in the region of Pilsen in Bohemia. The term *motorized* did not signify "armored" or, in fact, "without horse-drawn traction." An SS general named Hauser took command of this division. He went on to a career in the Waffen SS and became its head.

Stationed during a training period first in Würzburg and then in Münster, the second SS division was sent into the war in the West from the beginning of operations against the Netherlands, then against France in May 1940. Leaving Arras during early June, it crossed the Somme and Avre rivers, then was ordered toward Noyon, Château-Thierry, and Troyes; on May 20, it arrived at Le Creusot, where the Schneider factories as well as mineral deposits are located. Sent off immediately in the direction of Poitiers and Bordeaux, advance units reached the Spanish border on June 27. The Waffen SS troops had traced what was to become the Demarcation Line and were charged with its surveillance at the start of the Occupation.[14] During the campaign, this SS division was composed of three motorized infantry regiments (Germania, Deutschland, Der Führer) and support units. A regiment of field artillery, the music company [*sic*], and a few services were still horse-drawn in part or as a whole.[15]

Withdrawing from France and regrouping in the Netherlands, the division had its makeup changed. Some units were removed to form new divisions, in a customary practice of the German army; the Germania regiment became the basis for the SS Wiking division. Units often changed names and, at times, assignments. Returning to France near Vesoul at the end of 1940, the division was designated the Waffen SS Das Reich on December 21. It was composed then of three infantry regiments (Deutschland, Der Führer, and the eleventh SS, each of three battalions, for a total of sixteen companies), an artillery regiment with four battalions of mobile cannon, a unit of self-propelled cannon, a group of tank destroyers, anti-aircraft, reconnaissance, and "pioneer" units, a rear-echelon, and a field-police battalion.[16] We do not know their total strength, but estimating a company at two hundred men minimum and including the various command echelons, they must have been around eighteen thousand men.

After being stationed in Hungary in March 1941, the division took part in the Balkans invasion in April. This was a deadly campaign for the civilian population: the Yugoslav area of Banat underwent what was designated as a "cleanup." Before Belgrade was taken, fighting at Pancevo led to numerous civilian deaths: mass executions by shooting and hanging.[17] Sent to the Linz region of Austria, the unit was advance-positioned once again and was concentrated in Poland north of Lublin until the invasion of the Soviet Union.

The "Brutal" War in the East

Weidinger's "voyage to the East," which he undertook as an SS captain and then as major in the reconnaissance battalion of the Das Reich division, led to his attaining the highest Nazi distinction. He was in the last detachment of five thousand men in the SS division, kept on as a "combat group" until April 1944, taking part in the retreat from the Ukraine.

During World War I, the "brutalizing" of troops and civilians was a consequence of the very way fighting was carried out. With the orders of 1941, brutalization became the explicit intent. The dehumanization of warfare, well underway from 1914 to 1918, took on an aspect of deliberate extermination. Hitler had represented the coming war against "Judeo-Bolshevism" as an urgent necessity. It began in the form of a crusade with its appointed "sacrificial victims": Jews and Communists, indissolubly linked in the Nazis' thirst for vengeance.[18]

Bolshevism was the mortal enemy of the "German National-Socialist" nation. The objective was to exterminate it, totally and pitilessly. Out of this grew measures, qualified as "energetic," taken against agitators, partisans, and Jews, that were intended to "eliminate all active or passive resistance."[19] Since the causal link between Judeo-Bolshevism and the Resistance was a self-evident fact, as proclaimed by Hitler and the SS, an agreement between the OKW and the Central Security Office of the Reich gave carte blanche to special units of the SS—the Einsatzgruppen—to proceed in eliminating Communist officials and Jews. This was undertaken just behind the front lines.[20] In September 1941, SS General von dem Bach-Zelewski, the Obergruppenführer for the Central Zone in Soviet territory, commanded the police in newly conquered territories. As chief of staff he had a man named Lammerding, the future head of the Das Reich division in France in 1944. In a speech on "The Jewish Question and Its Link with the Partisan Movement," he drove home the point that "partisans are there wherever Jews are found."[21]

Ever since the War of 1870,[22] German military doctrine has traditionally recommended random preventive repressive measures against irregular troops. The Imperial army made broad use of these recommendations against the people in territories conquered and occupied during World War I. In 1941 the target was clearly designated. Massacres of Jews took place whenever a "commander" observed or merely suspected the presence of "bandits," the Nazi term for resistance groups, in his zone of operations.[23]

The violence was organized via four sets of instructions addressed to the troops. As early as March and April of 1941, the Central Security Office under Heydrich's direction set up death squads (Einsatzgruppen). SS officers, recruited from inside the SD, were instructed on the objectives to be achieved. Immediately behind the invasion troops but not under their control, special battalions were to operate in relative freedom. There were few protests from Wehrmacht officers, who theoretically were supposed to ensure the safety of the populace in occupied zones. Executions of Red Army "political commissars" and other communist officials were the responsibility of the SD. The Wehrmacht handed these prisoners over to the SD for "treatment" if they had not already been killed on the spot. In case of resistance, the "streamlining" of judicial procedures stipulated that suspects and those "aiding" them were to be killed by the army. In areas where the parties presumed guilty were not caught, collective measures were taken immediately against the civilian populace.

Directives for the conduct of troops in Russia provided for "pitiless measures"("harshness" was constantly recommended) against Bolshevik agitators, "guerrillas," saboteurs, and Jews. Violence, a form of discrimination, was used to segregate resistance fighters from the rest of the population. It was, in addition, intended to promote a sense of the "guilt" of the resisters being singled out.

From these orders, which increased the brutality of the war, there resulted a loss of moral guidelines among the troops, who were subjected as well to unremitting political propaganda. The enemy was represented as a "subhuman being" with whom all fraternization was forbidden. Even for officers with long-standing or traditional training, discipline took precedence over morality. Any moral lapses were in full accord with the Führer's wishes as passed down through the chain of command. Very quickly the soldiers grew incapable of distinguishing between matters of discipline and acts of barbarity. Segregation of the enemy in order to annihilate them, brutality, ruthless severity, the abuse of discipline, all gave rise to practices and behaviors that were to be repeated over and over again. The particularly brutal treatment of hundreds of thousands of Soviet prisoners of war who were starved, obliged to do forced labor, exhausted by the cold, deprived of food and clothing, shot or gassed to death would recur on a different scale in 1944 with the execution of Allied prisoners. Similarly, thousands of villages in the Soviet Union were burned to the ground and the populace shot to death because they were mainly Jewish; this foreshadowed random retaliations and collective executions in France in 1944.

There are abundant examples of this. In late September 1941, thirty-three thousand Kiev Jews were massacred in the Babi-Yar ravine. In mid-October all the Jews of the village of Smolevitch east of Minsk were executed "as a warning to the civilian populace and to convince them not to give aid to the partisans." A veritable murder frenzy was unleashed at Slutsk, south of Minsk in Byelorussia in the Central military zone, at the end of October 1941. This troubled one German official, a regional commissioner, who addressed a report to his superior:

> With indescribable brutality, by the German policemen as well but especially by the Lithuanians, the Jews and also White Russians were taken out of their lodgings and driven together. There was shooting everywhere in the city, and in the individual streets bodies of Jews who had been shot were piled up. . . . Aside from the fact that the Jews, among them also craftsmen, were brutally mistreated in a frightfully barbarous way before the eyes of the White Russians, the latter were likewise beaten with truncheons and clubs. . . . My own gendarmes were given the same task but because of the wild shooting often had to get off the streets in order not to be shot themselves. The entire scene was altogether more than ghastly. . . . I was not present at the shootings outside the city. Thus I can say nothing about the brutality. But it suffices when I emphasize that long after being thrown in the grave, some of those shot worked their way out again. . . . During the action the police battalion plundered in an outrageous way, and indeed not only in Jewish houses, but just as much in the houses of the White Russians. They took with them anything useful, such as boots, leather, textiles, gold, and other valuables . . . watches were torn from the arms of Jews publicly in the streets, rings were pulled off fingers in the most brutal way.[24]

Such "brutal action," among many others, aroused only selective indignation in this official. Would the ruthless treatment have seemed more acceptable to him had it not taken place in public? At this stage the violence had to be public in nature. It was a necessary display. A few months later it would take on a hidden form in the extermination camps, so as to be "administered" out of sight of the troops.

Collective massacres, arson, and pillaging were carried out by special units of the Waffen SS and Wehrmacht troops. They were expected to meet their needs through "levies" on conquered territories. The consequence was a profound disruption of discipline: a "perversion," as Omer Bartov observed.[25] It was not immoral to kill "subhumans." Nazi ideology, made up of expansionism, anti-Bolshevism, and racism, required it. Even more than the rigorous discipline based on various forms of terror and arbitrariness, this criminality, now so "ordinary," bound the troops together in the most difficult phases of the combat against the Soviet army. "The cohesion of the army of the East was maintained by a mixture of iron discipline in combat and extreme tolerance with regard to acts of barbarity committed against the enemy." The soldiers were able to accept the brutality of the discipline, the rigors of the climate, the violence of battle, because they had the possibility of transferring and reproducing the violence they had undergone on civilians and prisoners. "The recourse to brutality came to seem normal."[26]

The soldiers' convictions may be read in letters addressed to their families:

> The great mission that has been entrusted to us in the struggle against Bolshevism consists of doing away with eternal Jewry. When you take the trouble to look at what the Russians did in the way of oppression here in Russia, you know all you need to know about why the Führer began the struggle against the Jews. What evils our poor country would have had to face if those human animals had hung on to their mastery! We are still some way behind the lines and so we have not had contact with the Russians. But in the rear there is an assortment of rabble hanging around, scared of daylight, that could possibly turn out to be more dangerous to combat than the front. This is not the kind of enemy you encounter in open combat, but one that seeks its prey in the dark. Just a while ago, one of our comrades was found dead in the woods at night. Only a Jew could be hiding behind this crime. The raid we carried out as a result turned out very nicely. The people themselves detest the Jews more than ever. They are finally realizing that they are responsible for everything. This fight must be carried to the very utmost limits.[27]

The War in the East for the Das Reich Division

The commanders of the units involved in Operation Barbarossa knew the orders to be applied against Communist Party officials (the "commissars") and partisans. Incorporated into the central army, the Waffen SS of the Das Reich division went into action on June 26, 1941. Their eastward advance brought them to the region south of Minsk, then to cross the Berezina in early July. In this sector of Byelorussia, massacres of the populace started immediately.

The offensive along the Dnieper and toward Gorki, which the Soviet defenses made very difficult, caused grave losses in the SS division. A Soviet counterattack northeast of Smolensk around the town of Jelnja led up to an indecisive battle lasting several days. The German forces won a victory at Jelnja, and one unit of the division captured more than a thousand prisoners. Prisoners of war were treated pitilessly, without respect for international conventions. Several hundred thousand were shot right off and a great many others (around two million) starved or later froze to death: they were stripped, their boots were taken from them, and they were subjected to forced labor.[28] In the annals of the Das Reich division, the battle of Jelnja stood as the moment of its supreme military glory, an example that would constantly be recalled to new recruits later on. The eastward march continued in the direction of Kiev, where the encircled Soviet forces fought back in fierce combat. Once the city was taken, tens of thousands of Jews were massacred at the end of September and the beginning of October, notably in the Babi-Yar ravine on the outskirts of the city.

One survivor's story: "At about midnight the command was given in German for us to line up. I didn't wait for the next command, but threw my girl into the ditch and fell on top of her. A second later bodies started raining down on me. Then everything fell silent. About fifteen minutes passed, then they brought in another batch. Then more shots rang out and bodies of more dead and dying people fell into the pit."[29]

Mass executions behind the front lines fell under the jurisdiction of units specially organized for such slaughter. They were expressly authorized by a statement of March 1941: "The Sonderkommandos are authorized within the framework of their instructions and upon their own responsibility, to carry out executive measures against the civilian population."[30] These special units were supported and at times supplemented by units of Waffen SS and the army. To the surprise of some commanders of the special units, they went far beyond mere logistical support. "Armed forces agreeably well disposed against the Jews," a group chief noted in July 1941.[31] This collaboration held true throughout the chain of command, from top to bottom.

On October 10, 1941, Marshal von Reichenau, commanding the sixth army, sent a message to his troops telling them to treat partisans with rigor in this war between the Judeo-Bolshevik system and German culture: "Therefore . . . the soldier must have full understanding of the necessity for severe but justified sanctions against the Jewish subhumanity."[32] With violence authorized, given the rigors of battle and discipline, soldiers could act on their own initiative. Some officers noted excesses: "The fanatical will of Communist Party members and Jews to halt the advance of the German army at any cost must be broken in all circumstances. In order to ensure security in the rear zone of the armies, it is therefore necessary to take drastic measures. This task is entrusted to the Sonderkommandos. Nevertheless members of the armed forces regrettably have taken part in an action of this sort, in one locality."[33] There was no way excesses could be prevented—the preamble to the text cited above in fact forbade any return to norms—but more than anything, these excesses corresponded to the political wishes and intentions of the hierarchy of the Nazi regime.

The SS Das Reich division endured the mud of a Russian autumn, which bogged down the vehicles, but in mid-November 1941, freezing temperatures allowed it to continue its march toward Moscow. In battles early in the month of December the division neared the western outskirts of the Russian capital. The Germans' advance was halted at the gates to the city, and a pullback began at the end of December and continued in early January 1942. In military terms this was a withdrawal, except that the aggressors did not have "positions decided in advance" and the front was moving back. For the first time the Waffen SS was carrying on defensive combat, in retreat. The fighting throughout January underwent numerous reversals. The German troops loosened the vise and pushed back the Soviets, who in their turn retook territory and pushed the enemy back. In mid-March the Soviets attacked en masse, with tank formations superior in numbers and quality. Caught in a counterattack and decimated far to the west of Moscow, the SS division was withdrawn from the front. Transferred first to the camp at Fallingbostel, it then showed up again in France, quartered in the region around Rennes, to be reconstituted.

One infantry regiment, the eleventh SS, was taken away and transformed into a "mechanized" division. Some equally decimated units were temporarily joined to it, and a tank group was added, which would later become a regiment. The division took part in the occupation of the Free Zone.[34]

After several months' rest and "reconstruction," in January 1943 the SS division left France and was sent once again to the Russian front east of Kharkov. The following month the Soviet forces, continuing their offensive, pushed the SS division back. A withdrawal was carried out in order to defend the city, which they had been ordered to hold by an OKW order of February 13. On February 14 the Soviets broke through the German defensive front. Lost in February, the city would be retaken by the Germans in March amid great tank battles. A savage repression was unleashed on the populace. Photographs of executions by firing squads and collective hangings from the balconies of buildings and from city lampposts bear witness to this savagery.[35] The Waffen SS was to act in the same way in Tulle.[36]

In July 1943 the battle of Kursk began. The fighting, indecisive for several weeks, turned to the Soviets' advantage, and they began to advance in the direction of Kharkov once the German defensive front was broken. So there began for the Waffen SS of the

Das Reich division a retreat of several months' duration, which ended only with their transfer to France. For the majority of the troops, this retreat lasted six months, until mid-February 1944. On that date the division once again initiated a withdrawal to Fallingbostel, where it partially regrouped. Just one combat group (the division's operational remnant) was kept on the defensive front until the beginning of April. It was steadily pushed back by Soviet forces.

Lammerding, Bach-Zelewski's SS officer colleague, took command of the division's remnants before undertaking to rebuild it. An engineer without military training born in 1905, he entered the SS early on and made his career in it. Named an SS second lieutenant in 1935, he became a major in 1940, then chief of headquarters staff of the Totenkopf (Death's-head) division, the SS division of concentration camp guards. As an SS colonel he was called up to police headquarters staff of the Central Zone, that is, Byelorussia–Northern Ukraine.[37] From this post he is thought to have joined the Waffen SS Das Reich division in February 1944, as it was retreating west of Kharkov toward Vinnitsa. His command of the division, with the ranks of "SS-Brigadeführer und Generalmajor der Waffen SS" (SS brigade leader and Waffen SS brigadier general) lasted just over six months. Wounded in July 1944, he was replaced and became a member of the headquarters staff of the SS Reichsführer, which performed various functions in the Nazi regime's apparatus.

The Waffen SS troops who arrived in Oradour on June 10, 1944, were returning from the eastern front. The fighting image of their SS officers, SS noncoms, and some of the soldiers was permeated by this experience. The new seventeen- and eighteen-year-old recruits who arrived in France were about to discover, at one and the same time, both the imagery and the reality. They would be "shaped" by the educational principles formulated by Himmler at Kharkov: when the city had just been retaken by Nazi forces (before its definitive liberation a few months later), the SS Reichsführer gave a speech to the officers of three of the SS "historic" armored divisions, including those of the Das Reich division. "I ask you to be constantly shaping these young men for me and to inculcate in them our conception of the world. . . . I expect you to care for the very hearts of these young lads of seventeen or eighteen who come to us . . . to direct them, to not let go of their hands until they have been truly imbued with our spirit." And he went on: "While we were fighting to take Kharkov, our reputation went on before us: for we have a reputation for arousing fear and sowing terror; this is an extraordinary weapon and we must not let it weaken; on the contrary, we must forever enhance it."[38]

3 The SS Das Reich Division in France

In 1949 André Malraux recalled the fighting during the Liberation and his comrades in the maquis, "those who had known the snows in the brush thickets [known as maquis] of the Corrèze, where you advanced on all fours and which the Gestapo considered uninhabitable. Those who had slowed the advance of the Das Reich division."[1] The southwestern corner of the Massif Central, a hotbed of maquis and Resistance movements, was deeply scarred by the terrorist activity of the SS second armored division, Das Reich, which after sowing desolation in the départements around Toulouse in May 1944 left, the following June, a bleeding wound in the Limousin. A lightning strike of four days sufficed to leave an indelible impression in people's memories.

Fifty years later Henri Cueco, an artist from the Corrèze, wrote down memories of his adolescence: "In 1944 the shed was a hiding-place from which we could watch without being seen the German soldiers on guard a few yards away, on the sidewalk or the road. We could have touched them with our fingers, even stabbed them as they leaned against the door. After the landings,[2] the 'Das Reich' division was in a constant state of alert as it went up toward the front. They mounted roadblocks, with a tank or a half-track."[3] The flareup of violence to which the names Tulle and Oradour-sur-Glane bear witness left an enduring mark on local Limousin culture, to the point of elevating the SS division to mythical status: a symbol of barbarism.

Preparing for the "Invasion"

A war directive (number 51, dated November 11, 1943) anticipating the opening of a new front in the West called for reorganizing coastal defense arrangements. The directive stated: "The Reichsführer SS will test the preparedness of the Waffen SS units for combat, security, and guard duties. Preparations will be made to raise battle-trained formations for operational and security duties from training, reserve, and recuperative establishments, and from schools and other units in the Home Defence Area."[4]

The Nazi high command considered France an economic reservoir and R&R zone, or a possible combat zone. As an "invasion" seemed more and more likely, they quickly dropped the idea of actually attacking Great Britain and set about fortifying the coast. The unusually complex occupation arrangements, on the whole, corresponded to those objectives.[5] The military command organization for France (MBF) distributed Kommandanturen [command headquarters] among the département capitals. In 1942 the command organization was relocated to what had been the free zone of Vichy, essentially for economic reasons. The staff headquarters chain of command, in liaison with département and regional authorities, developed over the course of time. From 1942 onward, suppression of opponents and the Resistance fell under the command of the SS police, directed in Paris by General Oberg, assisted by Colonel Knochen, who controlled the regional branches. The Limoges branch was directed by an SS commander named Meïr.

The operational troops, concentrated near the coast, left practically open a vast area, the Massif Central. At the beginning of 1944, when the defense of the entire northern Loire region was entrusted to Rommel, there was a reorganization. A new group of armies, Group G, settled in Toulouse in May 1944 under the command of General Blaskowitz, with the first army in Aquitaine and the nineteenth in Provence.[6] An armored corps, the fifty-eighth, regrouped during the first quarter of 1944 and was to ensure protection of communications lines in the Garonne and Rhône valleys, with three divisions that had been brought back from the eastern front in bad condition. There were three armored divisions: the ninth in Nîmes, the eleventh in the Dordogne, and the second SS (Das Reich) in Montauban. These were the only armored forces in the entire southern half of France; they took their place in a defense system that was being restructured. Since a reserve infantry corps based in

Clermont-Ferrand, consisting of only a single division, was inadequate to contain Resistance activities in its sector (which extended as far as the Pyrenees), the German forces proceeded with combing operations in certain areas. The armored divisions were utilized within the limits of their capabilities.

Drafting Frenchmen from Annexed Alsace

The Das Reich division was partially assembled in late February and in March 1944, first at the camp of Souges near Bordeaux and then regrouped in the Garonne Valley when its "remnants" were brought back from the eastern front. It was also at this camp, known as a place of detention for Resistance fighters in the Bordeaux area, in which some had been executed at this very time, that new SS recruits arrived. Among them were Frenchmen from annexed Alsace, drafted by force, the ones who call themselves the "Malgré-Nous" [Against Our Wills].[7] Considered "Germanic," they were subject to the draft as a result of a decision by Wagner, the Gauleiter of Strasbourg (he was condemned to death and executed after the Liberation).[8] This decision followed on the failure of recruitment based on voluntary enlistment. In fact the Nazis obtained only 2,100 voluntary enlistments.[9]

One of these enlistees was Georg Boos, born in 1923 to a farm family in Keskastel, who joined the Waffen SS in April 1941. Assigned to the Totenkopf division, he attended school in Prague, then underwent brief paramedical training at SS centers in Oranienburg and Dachau. He joined the Das Reich division in August 1941. A year later he was a member of the Feldgendarmerie [field police] of that division and took part in the "retreat from Russia," all the way to Bordeaux. Transferred to the third company of the Der Führer regiment's first battalion, he took part in the massacre at Oradour, as we shall see. Fascinated by the Nazi occupiers (his parents had joined the Nazi Party and been granted German citizenship), Boos abandoned the Protestant religion in October 1942 and declared himself *Gottläubig,* without religion. During the trial hearings,[10] he would assert that he had "never been a Nazi."

Between a hundred thirty and a hundred thirty-five thousand Alsatian Frenchmen were forcibly drafted into the German army.[11] The total number of these involuntary French draftees in the Das Reich division remains uncertain. A report by an office of the judicial police dated April 16, 1948, identified one hundred twenty-nine Alsatians as having belonged to this division.[12] This may apply only to the Der Führer regiment, however. The number seems low, and the number of forced draftees must have been much higher. They were distributed about twenty per company in armored infantry units ("grenadiers"). Nineteen names of Frenchmen appear in a document listing the roster of Company Three, Battalion 1, of the Der Führer regiment.[13] Five of them would later be reported missing. At the time they were drafted, most of these men were eighteen or younger; 10 percent were over thirty. They had just undergone three months of compulsory labor in Germany. Called up by a draft board in February 1944, they were assigned to the Waffen SS and the Das Reich division, which they joined in Bordeaux. The new German recruits were the same age: eighteen, even seventeen. The SS unit was granted international recruitment status. A document dated June 21, 1944, for just Battalion 2 of the Der Führer regiment enables us to count thirteen different nationalities and two hundred forty "foreigners" (with Romanians and Croats, enrolled from 1941 onward, forming the largest contingents), plus twelve Hiwis, out of a total of seven hundred forty-eight men.[14] Including about one-third "ethnic Germans" recruited outside of the Reich's borders, to whom we may add those drafted from annexed territories, Alsace among others, the SS unit was anything but homogeneous. Furthermore, it was short of officers.

On March 15, 1944, still stationed in camp at Souges, the Der Führer regiment was missing two-thirds of its officers (there were 32 instead of 93), half of its noncoms (there were 349 as opposed to 742 under normal staffing), as well as 300 ordinary soldiers (2,515 rather than 2,814). But the distribution among the battalions was unequal. Battalion 2's lack of manpower precluded operational service. On June 8 it could not follow the division into the Limousin, and it did not join the formation again until July, once it had been partially strengthened. Battalion 2 had been "sacrificed," so the two others, numbered 1 and 3, ended up having a surplus of ordinary soldiers. These men, new SS recruits in training and clearly lacking officers, would run rampant in Oradour.

The defendants present at the Bordeaux trial described how they had been "instructed." They had learned how to handle weapons, but above all they had learned how to fit in with the platoons, where they seem to have been relegated to subordinate duties. Important positions in the units, such as firing machine guns, were not assigned to them. They loaded automatic weapons; similarly, they were rarely vehicle drivers or machine operators. "We were drilled; we were made to crawl in the mud," they would say. These drill techniques—violence both physical and psychological—tended to suppress an individual's capacity for independence, to mold him into absolute obedience, to make him malleable, to obtain reflexes and exclude reflection. Intimidation, arbitrary actions, and harassment by officers and noncoms were the daily lot of the soldiers, and at times of noncoms at the hands of officers. Physical tests of manhood and the fear inspired by the discipline were accompanied by political education. "Essential Principles to Observe for the Task of Education" were much the same for the officers in charge of National-Socialist propaganda (the Nationalsozialistischer Führungsoffizier) and the SS "educators." They emphasized above all the "role of the Jewish community in this war; requiring that every man be convinced that the enemy wants to take away our way of life from us; that this is a matter of life or death for us; that the intentions of the enemy aim at the disintegration of the German people; . . . every soldier must be educated so he is able to pursue our political struggle."[15]

Once they arrived at the unit in early March 1944, the new recruits saw action very quickly, as the division moved in around Montauban during the month of April. They took part in campaigns against the maquis in the départements of Lot-et-Garonne, Lot, and Haute-Garonne, in liaison with the SS police (SD and Gestapo) and the Milice.[16] The combing of zones, with police operations conducted over several days, prepared the "new" unit for combat situations. The unit was hardened by burning villages and by executing people presumed to be supporting the "bandits," who were harder to get at. The new recruits learned to kill and grew accustomed to blood and to death.

Thus in May 1944, when it was regrouped in the Garonne Valley, the SS division was a unit with reduced capacity, with insufficient officers and a significant proportion of new recruits, inadequately equipped with matériel often in bad shape.

"Segregating" the Resistance: The "Bands"

Although it was in the process of restructuring, the Waffen SS unit had to participate in maintaining communication lines between the Atlantic and Mediterranean coasts. Since this area was only very partially occupied, the combing of zones and the terror that the SS struck in the populace proved to be the only possible action against "the bands."[17]

A combing operation organized with the Gestapo and the Toulouse Milice took place from May 11 to 13, in which the mobile units of the DF regiment—not all of them were indeed mobile—took part.[18] They overran the town of Saint-Céré (Lot) at daybreak on May 11 and rounded up men aged eighteen to sixty in the town square. Jewish inhabitants were ordered to bring their jewelry and baggage. About thirty people, fifteen identified as "Jews," were taken away to Toulouse, then deported via Drancy along with others arrested that and the following days.[19] This is already akin to the preliminary stages of a massacre whose rituals have been interrupted.[20] The combing operation continued in Gramat, with about thirty people arrested, nine of them Jews, and in other villages: Blars, Cabrerets, Cardailhac, Lauzès, Orliac, Saint-Maurice, Terrou. In all of them people were assembled; there were arrests, houses burned, pillaging, and the execution of so-called fugitives and resisters. The next day the SS continued in Bagnac, Quezac, Saint-Hilaire-Bessonies, and Saint-Bressou, and in Figeac, where they stayed for two days. There a roundup of the inhabitants was ordered and almost eight hundred people were arrested; about six hundred of them were shipped out to Montauban and imprisoned; some of these would be deported.

On May 21 and the following days, another operation involved Battalion 1 (Der Führer) and, in particular, the company that perpetrated the massacre at Oradour three weeks later. In the Lot département, scenes of roundups, pillaging, arson, and murder were repeated at the villages of Blanquefort-de-Briolance, Devillac, Fontenilles, Lacapelle-Biron, Laussou, Montflanquin, Paulhac, Saint-Martin-de-Villerval, and Vergt-de-Biron. But the worst one, at least for this particular time, took place at Frayssinet-le-Gelat, where the third company, the one that later came to Oradour, commanded by an SS captain named Kahn, murdered fifteen people: eleven hostages including an adolescent killed by a firing squad, a woman shot dead with a revolver, and three others hanged in front of the villagers. This massacre had powerful repercussions, thanks to the terror it instilled in the populace; was this not its aim? The Waffen SS, the SS police of the Gestapo and Security Service (SD), with Milice support, brought to the war in the West the brutal methods used against partisans in eastern Europe.

Of course Belgium, France, and the Netherlands had not been totally spared at the time of the German conquest in 1940: the SS massacre of eighty people at Oignies in the département of Pas-de-Calais on May 21, 1940, is proof of that. To the Germans' amazement, however, the early days of the Occupation passed by without real opposition in countries stunned by defeat, until the summer of 1941.[21] But by the end of 1941 a wave of attacks reminded the occupying power of guerrilla warfare: the concept of "cowardly criminals" attacking "from behind" to commit "treacherous murders." Von Stülpnagel, the commander in chief in Paris, viewed the assassination of a noncommissioned officer at the end of August as "a Judeo-Bolshevik provocation going hand in hand with the plutocrats." Jews and Communists were considered responsible for the actions of the Resistance, and for the attacks. "The diatribes launched against Judeo-Bolshevism bear witness to the depth of the convictions anchored in the political imagination of MBF officials."[22] Criminalization of the Communists and Jews allowed the German authorities to choose hostages, starting in 1941, for the first massive executions in France.[23] Applying this criminalization to the "bands" would be the principal theme of SS General Lammerding in his orders to the Das Reich division in early June 1944.

On June 5, 1944, he proposed an often-quoted program of repression to his operational chain of command, which accepted it.[24] In it we find a critique of the methods—judged ineffective—of local occupation headquarters, and an outline of seven points for strengthening repression. In practice, the "Lammerding method" applied once again the measures put in effect in Eastern Europe and behind the front lines in the struggle against the partisans, beginning in 1941.

The first point summarized the method: "Counter-propaganda and segregation, starting immediately, denouncing the terrorists as Communist troublemakers, activity aimed at setting the populace against the terrorists." The action of segregation was to be accompanied by massive preventive arrests; the occupation of areas and the combing of zones (in which his division was already being employed); the requisition of vehicles (the division lacked them); rewards for information obtained (not money, but promises to free prisoners); and brutal sanctions such as those expressed in the sixth point: "Announcing and executing the measure that for every German wounded and every German killed ten terrorists will be hanged (not shot). Execution by hanging is not normal in the French system of justice. By applying it to terrorists, the latter will be segregated and excluded from the community of Frenchmen."

The ratio of Germans killed to the number of hostages executed might vary according to the intensity of national resistance and the degree of "subhumanity" of the population concerned: fifty to one in Greece, a hundred to one in Yugoslavia. But Lammerding recommended a measure that heightened the segregation: hanging. Used massively by the Nazis in the Balkans and later in the USSR, in particular at Kharkov, it was an ignominious and supposedly degrading form of execution, because it was "unmanly." Utilized in earlier times against or by women,[25] as in the time-honored image of the Burghers of Calais,[26] this method of killing was no longer used in France. "The neck in the noose" connotes humiliation, submission—this way of putting people to death smothers or breaks the victim's body, as opposed to the body being "pierced" by a blade or a firing squad. The SS chief's objective was for such treatment to segregate the "bandits" in the eyes of the majority of the populace.

During combing operations the Waffen SS did not try to get at the maquis directly, but to segregate them by overrunning inhabited areas. In the Lot département they did not launch actions specifically against the maquis located in the forested areas north or west of Figeac. They were concerned with the towns and villages; if they went to Figeac and the surrounding villages, it was to put pressure on the inhabitants.

4 A Hot Spot

THE MASSIF CENTRAL

The Resistance, inspired by General de Gaulle's Radio London declaration at the time of the Allied landings in Normandy on June 6, 1944, strove to liberate the country. Their long pent-up energy could finally be unleashed. Still poorly equipped—large quantities of arms would not be parachuted to them until July—they had no military coordination. From June 6 onward, parachuted teams of allied SOE and OSS officers made contact with the maquis, but unified command for the Resistance forces was not achieved until the beginning of August. The Resistance groups were not suited for "open" combat: Georges Guingouin, the head of the largest maquis group in northern Corrèze and eastern Haute-Vienne and a clear-headed strategist, was aware of this.[1]

The Situation Deteriorates

By late May the Wehrmacht high command (OKW) in Berlin was clearly concerned about the Massif Central.[2] Headquarters maps showed German troops scattered, with a large empty space throughout the zone where the maquis were established. One report, dated June 5, 1944, described the situation as critical, particularly in the Limoges area:

> Strong rise in Resistance movement activity in southern France, particularly in the areas south of Clermont-Ferrand and Limoges. Apparently identical behavior by resistance groups in their fight against Germany, by rejection of internal political decisions; announcement of numerous enlistments in the secret army, due in part to force and threats, in part to pro-

> paganda against mobilization for labor in Germany. Concentrations of armed groups near Tulle and in the mountains of the Massif Central near Saint-Flour. Great terrorist activity in the département of Corrèze. Frequent attacks on trains, unreliable towns, and French administrations, pillaging of French businesses, thefts of vehicles and fuel, release of prisoner convoy from civilian train following an armed attack. . . . Powerful counter-attack being prepared with necessary forces and air support.[3]

Orders were then given to dispatch the units that were in the best shape for intervention, but the units stationed in the Southwest had only limited mobility.

The Das Reich division lacked at least half its nominal quota of armored and other vehicles. All of the division's units were affected by these shortages. One document offers us a glimpse of this weakness, with an inventory of the forces immobilized on June 8, when the SS division moved out.[4] Of a total force of more than 18,000 men, 9,500 remained in quarters because they lacked means of transport and armored equipment.[5]

At the same time, reports by the regional préfet stationed in Limoges indicated increased Resistance actions. From March to May 1944 the increase was striking: 593 actions in March, 682 in April, 1,098 in May. The administrative region included the départements in the Limousin (Corrèze, Creuse, Haute-Vienne), that of Dordogne, and all or part of départements south and east of the Demarcation Line.[6] The report for May also mentioned increased repression: on May 2 preventive arrests of general and upper-level officers of the former French army took place in Limoges; on May 18 the occupation of the town of Saint-Junien (west of Limoges, the administrative seat of the district in which Oradour-sur-Glane is located) by "numerous German police"—actually by the SS. This same report noted tersely: "Jews were more specially targeted, as usual." It did not mention the raid, carried out by the Limoges SS police on April 7, of Jews who had taken refuge in Eymoutiers, a district administrative seat east of Limoges in the heart of a zone controlled by Georges Guingouin's maquis.[7] The préfet noted, in a paragraph devoted to "Relations with troops and operations": "Distressing incidents, though isolated in nature, are to be regretted here and there: rapes, thefts of varying importance."[8]

Starting in March, the climate hardened, particularly in the Dordogne. That month's report referred to a bloody repression that "literally terrorized the Brantôme, Mussidan, Terrasson, and Ribérac area:[9] shootings, arrests, fires, and pillaging followed one after the other. . . . Among the reports gradually reaching people in the area, a report of the double execution—as a reprisal—of twenty-five people interned in Limoges and twenty-three other detainees in Périgueux has stirred up very deep feelings. The details that are now known of what must be called mopping-up operations add to a disturbing reversal of opinion." The regional préfet indicated that he was not in control of the situation and that the SS, Gestapo, and SD were able to remove detainees from prisons and execute them as hostages. They were making no mistakes as to their targets: that was how Georges Dumas, the head of the Mouvements unis de la Résistance and the Libération-Sud in Haute-Vienne, was executed.[10] The local SS commands took over basic local authority, handing part of it over to the Milice, which, protected by the SS, arrested the Limoges superintendent of police and other officials in early June.[11]

The préfet regretted "proceedings against defenseless civilians."[12] Was this a premonition? He would soon face an extension of such "proceedings." New measures seemed necessary to the OKW, which from Berlin "gave the order to the command on the western front and the military governor for France, on June 6, to take measures to remedy this danger behind the coastal defenses."[13] The expected landings had not yet begun.

One of the measures concerned placing the former Vichy zone, declared a war zone, under German control. Public notices and orders from the préfets informed people of the new restrictions. The notices were dated June 10, 1944.[14] They would not be in time to arrive in Oradour. For the occupying forces, June 10 marked a new phase of combat in the West, putting into effect the methods used in the East. SS General Lammerding, who had arrived in France four or five weeks earlier, made it known that he was ready. And he was not the only one convinced that it was necessary to act "harshly."

Blaskowitz, a Wehrmacht general commanding army group G in Toulouse who was for a time Lammerding's operational superior, justified the new war methods intended to "segregate" the Resistance.

> The terrorists' fight against the German Wehrmacht and German organizations falls under the category of sniper activity; this has been noted unambiguously and brought to the public's attention by the Vichy government. The result is that there can be only one duty for the French people, which consists not only of distancing themselves, but of making it impossible for these groups to fight. . . . Disguised as peaceful citizens, terrorists act by surprise ambushes and sabotage. The German Wehrmacht must defend itself against this type of combat with all means in its power. If in so doing *it must resort to methods of combat that are new to* Western *Europe,* it must be noted that the terrorists' fighting by means of ambushes is also something new by Western European standards. . . . Complete prevention of innocent blood falling victim to bullets—strictly speaking, inevitable in such underhanded fighting, where it is impossible to distinguish friend from foe—will be possible only if the French authorities and French people, on their own, render the *terrorists' combat* impossible.[15]

This ponderous, pedantic note was addressed on June 17, 1944, to the regional préfet of Toulouse, Sadon, who had protested to the German authorities following a massacre of hostages committed on June 10 at Marsoulas, in Haute-Garonne, by a unit of Waffen SS troops (the Deutschland regiment). It was written after the Oradour massacre. On the morning of June 10 a unit swept an area on the border between the Haute-Garonne and Ariège départements. This small squad "visited" several villages in its own fashion. Arriving in

Marsoulas, it was greeted by gunfire from the church tower. The Waffen SS troops deployed immediately, flushed out the maquis fighters, and assembled the populace: twenty-eight hostages were immediately singled out and executed. Two of the three maquis members were killed, but the list of victims does not give their names.[16] The lone survivor, held responsible for the massacre by the local people, has been excluded from every commemorative ceremony held by the village since then. Might this not be taken as a sign of the effectiveness of the Nazis' "segregation"?

On June 7, 1944, the Das Reich division still had not moved. That day it received the order to move out. Toward the Allied landing front in Normandy, as was later believed? Not at all. On June 5, the fifty-eighth armored corps approved a note from Lammerding with the same date to "clean out the area where the bands are operating between Cahors, Aurillac, and Tulle."[17] Pending confirmation of this mission, the SS division busied itself around Figeac, south of Cahors, near Villefranche, and around Montauban: a house set afire here, a prisoner "interrogated," six houses dynamited, a munitions dump seized elsewhere. On the night of June 8, the SS division received orders to move out immediately:

> The development of the situation with the bands in the Massif Central requires undertaking an immediate, brutal strike with powerful forces. . . . The second SS armored division is to be assembled immediately and brought into the Tulle-Limoges sector. In this sector, apparently the creation of large bands. . . . Upon its arrival in the Tulle-Limoges sector, the division is to contact the command of the sixty-sixth reserve corps in Clermont-Ferrand and will receive further orders from them. In the framework of combat engagements, we particularly need to requisition motor vehicles and fuel reserves as agreed to by liaison headquarters, and to make them available for greater troop mobility. In the case of special situations that might arise, we ought to provide for the speediest possible return to active duty of all participating troops for other missions.[18]

The Das Reich division did not have all its equipment fully available; it lacked vehicles and fuel. The vague, operational chain of command, with the undefined reserve army in Clermont-Ferrand, gave the SS general sent to the Tulle and Limoges area considerable freedom in the application of his program. Might he have awaited orders—from a reserve general officer whose ineffectiveness he sharply criticized? Moreover, the division might be called on to change its objective at any moment. As of June 8, the Allies' landing in Normandy was not yet being considered the only new front. Was a trap not to be feared? While awaiting confirmation, the SS division had to clean up the "Tulle and Limoges" sector where the Resistance, starting a new phase, was coming out of hiding and going into "overt" action against occupation troop garrisons.

There was some urgency. On June 6, Saint-Amand-Montrond had already been liberated, but at first the Resistance fighters were facing only the Milice. On June 7, liberation actions were carried out at La Souterraine, where the German garrison was surrounded. Ussel, in Corrèze, was under siege. Guéret, the préfecture of the Creuse, Argenton-sur-Creuse (Indre), Confolens (in the "free" sector of Charente), Bellac, and Saint-Junien (Haute-Vienne) were overrun by Resistance forces. In Bergerac the military hospital called for aid. Issoudun, in the Indre, was liberated on June 9. For the occupation forces, the situation was growing worse on all sides.

Leaving the Montauban region on the night of June 8, a combat group of Waffen SS incorporating all the operational units of the Das Reich division, about 8,500 men, sought to comb a territory over two hundred kilometers long, from south of Cahors to Argenton. An advance detachment arrived in Tulle on the night of June 8.

Earlier the Der Führer regiment had been covering a broad sector. Heading north up National Road 20, the unit cleared a security zone sixty to eighty kilometers wide. This regiment had been reconstituted in order to be operational: only two battalions were available (the first and third), so Battalion 1 of the Deutschland regiment was added to them. Heading the column, this formation left behind a bloody trail. In Albussac, Bretenoux, Cahors, Carsac, Carlux,

Calviac, Cressensac, Gabaudet, Gourdon, Grolejac, Noailles, Peyrilhac, Rouffignac, Saint-Céré, Souillac (in the Lot, Corrèze, and eastern Dordogne départements), more scenes of violence than brief clashes took place: random executions, houses or hamlets set on fire, looting.[19] On several occasions Resistance fighters encountered the Waffen SS in impromptu engagements that they were unable to sustain.

Guingouin avoided confronting the German forces, except in chance encounters (the taking of an armored vehicle, the capture of an SS officer). But then came the shock of Tulle.

The Attack on the Town of Tulle

According to the département préfet, the area around Tulle "suffers directly from the state of anarchy that terrorism has plunged it into, and indirectly from the armed forces' repression."[20] At the beginning of April, the city and its surroundings had undergone a combing operation by a special formation that the préfet designated as "motorized division B." This was a group composed of an infantry battalion, the 799th (the "Georgians"), and a battalion of the 95th security regiment, commanded by a general named Brehmer. From April 1 to April 7, for the préfet "the bloody week," the Tulle area experienced almost three thousand arrests and one hundred fifty executions, including mayors and town clerks. There was a massacre in the township of Lonzac, with seventeen victims and twenty-four houses burned down. Three hundred people arrested in Brive were sent to forced labor in Germany. Was the capture on March 28, by men in Georges Guingouin's maquis group, of three German vehicles transporting inspectors of the Armistice Control Commission the reason behind the Brehmer division's combing operation? The Brehmer unit left the Corrèze in May after carrying out another hundred or so arrests and requisitions of vehicles.

The maquis fighters possibly imagined they were putting a stop to people's suffering. The attack on Tulle, where the German garrison consisted of only two companies (around 400 men), was within their scope. The FTP decided to attack on June 7. They were supposed to be joined by groups of the AS (the Secret Army), but these did not show up. Nonetheless the FTP, which outnumbered the enemy, took control of the town after a fight that was bloody for the occupation troops. They did not set up an external alarm system, however. In the heat of battle and taking power, they had no warning of the arrival of a Waffen SS unit sent out specially. Taken by surprise, they withdrew, abandoning the town. Tulle was then subjected to a repression like the ones in the East.

A notice from the SS general, who set up his field headquarters in one of the town's hotels, informed the inhabitants that, given the number of German dead, "120 maquis fighters and their accomplices will be hanged. Their bodies will be thrown into the river."[21] The SS chose hostages from among several hundred men whom they had herded into the courtyard of the arms factory. The hangings, in groups of ten, from balconies and streetlights, ceased at 99 victims. Was it the intervention of a priest, Father Espinasse, who was attending to the hostages, or perhaps the hangmen's fatigue that put an end to these executions?

The hanged men of Tulle were not those days' only victims: twenty men, railroad "line guards," were shot by firing squads. Of the 360 people arrested and taken off to prison in Limoges, almost 200 would be deported. But this was learned of only much later, in 1945. More than 200 inhabitants of Tulle died from the repression and its consequences. That might have set a gruesome record.

In a way the SS general achieved his objective, which was to segregate the Resistance and terrorize the populace. The préfet in Tulle wrote to the Vichy government: "The senselessness of the 'maquis' and its Tulle enterprise, which even the most moderate call folly, has earned deep resentment from every segment of the populace. Anger against the 'maquis,' which is guilty of drawing a bolt of lightning down on the community, is unusually strong; the horror inspired by the Germans' reactions has caused a rift between my citizens and the occupying troops that will be difficult to close. . . . A mindless choice has led to the slaughter of innocents, of Milice sympathizers, and even of Waffen SS candidates."[22] The "deep resentment" and "anger" of the people "against the maquis," considered responsible for the repression, would have been proof to the SS general if it was still needed that his methods were correct. He wrote this down the next day, and his troops demonstrated it once again. Once again he would become a "bolt of lightning."

In the chancellery of the Nazi Party in Berlin, the disturbances in the Limousin were taken seriously, according to a report of June 13, 1944: "From Limoges a significant deterioration of the situation in the area has been noted, due to an increase in terrorist activity. In the départements of Corrèze and Dordogne the terrorists have apparently gained the upper hand. The southern part of the Indre [département] and the town of Guéret have been taken over by 'bands.' In the cities of Périgueux, Brive, and Limoges terrorist attacks are expected imminently."[23] Once again there was a state of emergency.

The Waffen SS in Limoges

They arrived quickly. On June 9, they occupied the entire "Tulle and Limoges" zone, where they were to deploy for "cleanup." Der Führer regiment staff headquarters were set up in a hotel on Place Jourdan in the center of Limoges, with four "regimental" companies nearby. Three battalions surrounded the city.

The garrison's weakness was a source of anxiety for the occupation officials. A man named Speck is representative of the labor administration, run by an influential Nazi named Sauckel, which maintained a degree of independence. Its task—maintaining an inventory of workers to be assigned to businesses or sent off to work in Germany—was complicated by the upsurge in Resistance activities. A document dated June 15, 1944, gives us insight into Speck's state of mind, which may be supposed to resemble that of the other occupying forces.

> Railways have been sabotaged in various places, as have telephone and telegraph lines in hundreds of places. Recently terrorist bands have already been mobilizing their units. . . . With the onset of the invasion, they have been systematically attacking German occupation troops. . . . Bloody fighting has developed in sectors near Périgueux and Tulle. According to what we have been able to learn here, an attack on Limoges was planned for the night of June 10. Because of the presence of Waffen SS units relieving the city of Tulle, this announced attack was thwarted. . . . Since no troops—apart from a "home defense" company—have been quartered in Limoges itself, aside from a police battalion that has been constantly involved in combat against the bands in liaison with the SD, it would have in all likelihood been impossible to hold the city.[24]

We have to bear in mind that this garrison may have feared a maquis attack on Limoges during the night of June 10; the numerical weakness of the garrison, which was composed of older soldiers and staffed by elderly officers often from the reserves or recovering from wounds and "ready for discharge," would not have allowed it to hold out.[25] Examples from neighboring towns confirmed this pessimistic forecast. The poor state of the German garrisons aroused anger in the youngest, most dynamic SS general, Lammerding. He would show these "slackers" and walking wounded—unable, according to him, to hold on to their territory—how to go about it, and quickly.

On the night of June 9, the Waffen SS division received an order to go to the front opened by the Normandy invasion and to move out on June 11 at 1200 hours.[26] This order, which had been expected for two days, might have come at any time, but it complicated the SS chief's task: how was he to get to a front with troops divided into two groups several hundred kilometers apart? Even worse, more than half his troops lacked any means of transportation. As an added humiliation, these immobilized troops had to requisition or beg vehicles from local staff headquarters, for whom the

SS had the utmost scorn. A further cause of anger was that the vehicles and tanks of his combat group were experiencing breakdowns that were proving impossible to repair for lack of spare parts. In short, before leaving this region infested with "bandits," they had to wait for essential spare parts—motors, ball bearings, and so on—that the division did not have.

The SS division lacked fuel, which it found hard to get through the tangle of railway lines that had been cut, repaired, and cut again. Once it left for the "Tulle and Limoges area," the division did not have the reserves to make its way four hundred kilometers to Normandy. In addition to the confusion that is normal for any military unit, there were problems created by the "bandits," the lack of logistical planning by local staff headquarters, and the inconsistencies of the high command that had sent it to pacify an area.[27]

The impossible cannot be asked of a scattered division in the process of being reformed and with recruits in training. Since they had to wait and not move out for two days, at least they would try to clean up their current occupation zone. Angry to say the least, SS General Lammerding let this be known to his chain of command, which he held responsible for this negligence, and to make it quite clear, he sent a copy to the Waffen SS offices in Berlin:

> The division's combat potential has been disproportionately reduced by insufficient motorized equipment, extensive movement over quite unfavorable terrain, dispersal of units over three hundred kilometers, and insufficient coordination of planning with respect to operations and supplies. Sixty percent of our tanks and thirty percent of our tow-trucks and half-tracks are down. The majority of these out-of-service vehicles cannot be made mobile until we have received first-line replacement parts that are still missing despite repeated requests. . . . Sufficient fuel supplies depend exclusively on trains, which to date still have not put in an appearance. Transfer on time toward Normandy can be undertaken by the division only if it has rolling stock at its disposal. The condition of tanks and

> traction vehicles necessitates repairs that will take at least four days. As a precondition, the specially announced replacement parts must arrive by the morning of June 11. The complete paralysis of railway traffic that the terrorists have achieved by that very fact does not allow loading before such time. . . . The Figeac-Clermont-Ferrand zone is under the terrorists' firm control. Local German services and troops are shut in and besieged most of the time, in some places destroyed up to corps level.[28]

The terrorists had rendered the authorities of the French State completely helpless.[29] "The German posts' incompetence borders on the disgraceful. Unless someone takes firm control, the situation in this zone will be dangerous to a degree that has not yet been appreciated to its full extent as of the present time. A new Communist State is being created at this very moment in this zone; it is governing shamelessly and headed toward planned tax levies."[30]

It could not be better stated: lightning was going to strike somewhere. Numerous incidents and the fighting with the "bandits" explain the SS general's ill-temper.

Harassment and Repression

The record of engagements between German troops and the Resistance in the days preceding the massacre at Oradour is spotty. Several incidents are known. There was an attack on a truck on Route Nationale 147 northwest of Limoges. At Le Dorat (also northwest) fighting left German casualties. There was an encounter at Dournazac (south). At Sainte-Anne-Saint-Priest, a borough of Châteauneuf-la-Forêt, one armored car was captured, one Waffen SS soldier was killed, another was taken prisoner. Waged by various Resistance groups, these operations were motivated by a desire to fight and drive out the occupying forces. They constituted active, though not concerted or coordinated, replies to the appeal by General de Gaulle who, on June 6, had urged the French to carry out "harassing" combat "everywhere and on every occasion" in order to liberate the nation's territory. Because of the absence of coordination and, for some, a lack of experience in armed combat, Resistance fighters did not all have an equal appreciation of the risks, particularly those run by the unengaged populace.

An SS general under pressure could not be happy with a day like June 9, filled with unpleasant incidents. The next one promised to continue in the same vein and be just as difficult. The "Division Agenda for June 10, 1944," makes this clear:

> 1. The "bandits" are terrorizing the Brive-Clermont-Ferrand-Limoges sector, preventing German forces and the French State's organizations from functioning.
> 2. The division is cleaning the sector up quickly and lastingly, in order to free itself more quickly to get back to normal fighting order or full employment against the invasion.

Consequently, it was necessary to free up the main traffic routes, to ensure "clearing the territory situated between these routes of Resistance groups and supply depots of all sorts," and to destroy "parachuted troops." Allied SOE groups had recently been parachuted in to organize resistance and take delivery of weapons. Other groups (known as Jedburghs) specializing in sabotage actions were also arriving. The division had to get the German and French forces back into operation, a considerable task for an SS unit that was itself being "put back in shape." The agenda, three pages long, included an appendix concerning the "situation of the bands and the direction taken by fighting." It specified: "The bandits are in firm, complete control of the Figeac-Clermont-Ferrand-Limoges-Gourdon zone, only partially occupied until now by German troops. The bands located there are exclusively Communist in character. The small number of Secret Army forces also go along with the Communists. They are to be considered bandits. All measures, orders, and so on, must have as their *aim to set the civilians against the bandits* and to make our action stand out in the eyes of the French populace as one of pacification. *The danger represented by these bandits may give rise to effects of considerable scope, if we do not succeed in denying them any semblance of patriotism and marking them as highway bandits."*[31] This idea, repeated in the June 10 note already cited, included the entire Resistance in a bloc as "Communist bandits," to be segregated as criminals responsible for uprisings and therefore for reprisals.

On June 9, Battalion 1 arrived in Rochechouart, the sous-préfecture of western Haute-Vienne, and in Saint-Junien, the département's most important town after Limoges (as already noted, before the war it had a Communist administration). Saint-Junien had been under siege since the day before. A Wehrmacht unit that had come from Limoges on June 8 was quickly relieved. Its arrival in a city without permanent occupation troops had been prompted by the appearance of about 300 maquis fighters, who occupied the city for a few hours and derailed a train on a bridge over the Vienne. With rail traffic shut down, travelers had to walk to the station to continue their journey. German soldiers, probably transferred from Angoulême (the administrative seat of Charente) for health reasons, were greeted with machine-gun fire as they got off their train. At least one soldier was killed, but the exact number is not known, as they gathered up the dead and wounded. When the liaison staff in Limoges (the equivalent of a command headquarters) was notified, it sent a security unit. After they left, the Waffen SS took over the city and patrolled the streets. After establishing a curfew, they shot at will at anything that moved. Great tension reigned in the city. "The night was often disturbed by patrols and shots being fired," noted a secret police report.[32] On the morning of June 10, an SS soldier of French origin went with a noncommissioned supply officer to buy Michelin maps.

Other units of the Der Führer regiment were sent on June 9 toward the "hot spots" on the outskirts of Limoges. A scout company raced north to Argenton-sur-Creuse and drove out the Resistance forces. The number of casualties of this lightning strike came to thirty-three inhabitants killed on the spot and fourteen prisoners taken to Limoges and executed in a place known as the Malabre

Quarries. South of Limoges we find Battalion 1 of the Deutschland regiment temporarily attached to the Der Führer regiment; it arrived at Nexon with the intention of taking away the camp's internees.[33] The Waffen SS arrived too late: the camp had already been overrun by a Resistance group that had freed the detainees.

East of Limoges, Der Führer Battalion 3 moved out toward Guéret to recapture the town: a Wehrmacht company from Montluçon had been beaten off. On June 9 an entire battalion returned; with aerial support it managed to take control of Guéret. When the Waffen SS arrived the town had calmed down again; since their presence seemed superfluous, they moved on without doing further damage—as they were to do elsewhere. The Resistance had, in fact, withdrawn and taken along part of the German garrison. Since they could not have left the sector, search efforts began. During the combing operation that ensued, the Waffen SS came across a truck with a group of Resistance fighters. Inside the township of Janaillat in the Creuse département, on National Route 140 twelve kilometers north of Bourganeuf, at a place known as Poteau de Combeauvert, twenty-nine members of the maquis were shot by an SS battalion Commanded by SS Commander Kämpfe.

After this execution was carried out, was the commander in a hurry to get back to Limoges? He left by himself in his vehicle—a requisitioned convertible—ahead of his troops. At a crossroads, totally by surprise, he came across a car full of maquis. They captured him to take him to their leader. The group, part of Georges Guingouin's maquis, was commanded by a sergeant named Canou. For lack of a second driver, he had to abandon the convertible. French military justice later investigated this affair: "At nightfall, SS Commander Kämpfe, the head of the 3rd Battalion, ventured out alone in a small car ahead of his convoy. On arriving at the village of La Bussière, about twelve kilometers north of Bourganeuf on RN 140 in the Creuse département, he was captured. . . . He was taken to the nearby town of Cheissoux and executed the next day, June 10. . . . Commander Kämpfe's capture served as a pretext for a whole series of reprisals."[34]

The SS battalion's war diary rather tersely noted the circumstances of its commander's disappearance: "An SPW found the commander's vehicle on the right-hand side of the road, completely stripped, with the ignition light on. The commander had a ten-minute advance. Immediate action by reconnaissance patrols proved fruitless."[35] The account does not mention immediate random reprisals that cost the lives of two peasants seen nearby.

Search operations resumed the next day, aimed at finding the men of the Guéret garrison also. An exchange was considered: detainees from the Limoges prison for the Waffen SS officer. The go-between, a truck driver from Eymoutiers, was sent to contact Georges Guingouin, identified as the only man capable of interceding, but he did not succeed in negotiating with him. The maquis leader ordered the execution of the Waffen SS officer, who had been responsible for numerous harsh measures.[36] An SS captain named Werner, an adjutant of the SS colonel commanding the regiment, quickly replaced him as head of the battalion on June 12. In the Das Reich division's saga, Kämpfe would be considered as "fallen in France."[37] His body was never found. As they were leaving for Oradour, the Waffen SS officers told their men they were going to look for an officer who had disappeared; this reason was repeated before witnesses by Waffen SS men on the outskirts of town.[38]

The day before, on the afternoon of June 9, an SS supply officer and his escort arranged billets west of Limoges in the Nieul sector about ten kilometers northwest between Limoges and Saint-Junien. (These were the billets that would be occupied by Battalion 1, coming from Saint-Junien, starting at 10 o'clock that night.) In Peyrilhac, a village near Nieul, the SS officer encountered a GMR detachment from Limoges, which captured him. They were deserting and joining the maquis in the Monts de Blond, south of Bellac and north of Oradour. Along the way, taking advantage of the GMR men's lack of experience, the SS officer, who himself was quite experienced, managed to get away. By following a rail line, he arrived in Limoges at dawn. He would tell, or more likely he was asked to tell, of a route that had him passing through a town named Oradour (there are several of them in Haute-Vienne). This story—known as "the Gerlach affair" from the SS man's name—would fill in the cracks of an argument that, according to the Nazis, could "justify" the massacre. It would later be the source of certain rumors.[39] However, not one statement by those accused in the affair mentions this reason, at the time they left Saint-Junien.

Preparations for a "Brutal Operation"

For SS General Lammerding and his Waffen SS, the situation in Limoges and the surrounding region must have seemed unmanageable, with the endemic weakness of the German troops (except for the all-too-aggressive SS police), the powerlessness of the Vichy forces, and the constant threat of Communist-tendency "bandits" joining together (preparing to govern, according to the Nazis). Furthermore, Lammerding had orders to withdraw and go to the front. Since the local troops had reached a "disgraceful" level of ineffectiveness, was it not obviously his duty as an SS officer and party member to show them the road to follow and the validity of his method? "Without a brutal operation" there would soon be a "Communist state." And so he must act as he had in the East. The feeling may well have been widely shared at various upper echelons of the Waffen SS chain of command, which must have found it hard to resist the pressures on them. A "brutal operation" did not require any specific order. Presented as necessary, it was ipso facto authorized: it was in line with one of the chief's wishes. And so, as in the East, it depended on a unit commander's decision, in accordance with the circumstances he encountered or created.

The massacre at Oradour was prepared in advance. From the story told by a Milice man on duty in Limoges, we know of three meetings.[40] Camille Davoine, a young Milice member from the Nord, born in 1918, was for several months in the entourage of Darnand, the head of the Milice, who had been named Minister of State for Maintaining Order.[41] As a member of then-Lieutenant Darnand's company he fought under his orders on the front at Forbach.[42] He was a hairdresser in Nice when Darnand, as Secretary General of the Milice, called him to Vichy in April 1943 to serve as his orderly. Davoine came to Limoges as a Milice member and Police Inspector for Jewish Questions in May 1944. During the same period, Darnand, on a visit to Limoges, had a man named Jean Filliol released from the camp at Saint-Paul d'Eyjaux, southeast of the city, where he had been interned on orders from Laval.[43] Darnand then named Filliol head of the second section of the Milice—the "action and intelligence" section. Filliol became a representative of Maintaining Order in Limoges.

In May 1944, under the orders of his "chief" at Jewish Questions and with his "colleagues," Davoine directed and carried out confiscations "during our operations against the Jews." At the same time the SS police—with whom Jewish Questions closely collaborated—received from its Paris hierarchy (Brunner's service) an order to close down the office of the Union générale des israélites de France, which was still operating in Limoges.[44] On this occasion it was recommended to turn the office into a trap to capture people who showed up. "Check whether the office still exists and if so, arrest the Jews and transfer the files found there to Drancy. It would probably be a good idea to stay in the office for a few days, to catch any Jews who show up."[45] Throughout the month of May 1944, panic reigned among the Jews of Limoges.[46] The Milice helped this along by unannounced "visits." They threatened or expelled people in order to "requisition" their lodgings, which they then kept for themselves.

Davoine, a twenty-five-year-old member of the Milice and Inspector for Jewish Questions, attended one "Friday evening meeting on June 9, 1944, around nine in the evening, [when] chief 'Falchi' [*sic*] of the second service of the Milice assembled us, and at the 'Havillon' (read Haviland) police station assigned us to go with the Germans right the next morning. It was Deschamps, in reality Fiol [*sic*], more particularly in charge of tracking down parachuted war matériel, etc., and arresting Gaullists or maquis types, who did the talking. In substance he said: 'There will be an operation in the area carried out by a German division. We are going to split into four groups[']—as far as I can recall exactly—[']with our mission to make sure the German troops don't go overboard.'" In December 1944, Davoine, held in the Limoges prison, was interrogated as witness to an affair where he had every interest both in being confused and in downplaying his participation, revealing only bits and pieces, hoping they would not end up being used against him. His interview tallied fairly well with those of a Gestapo collaborator named Patry, who would confirm the sequence of events. Patry, born in Alsace in 1915 and a former member of a GMR from which he had been expelled, was at the time of these events a paid interpreter for the SS police and liked to strut about in a German uniform.

The day after this meeting, at nine a.m. on June 10, a squad of five Milice members pulled up in a vehicle outside the building where the Der Führer regiment's staff headquarters were located. There they found some SS policemen who had come to set up the operation with the Waffen SS, and also Patry, attaché to an SS police lieutenant. At 10 o'clock they moved out together on the road to Saint-Junien in an escorted convoy with several trucks. Davoine, of course, "did not know" this SS officer "in uniform." Patry later said it was a Gestapo official named Kleist.[47] Arriving in Saint-Junien, the SS policeman went to consult with the Waffen SS officers of the battalion in a hotel across from the railroad station. The collaborators claimed they waited for orders without taking part in the meeting, which allegedly lasted "around two hours." As he left, Kleist, the SS man who according to Patry came to "get instructions from SS headquarters, [allegedly stated that] the 'maquis' had attacked a vehicle with twelve SS men in it, including a lieutenant who was taken prisoner; they were taken to Oradour-sur-Glane and hanged, except for the lieutenant, who managed to escape."[48] It is obvious that Patry was making things up. His depositions show that he did so habitually, and his stories need to be checked out: the account in fact contains distorted elements of the "Gerlach affair." He added that he "did not want to follow the commander of these SS men because he intended to go and exact forty hostages at Oradour-sur-Glane, and did not want to be present at these executions. It had been arranged that our car and the one with the four (or probably five) Milice men in it would follow the SS detachment on that occasion." For his part, Davoine saw the "German column . . . ; the troops were in field uniform with their sleeves rolled up, armed with various kinds of equipment, wearing camouflage raincoats."[49]

Around 1:30 p.m., two Waffen SS columns left Saint-Junien. The larger one headed east. A French forced draftee told this story: "On Friday, June 9, we arrived in Saint-Junien with the entire battalion. In the town we were told that the maquis were going to attack and so we had to patrol it all night. On the morning of Saturday, June 10, we took it easy in a hotel. We had our noon meal and around one p.m. we were ordered to fall in and sent off in a convoy toward Oradour-sur-Glane. Sturmbannführer Diekmann, the head of the first battalion, was in command of our company. He sat in an armored half-track (SPW). He headed up the convoy, and next to him was Hauptsturmführer Kahn, who commanded our company, the third."[50]

Another battalion company, the first, left heading west and arrived in Saillat, about ten kilometers from Saint-Junien, on the border of the Charente département. The SS policemen and Milice later said they went to Saillat, where there was a paper mill. They did not specify that "drafted" foreigners were working in a Foreign Workers' Group there under Vichy supervision. According to Patry (who tended to "embellish"), "the troops surrounded the town. A decision (without further details) had been made that workers in a small local factory would be executed because the director of the factory had been reported supplying gas and oil to the 'French maquis.' . . . Eventually men and women workers were assembled and interrogated. The director and a young man were beaten by the SS men and a man named Simon (a Milice member), in particular the young man, who lost a lot of blood."[51] Other "witnesses" added that there might have been at least one dead among the workers. This was confirmed by an SS soldier responsible for surveillance at the factory, who added: "In any case, I know that this factory, a paper mill, must have employed around 150 workers, of whom 75 were connected with the maquis. I saw one of them killed by a burst of machine-gun fire right in the gut . . . and another worker severely wounded by a rifle bullet in the back."[52] It is not known who informed the SS soldier of the paper-mill workers' resistance activities; on the other hand, he did see the dead and the wounded.

The expedition ended around five p.m., and everyone returned to Saint-Junien except part of the first SS company, which was sent from Saillat to Aixe-sur-Vienne.[53] Why did this town get a brief "visit" from the Waffen SS troops? The next morning they left for Nieul without carrying out any acts of violence against the people, at least as far as our documentation shows. As in Saillat, there was a Groupement de travailleurs étrangers [Foreign Workers' Group] in Aixe-sur-Vienne. The GTE in Aixe had a particular history: it had been created by the transfer of the one from Oradour-sur-Glane. Foreign Jews who were assigned to Aixe and to Sereilhac might still have had links with the village of Oradour.[54]

Could this method used by the Waffen SS, of tracking foreigners in the places where they were assigned residence, be an indication of what they were looking for?[55] The population of "draftees"—an administrative term used by Vichy offices—in the GTE of Haute-Vienne was mostly composed of Spanish refugees and Jews of various nationalities, or who had been deprived of their own. These refugees fitted in with the Nazis' idea of Communist "bandits" and Jews, to be segregated—those who, making up "criminal bands," must be "cleaned out," liquidated, or sent to work in Germany.

On their return to Saint-Junien, the Milice checked passengers at the railroad station and on a train, then went to a café with the SS police and their interpreter: standard procedure. Then the squad awaited the order to move out for Nieul, where the battalion regrouped for the night with the unit that had gone on its "mission" to Oradour. They arrived very late; since the battalion was short of trucks it had to requisition some on the spot to transport the kitchen, supply corps, and other services. The requisitioned trucks ran on wood-gas and were slow. If these trucks did not pass through

Oradour on their way out, as they would do empty on their way back, did the Milice pass through there at night? They later claimed they did not: they had not gone via Oradour. But a gap in their evening schedule remains unexplained. Patry contradicted himself several times. For his part, Davoine was cautiously vague. However, a farmer from La Barre (between Oradour and Saint-Junien) saw civilians riding in a sedan-type vehicle in a convoy coming from Oradour that evening.[56] The convoy was headed for Nieul, where the troops were billeted and where the Milice members stayed until the Waffen SS troops departed the following Monday morning.

Patry indicated that he had gone to Oradour with an SS policeman once in the afternoon and once in the evening, which might seem contradictory, given the distances to be covered; during the course of the inquiry he first confirmed and then denied this. A policeman, the boyfriend of a teacher who died in the massacre, happened upon him the following August in a Limoges café, commenting on pictures of the mass graves in Oradour.[57] Patry was a braggart and not too aware of the spot he was in; his defense strategy seems very weak. There was no need for proof of any sort of participation in the massacre for him to be convicted. The Limoges Court of Justice had an indictment file against him. He was sentenced to death on July 10, 1945, and executed in September. Davoine, sentenced to death by the same court, was later pardoned. After being set free, he disappeared.[58]

Three preliminary meetings have been identified and are known about from testimony included in police investigations. Particulars of the meetings (who participated, how many were there, what they said to each other) are still unknown, with the exception, however, of two things: the demand for hostages—a figure of forty was given after the Saint-Junien meeting—and the search for a missing officer. Supposedly the Waffen SS unit was to move out the next day, but as of 1:30 on the afternoon of June 10, it had been given neither its destination nor its itinerary. In any case, the SS chief did not appear ready to leave the region without "cleaning" it up in a "brutal operation."

As of June 10 the SS division had not yet received the spare parts requested. At 6:35 p.m. on June 11 "it is ready to start moving. The trainload of tanks is leaving from Périgueux. As to wheeled and half-track vehicles, travel by road is envisioned. Questions concerning the destination and route are as yet unanswered." At 9:36 p.m., they thought of loading the half-tracks on trains because of a lack of fuel, but the destination and travel route were still not spelled out. At 10:14 p.m. the spare parts were sent to Tulle; the stated time needed for repairs had to be taken into account before setting out. Information about the travel route was received at 10:32 p.m. on June 11: "For wheeled vehicles: Tours, La Flèche, Laval, Fougères. . . . The unit commander is to report to high command of the seventh army at Le Mans."[59] The division, at least those units stationed in the Limoges area, moved out on the morning of June 12. That same Monday morning, the Milice collaborators who had spent the night in Nieul returned to Limoges. General Krüger, commanding the eighteenth armored corps, sent his regards to Lammerding: "Most sincerely, my best regards to the renowned 'Reich' SS. I hope we shall meet again, to work together in the future once more."[60]

But almost 9,000 Waffen SS troops were still immobilized in the Toulouse area, where liaison staff headquarters employed them for combing operations.

The Waffen SS Butchers Leave for Oradour

The story told by one SS trooper: "We were ordered to move out, the entire company, not knowing what direction we would take. But they repeated we were to look for the chief of the third battalion, who had been captured under circumstances I'm not aware of. It was on arriving near a village that I saw a sign saying 'Oradour-sur-Glane.' . . . The battalion chief took over the operations himself, it was Diekmann (thirty-two years old), recently promoted to Sturmbannführer; Obersturmbannführer Adjutant Lange, a lieutenant . . . Captain Kahn, thirty-eight years old, heavy-set, with a proud bearing, a long face, cold stare, apparently from Hamburg. . . . The company was divided into several groups, each commanded by a non-commissioned officer and other ranks. My group chief was Tscheyge. The other noncoms were Rennert, Maurer, Nell . . . and Sergeant Boos, who was the only Alsatian noncom in the company and maybe the battalion, but also the meanest, and he seemed to have deep Nazi convictions."[61] By the time of his hearing in December 1944, this man, a forced draftee taken prisoner by the British and sent back to France with other Frenchmen in the same circumstances, had joined the Forces françaises libres [Free French Forces].

There were several in similar circumstances who were heard as witnesses. They described the officers: Second Lieutenant Barth, "twenty-five years old, fat, heavy-set, about five feet six, very knock-kneed, a really mean officer," who commanded the first section; and another second lieutenant named Klar, "twenty-eight or twenty-nine years old, about five feet five, sturdily built, tall, with a slight limp," who generally commanded the second section. But on that day, this SS officer was at regimental headquarters, which in order to function needed officers from the combat companies. He had been replaced at the head of his section by a noncommissioned officer. "On our way to Oradour, our company had 120 fighting men; the rest of the company was noncombat personnel, munitions men, clerks, cooks who had gone directly to Nieul." The total strength of the third company was 207 Waffen SS men, with a combat strength of 137 men divided into three sections.

The first section, commanded that day by Barth, comprised a command platoon and three combat platoons of thirteen men each. Each group had a chief with his adjutant as well as his driver, gunners and servers for two light machine guns (MG 42s), a sharpshooter with a rifle equipped with a telescopic sight, a gunner with a smoke-bomb launcher, and four men armed with carbines. The total was forty-seven Waffen SS soldiers.

The second section, commanded at Oradour by Staff Sergeant Töpfer, was made up of four platoons plus the command platoon. It had the same weapons as the first section, but with grenade-launchers replacing the smoke-bomb launchers. The fourth platoon, designated a "scout" platoon, was commanded by the French sergeant, Boos. The section total was fifty-eight Waffen SS soldiers.

The third section was commanded that day by Sergeant Rennert. It had heavy machine guns, higher-performance weapons with a greater range. There were only two platoons of heavy machine guns, each gun served by six men. The section total was thirty-two Waffen SS soldiers.

We must also include the command section of the company in whole or in part. We do not know its exact strength. Boos, who turned up as a prisoner in Great Britain in April 1947, indicated that about sixty men stayed behind in Saint-Junien. Since the full strength of the third company was 207 Waffen SS, we can infer the existence of a command platoon accompanying the SS captain. This platoon was commanded by an SS adjutant named Gnug, an explosives expert, who would play an important role. The company of Battalion 1 arrived at Oradour with around 150 Waffen SS men.

This was not all. There was also the battalion commander and his adjutant officer, SS Lieutenant Lange. These two officers did not move about unaccompanied. In "real strength," the command company of the battalion numbered five officers, twenty-two noncoms, and eighty-five soldiers: one hundred twelve Waffen SS men, of whom between a third and a half may have accompanied their commander.

So there were about 200 Waffen SS soldiers who suddenly appeared on the scene at Oradour. This figure seems to us closer to reality than the figure usually given, the 120 stated by the government commissioner to the military tribunal in Bordeaux in 1953.[62]

As they set out, with the troops surprised at leaving without their packs for a destination that had not been spelled out, Barth is said to have told the SS soldiers as they climbed into the trucks: "It's going to heat up; we'll see what these Alsatians can do!"[63]

5

Was Oradour Just an Ordinary Village?

It is not our intention to write a monograph on the village that disappeared.[1] *Using archives, we have been able to shed light on elements of the past that were marked as unimportant, were forgotten, or were overshadowed in the story as told by the "Oradour community." We have retained these elements because they set the village in the context of the times and constitute the markers for memory. When we set up the permanent exhibition at the Centre de la Mémoire, there was an agreement with representatives of the Oradour community that the expression "an ordinary Limousin village" might be used to characterize the former town. By "ordinary" we should understand "like other villages nearby," from which there were no major differences. This "convention" seemed essential in order not to alter the traditional reading. As to rural and Limousin references, they have the advantage of accounting for geographical reality; but they also denote the imagery of a certain culture, along with its economic, political, and social components.*

"It Is a Verdant Hollow by a Murmuring Stream"

Coming from Limoges we see the village on a hillside. To enter it you have to cross the bridge over the Glane.[2] Even if you do not see the stream right away, when it is hidden by trees or is too deep within its banks, you feel its presence and hear the sound of the water, over rocks worn by the current. Dammed here and there by a mill, it broadens out to follow the gentle curve of the hill. Thus the stream alternates lively movement and calm: in some places there are trout, perhaps pike, elsewhere tench, carp; there are small fry and at times crayfish everywhere. Fishermen of all ages have long known the paths along the banks, which are haunted by equally placid strollers as well. In the heat of summer people come to picnic and bathe—or rather, used to, as the custom seems to be fading today. On Thursdays children used to put broken bottles in the current to catch minnows.[3] Some people still come to fish, looking busy and a bit silent. Often they have enthusiasts' gear worthy of professionals. Fishing, the anglers' club, contests, and post-contest banquets mark local life. More than the Vienne, whose waters have for a long time been polluted, the Glane and its neighbor a little to the north, the Gartempe, have earned a solid reputation for good fishing. Keeping an eye on currents and eddies, anglers enjoy the scenery and seem to be listening to the silence, unlike the hunters who shatter it with their shots. Fishing, a solitary passion if not a passion for solitude, keeps its distance from noise and intruders. This is perhaps the prime source of Oradour's reputation for "peacefulness."

The Glane flows through a landscape that has remained much the same since the nineteenth century, as it was known and painted by Corot. Saint-Junien boasts of having a "Corot site" whose authenticity is vouched for by the town. Might one of the artist's drawings perhaps represent the "village square" of Oradour?[4] It has a curving perspective with a great oak tree in the foreground. This is unfortunately impossible: the great oak in Oradour was planted as a "Liberty tree" after the Revolution of 1848. It would not have had time to grow by Corot's day. He was probably drawing an "ideal" village.

Might nature be just "order and harmony," as Senancour asked? The question fits the natural environment of Oradour quite well. But he added, in *Oberman:* "Nature is felt only in human relationships. . . . The fertile earth, the immense skies, the fleeting rains are merely an expression of the relationships that our hearts produce and contain!"[5] Is it not our eye that creates a landscape? And do not the feelings that attract us to it make us see it, or see it again years later, as attaining perfection? The emotions of people who talk of the lost town are never feigned. They are not speaking only of Oradour, of course, but of what they lost there; even more, they are speaking of themselves in these places, whether they have dwelt there since childhood or only in passing. They see people on the doorstops or leaning on the windowsills, they hear the sounds of the village, the church bell ... Oradour belongs to those who remember it, then. It would have remained almost unchanged, for decades and decades, were it not for the ruins and the shifts in perspective they force us to see.

The landscape limits the horizon to the nearby hills, which are sliced through by the "tramway" as they are by the Glane. An "umbilical cord" with the city, the département railway set the beat of village life: everything arrived by it. A crossroads of memory, as much as the Glane, it entered service in 1911, later than in the neighboring départements, where it was powered by steam locomotives that were used until the lines closed. Haute-Vienne went immediately to electric power, a major step forward. This alternation of an archaic situation with another determinedly modern one is typical of the Limousin,[6] which is poor and isolated, far from important economic centers and without great appeal for those in power, but which recorded economic and social advances as a result of political struggles, strikes, and workers' solidarity.

At the northernmost limit of Occitanie, where the languages of *oc* and *oïl* meet, the Limousin is also a border area in its northern part, known as "La Marche."[7] In the days when the dukes of Guyenne and the kings of England contested the king of France's crown, mercenary bands stormed across the entire region. A king of England, Richard the Lion-Hearted, was killed in 1199 in the siege of his castle at Châlus in southern Haute-Vienne. A "Black Prince" mercilessly slaughtered the inhabitants of Limoges and the region in 1536, leaving marks passed down by local lore. These ancient barbarities faded away and are buried in the memories of the people. Does their distance in the past confirm the peacefulness associated with the environs and the village of Oradour? At the time of the Fronde, a lady of the court sought refuge "in her Limousin." Tallemant des Réaux recounts her "little story," as well as one about a certain "Monsieur d'Oradour" who was "also of the sect": the Oradour family were Huguenots at the time.[8]

Because of its border location, Oradour for a long time wavered between Aquitaine, Poitou, and the Limousin. The ancien régime retained complex powers by dispersing them as widely as possible; the Revolution brought order, rationality.[9] When it created the département of Haute-Vienne, the French Republic gained its inhabitants' loyalty. But the most important cultural heritage—along with language, which indelibly marked regional society—was its family organization, dominated by what is known as the "linear family."[10] This is characterized by the several generations living together under one authority (male or female) capable of assuring the transmission of property, without there being equality among the heirs. A "communitary" form of family organization, less often noted, complements the linear family in the region. Here, the authority of a parent over the family group is its principle, as well, but with one fundamental difference: equal sharing of the inheritance among the heirs. The Limousin and the border country where Oradour is located cling to these forms of organization of private life, based on respect for authority.

These authoritarian family structures allowed for development of "new ideas"—anticlericalism, pacifism, trade unionism, socialism, and later communism—in a rural setting that was not a priori very open. The culture, promoting an "among ourselves"[11] spirit that is powerful in the Limousin, was strengthened by these ideologies, and they themselves in turn adapted to this local feature. We will rediscover these components of social life—the principle of authority, the "among ourselves" spirit—reflected in the construction of the memorial center after the tragedy.

Denise Bardet, who was born in 1920 and died in the massacre, was a schoolteacher in Oradour, though she did not live there. She left fragments of a personal diary.[12] Among the primary themes she dealt with in it were nature, in which she loved to take walks, usually by herself or in the company of a quiet woman friend; the family, limited to close relationships with her mother and her brother; pacifism, which she hoped would emerge victorious thanks to the German authors persecuted by the Nazis; and decency, on which love and work have to be founded. An active young woman, she turned down marriage offers out of "decency" but also as her rejection of "authority." The young schoolmistress must have been totally opposed to the Vichy regime and the hopeless images of "Here we are, Marshal Pétain!"[13] An intellectual, decidedly modern in her approach to authority and her will to rise above the period of conflict with Germany, Denise Bardet counted on postwar reconciliation with the writers and artists she felt were the true representatives of the German people: "We must not confuse Nazi barbarity with Germany. . . . We must speak up for the names of today that are the hope and a hymn for the future: Thomas Mann, Bertolt Brecht, Anna Seghers, Lion Feuchtwanger." The list coincides with that of the writers expelled from Germany by the Nazis.[14]

Yet Germany represented the ancestral, hereditary enemy, an object of absolute hatred. The people of the Limousin were able to express an ineradicable "anti-Boche" culture.[15] First had come the Franco-Prussian War, then the Great War. How could they forget the ninety-nine Oradour-sur-Glane men who died in World War I? Could anyone have imagined worse? "In the prime of life," they were sorely missed. The village, like so many others, never recovered from it. The 1914–1918 war started a decline in the population and local agricultural economy. Surrounded by fiercely anti-German public opinion, Denise may have felt herself rather isolated. Among the people of Oradour she appears to be an exception. A "product" of Republic schools, she shows subtle signs of being an "emancipated woman" at a time when women had not yet gained the right to political citizenship in France.[16] She had acquired her convictions through work, clear-headedness, and precise thinking.

On the morning of June 10, Denise Bardet held class for her pupils. No teacher would have abandoned children in danger, so she remained with them. Her corpse was never identified. Camille, her younger brother, was in Limoges, awaiting the results of a competition to enter the département's Normal School. He was successful and later became a teacher in Oradour.

Economy and Politics in the Village

There were two main elements influencing the life of a town like Oradour-sur-Glane in Haute-Vienne in the years between the wars: the agricultural crisis, with its resulting decrease in population, and political stability under Socialist leadership. World War II altered both of these. Family subsistence agriculture played a role in non-market food supplies for city dwellers, and the Vichy government dismissed Socialist mayors—the Communist mayors had previously been relieved of office by the Daladier government—and replaced them with prominent pro-Pétain figures.

The agricultural land of the Limousin was poor. Unfertile soil produced meager cereal crops. Cattle raising was predominant on small-scale plots and minuscule landholdings. In the center of the township, the village grouped public and private services, shops, and craftsmen. Agricultural concerns were scattered throughout the small villages, run by farmers or tenants rather than owners. Fairs and the monthly markets set the rhythm of village life. They were a meeting place for farmers who came from outlying areas, walking in with their animals and carts to buy and sell. Fairs, a time for rewarding labor—or not rewarding it when prices fell—brought excitement. Ten or so cafés, restaurants, and hotels played an important part in the town's reputation. A drinking culture, with numerous cafés, some more elaborate than others, was a constant of village social life. For one whole day, labor in the fields was abandoned, though not in the stables, which had to be taken care of before dawn or upon return. The work of the soil required a large number of laborers—free of charge when it came to the family, and with very low wages where hired workers were concerned, since food and lodging figured in their salary. World War I losses deprived agriculture of these workers; the farmers' and tenants' inability to invest prevented making up for them with agricultural machinery. Livestock, in particular oxen and some horses, remained their source of draft power.

The economic crisis of agriculture in the 1920s and 1930s led a family-structured agriculture, generally at subsistence level and therefore uncompetitive, to adapt to markets and productivity. It brought about the disappearance of farmers who could not keep up. The villages, as the hamlets surrounding the towns were called, were steadily drained of their population, whereas the town centers remained stable or grew slightly. Oradour township's population dropped from more than 2,000 inhabitants around 1900 to 1,574 according to the 1936 census. This decrease was not a sign of good economic health.

The Socialists, and then from 1921 on the Communists, took up the defense of this rural world in crisis, a crisis that intensified between 1930 and 1935. It was not the falling price of wheat that most affected the Limousin farmers, since they did not produce much, but that of livestock raised for meat, because of the importance of cattle breeding. Over five years the price of beef cattle was cut in half; that of hogs fell by three-quarters. There were regularly between 6,000 and 7,000 unemployed workers in Limoges during this period, but the farmers' situation worsened even more dramatically. It was "the great poverty of the countryside," as Socialist député Vardelle, representing the second district of Haute-Vienne, wrote.[17]

The farmers went along with the words of the Socialists, who got a foothold in the municipalities of Limoges and Saint-Junien from the end of the nineteenth century onward. They developed union organizations and cooperative solidarity groups, which they accompanied with arguments for pacifism. International pacifism was to reconcile the national working classes. We know what came of that and how national bourgeoisies decided otherwise, for everyone. But the Socialists of Limoges maintained a critical stance toward the "Sacred Union" during World War I.[18] This pacifism persisted: another war was unimaginable. Complemented by references to the defense of agriculture, pacifist statements appealed to country folk, who were used to talk of the antagonisms between "small" and "big"—people who labored vs. those who did not (priests, nobles, absentee landlords, and so on), the "castle" vs. the others—much more than of ideology and the search for new groupings.

From the 1920s onward, as they undertook the conquest of rural townships, the Socialists found themselves competing—always doggedly, at times violently, at least in words—with the Communists. The Socialists manifested an unsubtle anti-Communism; and for Communists, the right wing began with the Socialists. The first antifascist committee appeared in Limoges in 1932 and was exclusively Socialist; the Communists organized and demonstrated separately. Their first unified demonstration took place on February 12, 1934. The Common Front of July 1934 did not arouse much enthusiasm among the Socialists, and the Communist Party's leadership criticized local officeholders who did not follow the Central Committee's line closely enough. Thanks to the Common Front, the local Communists' main interest was in getting incumbents reelected. The Socialists kept their majority in the département's general council.[19]

Withdrawal from candidacy among the parties of the left, in the municipal elections of 1935, resulted in the reelection of the incumbent mayors of Limoges, Saint-Junien, and Oradour, among others. As a result, all the Socialist candidates in the next senatorial races were elected. The legislative elections of the Popular Front sent all the Socialist candidates to the National Assembly. Their dominant position was strengthened even further in the 1937 local elections: of twenty-nine positions, the Socialists had fifteen town councillors, the Communists four, and moderate Radicals ten. A breakup of the parties of the left came in 1937 over questions of international politics and the expression of "absolute pacifism" by the Socialists. The far right was not absent from the local political landscape: Colonel de La Rocque came to Haute-Vienne in 1935. On June 2, he was in Aixe-sur-Vienne. The Croix-de-feu organized marches against the Communist municipalities of Eymoutiers and Saint-Junien, and a meeting in Limoges on November 16, 1935, ended in a pitched battle with shots exchanged.[20]

For decades members of the Desourteaux family had taken turns as mayors of Oradour. From father to son they seemed an obvious choice, as prominent doctors and conservative Republicans; campaign broadsides characterized them as "ministerial Radicals" favoring the governments of the Republic.[21] They probably showed moderate anticlericalism—no one could be elected in the Limousin without such a label. The Desourteaux benefited from a "political heritage" that let them succeed one another as mayors. Such was not the case of the man who beat Paul Desourteaux in the elections.

Some Socialists came on the city council in 1908, but they remained a minority until one of them, Joseph Beau, was elected in 1919. The new mayor was first a clogmaker then a grocer in town, and he published and sold postcards of the village.[22] He was not drafted during the war because of family responsibilities, as opposed to Paul Desourteaux, who headed a field hospital and was decorated with the Légion d'honneur. Joseph Beau was not a veteran, and this would have repercussions during the Vichy regime.

The new mayor was in the mainstream of Socialist officeholders: nonreligious, pacifist, and anticlerical, often Freemasons (a common way of selecting Socialist officeholders in the Limousin). Logically enough, he gave priority to the Republic's (that is, public) school, but the township's limited financial means did not allow for building a school complex.[23] The schools, scattered through the town, were given a movie projector, however, a sign of "modernity." The defense of nonreligious schools was rooted in straightforward anticlericalism. A veritable culture of anticlericalism opposed the mayor (with the majority of the residents) and the village priest. He, as it happened, was an old conservative priest who, it was said, viewed the coming of Marshal Pétain's regime as a blessing in a largely dechristianized rural milieu. The opposition between the two "clans" was not a harmless one.[24]

The township's annual holiday, *la frairie,* enjoyed considerable renown in the environs. It was traditionally held in August, with a great many festivities: merry-go-rounds, concerts, costume parades, uninterrupted dancing night and day, a bicycle race, a hot-air-balloon launch (clear signs of a certain paganism), without the Church appearing at any time. Limousin tradition, ignoring the Catholic church and mingling folk jubilation with symbols of progress, seemed solidly rooted and widely accepted. The August 1939 *frairie,* scheduled to last two full days, was canceled at the last minute. The next day the government declared war on Nazi Germany, which had invaded Poland. Mobilization immediately followed.

Whereas war memorials had been erected just about everywhere during the 1920s, several Limousin towns refused to do so. Some, out of pacifist ideology, conceived of memorials without any patriotic reference or at times with antimilitary connotations.[25] Oradour-sur-Glane, a Socialist town, did not construct a war memorial; was this meant to signify that the war was foreign to the local situation? As in Saint-Junien, a Communist municipality, reverence for the dead, called for with considerable pressure on the towns from the central power authorities, was dealt with by a plaque in the church.

The militant activity of the Communist Party—involved in a struggle for peace through mobilization against fascism—tipped the Socialists' pacifism, particularly in the Limousin, from internationalism to nationalism. The area's Socialists were partisans of nonintervention in Spain, where the Republicans were fighting on unequal terms against Franco's troops. The same attitude was repeated toward Nazi Germany's annexation of Austria and then the Sudetenland.[26] The Haute-Vienne Socialists gained broad dominance over public opinion during the 1930s. The electoral victory of 1936 was celebrated in Limoges with the participation of a new minister, Paul Faure, the former editor in chief of the Socialist daily *Le Populaire.*

Faure, who was very influential in Limoges, opposed Léon Blum particularly on the question of military support for the Spanish Republicans, and he then became a partisan of "Munich."[27] The Munich accords were enthusiastically received by Limousin Socialists. A September 1938 petition called for "the government to make all necessary concessions for maintaining Peace and rectifying borders according to the peoples' needs and wishes." For the Communists, this was not admissible. The federal congress of Haute-Vienne Socialists unanimously approved a motion offered by Paul Faure, and on October 3, 1938, Le Bail wrote that "for the first time Peace has been concluded without victors or vanquished."[28]

So the dominant position of the Socialists in Haute-Vienne was won not only against the right but also against the Communists. It escaped nobody's notice that voters on the right preferred to vote Socialist, so as to eliminate the Communists.

The right disappeared from Oradour-sur-Glane's municipal council in the 1935 elections. Its candidate, Paul Desourteaux, was not reelected even though he was the sole incumbent opposition councillor. There was no longer any opposition on the right. This did not cause the diversity of political opinions among the township's populace to disappear; one could find a spectrum ranging from the far right (the Croix-de-feu, though a small minority, were not absent) to the Communist far left. Oradour's Communist Party cell numbered about ten members, who influenced some fifty voters in town and legislative elections.[29]

The declaration of war disrupted life in the town. The suppression of the *frairie* is just a trivial detail compared with the mobilization of 168 men, more than 10 percent of the population. After the June 1940 armistice, 113 men returned to the village. Some who had escaped from prisoner-of-war camps settled back in their homes under the protection of the inhabitants, despite their "irregular" situation. Fifty-five men from the commune remained prisoners until May 1945.

Did "the strange defeat," the collapse, the exodus preceding it, with the arrival of hordes of displaced persons,[30] experienced in Oradour as in the rest of France, mean the end of a world, the end of living peacefully, of enjoyment among one's own kind, the end of "happiness in Oradour"? Not really. During those dark years, the village of Oradour became known for a new reason: city dwellers [from Limoges], hit by food shortages and rationing, came to shop in a village that was easily accessible by "tramway." Under highly unusual circumstances, subsistence agriculture, which had been condemned to economic death, became competitive once again. At the same time shops, particularly the butcher's and wine merchant's, experienced considerable activity, both legal and illegal. Pierre Poitevin could write in the introduction to a book he wrote after the massacre: "Before the war, no poverty was known of in Oradour."[31]

Marshal Pétain's speech of June 20, 1940—"After the victory a spirit of pleasure won out over sacrifice"—passed unnoticed. No one ever referred to an appeal by a French general on English radio.[32] Stunned, the people could only follow events from a distance. It was not a time for criticism, even less for a spirit of opposition. At the time no one, the Communists even less than the others, imagined any possible "Resistance." Marshal Pétain's regime had widespread approval. On July 10, 1940, the parliamentary delegation for Haute-Vienne (all Socialists) voted him full powers in Vichy—all but one of them, that is. Léon Roche, who represented the district including the town of Oradour-sur-Glane, one of eighty members of parliament who voted no, is forgotten in Haute-Vienne, where there is no symbolic marker to commemorate his vote.[33]

The dark years begin in Oradour, almost unnoticed, in January 1939 with the arrival of foreign refugees.

The Refugees

The collective memory of Oradour's residents identifies three successive waves of refugees starting in 1939: Spaniards early that year, Alsatians that summer, then people from Lorraine in the summer of 1940. There are no clear recollections of a fourth and vaguely defined "set" that, unlike the other three, had no real identity. These last arrived a few at a time, over the course of several years, and grew in size or faded away depending on the activities of the Vichy administration, and later the German occupying forces. Among them were some Jews. The presence of Jews—foreigners of various nationalities or Frenchmen from several different regions—was a subject of controversy, indeed polemics, particularly when that presence was organized by Vichy.

At the beginning of 1939, Franco's victims arrived. By that summer there were 2,257 Spanish Republicans in Haute-Vienne, distributed through host towns that welcomed them with varying degrees of goodwill. The Spanish Republic had been abandoned by the democracies, and the refugees were victims of fascism. They arrived in rags, completely impoverished.

At first there were about twenty. Primarily young people, they were settled in La Fauvette, not far from town along the road to Confolens, where they built a camp of huts made of branches.[34] They were tolerated rather than welcomed. The arrival of entire families posed the usual problems of lodging: there were few vacant houses in town but more in the outlying hamlets. Despite encouragement to return to Spain, where the Franco regime promised they would be "received with profoundly Christian leniency and brotherhood," the Spanish refugees settled in.[35]

They were politically active: anarchists, Communists, Socialists, tendencies that had all been suspect since June 1940, if not before. Some of them were drafted into the Compagnies de travailleurs étrangers [Foreign Workers' Companies], which later became Groupements [or "Groups" (GTEs)]. GTE 643 was set up administratively in Oradour. Fearful of internment in camps or of enrollment in GTEs, some men went into hiding, and a fair number of them joined the Resistance. Police surveillance records noted clandestine activities—the distribution of tracts, "escapes" from GTEs and other places meant to keep track of them.[36] A note dated September 12, 1942, from the Limoges SRPJ [Service régional de la police judiciaire (Regional Service of the Criminal Investigation Division)] to the regional préfet requested "administrative" internment in the Saint-Paul d'Eyjaux camp for six Spanish refugees enrolled in GTE 643 at Oradour-sur-Glane, as a result of searches carried out in the GTE. The note pointed out that one of those enrolled at Oradour had been arrested in Toulouse in the company of another Spaniard, assigned to GTE 644 in Saillat, and that they were in the hands of the law. As far as Spanish refugees in Oradour are concerned, only women and children remained in 1943 and 1944: twenty-two on December 31, 1943.[37] Fifteen of them died in the massacre.

In September 1939, Alsatian evacuees arrived, supposedly sent away from the dangers of the presumed battlefield. Those from the

Bas-Rhin were sent to three départements of the Southwest including Haute-Vienne. "Crowded into railroad cars, the refugees spent several days and nights in primitive hygienic conditions, with an unspoken worry in their hearts: what would become of their abandoned houses, the property they had left behind?"[38] Thus about fifty residents of Schiltigheim, an industrial suburb of Strasbourg known for its breweries, arrived in Oradour.[39] For them, the France that they called "the interior" (as compared to their border location) was a terra incognita whose language they did not all speak fluently.

Arriving in the Limousin, the Alsatians were changing worlds and facing a culture that was very different from their own. They found lodgings with minimal facilities, far from what they were accustomed to. The absence of heat and running water (there was no village water supply), cooking that might still be done in an open fireplace, and outdoor privies constituted a series of unpleasant surprises. They were faced with a certain laxness on the part of the local people, who did not sweep their courtyards or have flowerboxes in the windows. The local people did not like to hear these Alsatians speaking what sounded like "Kraut," the hated enemy language, among themselves.[40] Their confusion of the Alsatian dialect with German led to hasty identification of the Alsatians with the Germans. At this point in time, under their present circumstances, the Alsatians' language was a last cultural refuge, the expression of their emotional link with Alsace.

The majority of Alsatian refugees started home in the summer of 1940. The German occupying forces encouraged them to return; some went back happy at the idea of going back home. Not all of them did, though. One clearheaded refugee in Limoges urged his compatriots through posters not to leave, emphasizing the risks they were sure to run under the Nazis. Those who gave up the return to Alsace did so out of fear, out of conviction (such as one seminarian called Neumeyer, who stayed along with one of his sisters and was known for his opposition to the regime), or because they knew that as Jews they were undesirable. The Germans forbade the return of any who were not born in Alsace, those for example who had arrived during the 1930s and were granted French citizenship, as was true of several evacuees. The Alsatian and Moselle départements' annexation was felt to be a capitulation. This feeling was reinforced by a general silence, particularly on the part of the "interior" clergy.

In June 1944, the regional préfet headquartered in Limoges was the son of a Strasbourg pastor, born in Schiltigheim in Alsace. On the other hand, some Alsatian refugees joined the Limousin Resistance. But a decisive factor for the inhabitants of Oradour was to be their discovery in 1945, after the writing of the official remembrance committee's book,[41] that among the perpetrators of the massacre were some Alsatian forced draftees, some of them from Schiltigheim. Might they somehow or other have been the reason the Waffen SS came to Oradour? The question has been asked.

Nine of the massacre victims were from Alsace.[42]

In August 1940, the Nazis annexed Alsace and the Moselle, expelling French speakers. The situation of people from Lorraine was very different from that of their Alsatian compatriots.[43] They were expelled in the context of an annexation and consequently a "depopulation"—a "Nazification" that today would be called a "campaign of ethnic cleansing." The Moselle residents were expelled with no hope of return. The suddenness of their departure meant they took only minimal baggage with them: they were leaving their homes forever. About eighty people from Lorraine arrived in Oradour, coming all in one group from a village called Charly.[44] Very ill-equipped, they were accompanied by a teacher and a priest, an individual qualified as "anti-Nazi" by his nephew and, according to this nephew, little inclined to go along with the regime. They had their own school in town, attended also by three children who were born in Alsace of immigrant parents. Since they were French speaking they were well accepted, and there was no problem integrating them. The town was short of laborers, so they went right to work.

Forty-four of the people expelled from the Moselle died in the massacre. After the war their village took the name of Charly-Oradour.

The "scattered" refugees arrived with the "debacle."[45] Their number varied and is not very certain. A prefectoral document of January 1943 refers to thirty-one refugees from the "forbidden zone" (mainly from the Nord and Pas-de-Calais départements), four from the "authorized" zone (these may have been National Child Care children from the Paris area).[46] Those who managed to come from the "free zone," particularly Montpellier or Avignon, must also be added, though they were not counted—as some Jews from the Paris area or Meurthe-et-Moselle, who did not always live within the village precincts, also were not accounted for.[47] They may have sent some children to the town schools and hidden some in outlying farms. Their identity was sometimes falsified. No account was made, either, of refugees who were taken in by relatives or stayed in hotels in town. This was the case of the family of Jean Pallier (his testimony will be quoted in the next chapter), who lived in Paris and whose wife, née Metzger, was from Franche-Comté.[48]

A Bayonne family took refuge in town in April 1943.[49] The head of family, a Sephardic Jew named Robert Pinède, had been stripped of his "Aryanized" tannery business and vainly sought employment in Saint-Junien, a leather-goods town. Deeply involved in his community, a Freemason and a prominent "legal expert," he had previously been a delegate to the Union générale des Israélites de France [UGIF] for Bayonne and the Basses-Pyrénées département. Starting in October 1943, he became an officer in the Brive and Limoges UGIF bureaus, in charge of accounting, and then "loan manager" (a financial administrative post) for a section of the civil organization, with responsibility for the entire southern zone. His job was to distribute aid to indigent Jews interned in camps or GTEs, usually through the intermediary of rabbis. This activity required trips to Brive and Limoges and involved considerable correspondence, maintaining a postal checking account, and using the town's telephone booth (the latter with the knowledge of the postmaster).[50] This situation must have been known to the mayor's office, or the German authorities and Vichy's Jewish Questions police.

This family of six had ration cards stamped "Jew," a status imposed by the regime that does not seem to have made for problems in town, even among Pétain supporters. Since Jews had been arrested in August 1942, people's attitudes had changed. The fact that it was a French family may have fostered their acceptance. Belonging to the Sephardic community, as well as his legal status as a UGIF official, probably ruled out the possibility of contacts with other Jewish refugees of Ashkenazi origin, who no doubt wanted to avoid the UGIF.[51] As a precaution two houses were rented, so as to separate the three children from their parents and a grandmother. The three adults were to die in the massacre.

At least until the summer of 1942, the presence of Jewish refugees was not looked upon by most people as being a consequence of racial persecution resulting in creation of a special status, deprival of rights, exclusions, confiscations, and finally arrests. "Just passing through," these refugees arrived and departed, as they had come, amid indifference. They were not considered undesirables, but they obviously were not particularly desired either; such is the status of all refugees. Neither the camps in the area nor the other forms of administrative constraint imposed by Vichy were seen for what they were, at that time or afterward. "Not only was the Jews' fate not regarded as a central and crucial question, but . . . it was not even the subject of any special attention."[52]

Town officials' involvement could vary from one place to another, however. One township near Oradour, Saint-Victurnien, immediately adopted an attitude of support for the Jewish refugees, thanks to its mayor, a man named Bardet, assisted by his town clerk, Dugot. A marriage was celebrated by Rabbi Deutsch from Limoges on town hall premises in December 1940. The mayor's office then supplied them with papers and information concerning police activities.

Interventions by Vichy

At the time such interventions took place, they were not regarded by people as a coherent set of measures. Consequently their role or their influence on village life may have been diminished or even overlooked. Any opposition they might sometimes have aroused stemmed from the fact that they were imposed by a central power, the most noteworthy examples being food supplies and forced labor.

The local section of the Légion française des combattants et volontaires de la Révolution nationale [French Legion of Veterans and Volunteers of the National Revolution] was created, as it was everywhere, by the obligatory consolidation of veterans' associations. The Oradour section was led by a team of prominent conservative citizens (opponents of the Socialist mayor) who were appointed at the département level; its president was an agricultural products and grain merchant, and Paul Desourteaux (the ex-mayor) was one of the vice-presidents. This section of the Légion did not show very much militant activity but took part in a number of significant events, for example Marshal Pétain's visit to Limoges and Saint-Junien on June 19–20, 1941. For the town, the most important event came when the leadership of this local Légion section replaced the town council by order of the préfet. Questions may at least be asked about its participation in an operation denouncing "foreign Jews," in reaction to the presence of the GTE. Whatever the case, the activity of local sections of the Légion diminished from the winter of 1942–1943 onward and practically disappeared after that.

The local government managed to avoid being dissolved. Since the town fell below the threshold of two thousand inhabitants, the team led by Joseph Beau remained in charge of its own affairs. The administration, when it thought to set up a GTE in the winter of 1940–1941, may not have considered the Socialist mayor and his councillors reliable or favorable enough to the measures it was taking. The mayor was removed from office in April 1941. It is thought that this was motivated by some business concerning the distribution of army surplus shoes, which the administration did not find in conformity with regulations.[53] The incident had no legal consequences, though. Dissolution of the council as a whole shows that this was a collective measure reflecting considerations that are not a matter so much of detail as of a more general scope. Prefecture authorities appointed a "Special Delegation," presided over by Paul Desourteaux, that was made up of prominent citizens, craftsmen, and merchants. With the exception of its president, who otherwise might act as political liaison, this selection corresponded to the leadership team of the local Légion section. Paul Desourteaux had, in the minds of most residents respectful of authority, a legitimacy as a war veteran that Joseph Beau lacked. He also had a background in politics, and he once again became mayor. The right, which had opposed the Socialists in vain, thus now took back power in town. Both mayors, the last one elected and the former one restored to power, died in the massacre.[54]

The police were keeping their eyes on the alleged activities of the former Communist cell members and of the Spaniards drafted into the GTE.

In November 1941, an anonymous denunciation sent to Vichy triggered a police investigation concerning the activities of militants from the disbanded Communist Party cell in Oradour. In his report the investigating officer did not fail to mention that the special police in Limoges had already carried out an investigation of the people who had been fingered. A regular watch was being kept over the Oradour Communists, like others in the département. The note from Vichy asked for reports, which the officer provided. The president of the Special Delegation had been cooperative: the report emphasized his anti-Communist and anti-Socialist sentiments. The police were focusing on sixteen men, including Santrot and his son (the latter the local agent for *L'Humanité*) and Aimé Faugeras, the cell's secretary.[55] But despite nine examinations and searches, it proved impossible to find any concrete facts: of course former Communists (or people taken as such by the police) met at the café or went fishing; dogs barked at night ... The police recommended keeping an eye on five people in particular, who "must be immediately apprehended at times of social tension, including one Martial Machefer, a town resident, well-known Communist and strike leader." No leaflets or propaganda materials were found in Oradour, but since the Communists knew they were being watched, they were on their guard. The police saw no cause for alarm: "The Communist Party was in an embryonic state in Oradour before the hostilities; the great majority of voters leaned toward the Socialist SFIO [Section française de l'Internationale ouvrière (French Section of the Workers' International)]. Moreover, Monsieur Beau, who was recently stripped of the mayor's office, had been reelected uninterruptedly for twenty years under the SFIO label." As a practical measure, the report proposed taking a company-provided motorcycle away from a town resident named Leboutet, "the soul of the party," an employee of the département railroad. He was suspected of using the machine to deliver communications. The police ran up against the neighbors' unwillingness to talk: they had an abiding hatred of all representatives of central authority.[56]

GTE 643, as we have seen, was organized in Oradour-sur-Glane during the first half of 1941.[57] It remained there until its transfer to Aixe-sur-Vienne, southwest of Limoges, on October 25, 1942. In May 1941 it numbered a little over 200 recruits, or the equivalent of a military company. Only two sections were based directly in Oradour: an administrative section of some twenty men with their "commander," a soldier in the reserves, and a "temporary" section for the sick or for men declared unfit for work. There were two sections of "foresters" (sixty men at Thouron near Nantiat and Nieul, forty in Saint-Martin Terressus near Ambazac). Finally, another section was spread over the district of Saint-Junien, which as we know includes the township of Oradour-sur-Glane. Although this GTE was used at first for Spanish refugees,[58] the administration gradually drafted foreign Jews who had come to the southern zone, usually after clandestinely crossing the Demarcation Line not far away. The presence of this "group" in town does not always seem to have remained unseen. There were assemblies on the fairgrounds at which the recruits were made to watch the raising of the colors.[59]

Foreign refugees may have been accepted individually as farm workers, but the "groups" were much less welcome. During the second quarter of 1942, local sections of the Légion made a point of denouncing the presence of foreign Jews during a campaign that, as far as the documents show, seems to have been coordinated. The Légion echoed local antisemitism; the Vichy regime authorized its open expression. Did the president of the local section of the Légion take part in this denunciation campaign? The probability of this seems to us to be confirmed by an August 1942 report from the sous-préfet of Rochechouart. In this monthly report to the département's préfet, the sous-préfet recalled earlier statements in which he brought to the préfet's attention the anxiety of the residents of towns where the number of Jews might be too large. As examples he gave the towns of Saillat and Oradour-sur-Glane:

> The problem of the Jews. Numerous foreign Israelites are crossing the Demarcation Line clandestinely every day. In my area they add to the number already there. Since they have the financial means, throughout the countryside they cause the disappearance of goods needed by the populace, by buying them at any price. This stirs deep resentment, which can only grow stronger. . . . The region is too close to where they cross; it is in danger of being overrun by such undesirable elements. These arrivals increase the problems that have been noted in my reports, caused by the presence of Worker Groups in Saillat and Oradour-sur-Glane.

The sous-préfet cited five reports addressing this question between May and July, and added: "In all the localities where the number of foreigners is great enough to bring about the problems indicated, the people keenly desire their departure and shipment to concentration camps."[60]

A member of the higher administration might accuse "the Jews" of being responsible for the black market and demand they be sent to concentration camps. Two elements strike our attention. The first is the coupling of Saillat and Oradour-sur-Glane, the destinations (as indicated in the previous chapter) of the two Waffen SS companies that left Saint-Junien on June 10, 1944. In both towns there were or had been GTEs.

The second element would be the existence of complaints by residents of those towns or, in administrative language and euphemistically put, of a desire to get rid of the foreign Jews—"the people keenly desire." Of course, members of the Légion were part of the population, so it is possible to attribute the origin of this desire to them. In addition, we know that some local sections of the Légion had sent mail denouncing the presence of foreign Jews, or "undesirables," to their département head. Did the president of the Oradour Légion write "his" letter, like the presidents of neighboring towns? We do not know, because in the current state of our documentation we have not come across a letter that the sous-préfet's report would lead us to believe exists.

However, we have come across a file that deals with this topic. It dates from June 1942 and concerns Mézières-sur-Issoire, the seat of a district in Haute-Vienne that is west of Bellac and north of Oradour. The town of Mézières was in the zone of influence of GTE 313, of Saint-Sauveur-de-Bellac.

> **A Tragicomedy** (excerpts from the file):
> A letter from the local Légion president to his département head in Limoges:
>
> > "at a time like the present it is growing scandalous to see all these people, especially men in the prime of life, pass the time strolling about the countryside in search of goods (poultry, eggs . . .) that they snatch up at any price and get away with it, living off the fat of the land in sheer idleness. The spectacle is growing increasingly revolting."
>
> A dispatch from this head to the préfet:
>
> > "I believe that these facts, which have already been brought to my attention by several of my presidents, deserve your attention because our rural residents no longer understand

how it can be that these Jews enjoy such an enviable position at the present time."

A report of an investigation by the Police for Jewish Questions:

"the presence of all sorts of refugees in all these towns, passively waiting on events and not trying to rehabilitate themselves, because they think they will soon take up their businesses and the same old habits again, has a distressing effect . . . until (some) *radical measure* is taken, we will continue to see these individuals, who all have resources allowing them to live as parasites, pursuing their own little personal affairs without troubling themselves over the Country's general interests."

A comment from the head of this bureau:

"I am in complete agreement with conclusions."[61]

Phrases such as "increasingly revolting spectacle" and "such an enviable situation" are signs that the antisemitic doctrine of Marshal Pétain and his government could be freely expressed, at least among his supporters. Could this daily diet of the Légion not have affected the president of the Oradour section? The "radical measure" completed (or attempted to complete) the process of elimination that was already being prepared.

The "radical measure" desired by the Légion and awaited by the Jewish Questions police and the sous-préfet (who could not fail to have received the circulars preparing it) arrived on August 26, 1942. It principally concerned foreign Jews interned in camps and those enrolled in the GTEs, lists of whom had been drawn up by the administration.[62] Despite the complex of recommendations and precautions taken by the administration (to act as a group, be polite, avoid talking to neighbors, prevent escapes, noise, suicides), the forces of the gendarmerie and police did not arrest the anticipated quota of foreign Jews. Still, more than 480 people were taken in that day and brought temporarily to the camp at Nexon.[63] It had previously been emptied of its internees for that very purpose.

At first a "center for preventive detention," the Nexon camp later became a "screening center for foreign Jews" and the holding area for the camp at Drancy, from which trainloads of deportees left for Auschwitz. That is how people arrested in the Oradour GTE on August 26, 1942, were "sent to the occupied zone" (a euphemism employed by the administration in its reports, meaning they were handed over to the SS) and to Drancy, where they arrived on August 29, 1942: 446 came from Nexon by the sixth train from the southern zone. In train number 26 leaving Drancy on August 31 with 957 deportees, 82 people came from Haute-Vienne and 3 from the Oradour GTE, according to documents; they arrived in Auschwitz on September 3. Were the arrested people from the roster of GTE 643 living in Oradour itself or in other GTE sites? We cannot say exactly. Would such precise data change anything for the inhabitants who "saw nothing"?

The name Oradour,[64] which in this context we are not confusing with its residents, is symbolically linked to a crime against humanity, committed with the complicity of the French State.[65]

The local people's reactions have been the subject of studies that we will not recall here. We do know that there was real indignation after this roundup. Public reaction by prelates, those of Montauban and Toulouse, is well known. That of the bishop of Limoges, Louis Rastouil, has not been recorded, perhaps because it was less public. He received Marshal Pétain in the Collegiate Church of Saint-Léonard de Noblat in June 1941, but he later made it clear he was distancing himself from the regime. After the Oradour massacre he played an important role in shaping the memorial process. Earlier he expressed disapproval of the arrests of foreign Jews and asked the priests in his diocese to resign from the Légion, as the préfet informed the government.[66]

Laval devised a complicated process called "relief," which was to allow the return of prisoners in exchange for workers sent to Germany. The failure of this procedure, based on voluntary service, along with pressure from the German occupiers, caused Laval to decree a form of mobilization for work in Germany: the Service du travail obligatoire [(STO), Obligatory Labor Service]. We know that the STO indirectly steered men toward the maquis, particularly young men who refused to go. The law on obligatory labor of February 16, 1943, was announced to Haute-Vienne towns at the end of the month. In 1942 the process had sent only 364 volunteers from the département; in 1943 it affected more than 7,400 young men. With this change in scale, the danger grew clearer: the German authorities were requesting more than 1,100 workers from Haute-Vienne.[67]

The ins and outs of exemption permitted the authorities of the Saint-Junien district to call up 134 young men and, finally, to assign 81 of them to work in Germany. Many showed a good deal of imagination in avoiding call-up. Some youths of the Oradour township claimed duties essential to the area's economy; some took precautions against further call-ups; they staked out hiding places and other means of concealment in the neighborhood. Heading out for the maquis does not seem to have been contemplated as a solution at that point. But some did leave.[68] Such was the case with the town clerk: the president of the Special Delegation did not protect a clerk recruited by his Socialist predecessor. Those young men drafted for the STO returned home in May 1945.

Food Supplies, the "Gray Market," and the Black Market

The search for food was the main item of business during the Occupation. Faced with a breakdown of the economy and the German authorities' requisitions, the government imposed administrative regulations on the market. The General Food Administration inspired total rejection by consumers and producers and the spread of parallel markets. In cities the food situation did not allow for adequate distribution of supplies, and indeed people had to wait in lines at the stores and often ended up frustrated. In rural areas people did not experience pressure in the same way, since it was easier to find essential items. Farmers, forced to make obligatory deliveries to the administration, found new outlets via a "gray market" (the expression "black market" was more applicable to the business world). The economy of a town like Oradour seems to have reflected aspects of both.

Oradour's obsolete agricultural methods were an important part of the city dwellers' food supplies and the village's reputation. From the fall of 1940, the German army's massive fodder requisitions led cattle breeders to sell off quickly animals that they could not hope to keep for fattening. The price of cattle for slaughter plunged without being carried on to consumers, and so the grumbling began. The situation did not improve: the combination of German levies, mandatory deliveries to the General Food Administration, and prices that were too low led people to conceal crops and animals. During the winter of 1943–1944, farmers preferred to fatten hogs and piglets, which were more in demand because they were easier to transport; not to deliver either milk or potatoes; and to keep grain for their poultry and produce eggs, which could be sold outside the regular market. City dwellers came for food supplies to Oradour, as they did in all rural areas. The "tramway" made the trip easier.

People listened politely and with visible indifference to the "lectures" organized by propaganda envoys and sous-préfets, with the help of the presidents of local sections of the Légion. The sous-préfet came to Oradour several times up to March 20, 1944, for lectures concerning the shortages facing the poor city dwellers. He asked for help in bridging the gap between wheat deliveries, but at that time the market for grains, potatoes, and cattle was in disarray. Georges Guingouin had understood the weakness of the system ever since the start of the Vichy regime. He had acted to sabotage and limit requisitions. Setting himself up as the "maquis préfet," he posted maximum produce prices. The directors of the General Food Administration feared Resistance interventions.

The regime could not control the market, despite repressive actions that sometimes managed to achieve their aim. The "black market internees" at Nexon found internment in camp, where they had to rub elbows with Communists and foreigners, hard to bear. As early as 1942 the regional préfet noted: "Businessmen are clearly at an advantage, since the practice of barter allows them to procure many items; their attitude is very cautious. They are concerned about order, which is indispensable if their business is to flourish. And it has, this year (that is, 1942), brilliantly. All the food stores, especially butchers' and wine merchants', have been making often scandalous fortunes."[69]

The town of Oradour boasted four grocery stores, three butcher shops, one of them also a delicatessen, two bakeries, one pastry shop–café, one wine merchant's, about ten cafés, five inns with restaurants, three hotels, dry-goods and haberdashery stores, a collection of stores where people learned to "adapt" to the situation.[70] The people in Oradour, like those in many other villages, adapted to the constraints of food shortages; they sought either to overcome them any way they could, which is easier in the country than in the city, or to take advantage of them.

"Clandestine slaughtering has given rise to a 'gray' market that is used by certain butchers and a great number of producers. Many families get their food this way and it is impossible to take effective steps against it." The regional préfet noted the failure of "administered" agriculture and the necessity for the parallel market.[71] There was nothing to be done: the distribution system was ineffective, and so was enforcement: "Activity against clandestine slaughtering, the black market, and the cattle dealers' schemes has not had full effect during the past month" (April 1944).[72]

In March 1944 the sous-préfet in Rochechouart noted that "rural people are not as well disposed as in the past to sell to the General Food Administration." He blamed this on "foreign propaganda" and acts of sabotage. He also pointed out "the lack of sanctions against poor deliveries. . . . The bureaus' excesses and the exorbitant prices at which certain products are sold officially or clandestinely also explain their disappearance. Clandestine slaughtering has recently reached proportions unheard of until now, to the extent that many butchers sell meat to their customers without paying attention to established rationing. . . . These past months I have often been able to note how white the bread was that farmers were eating. It must be assumed that there are many barterers who consume much more than regulation rations."[73] What we see here is probably much like the situation in Oradour, where differences of means—between landowners and farmers, shopkeepers, professionals, and wage earners, between refugees who were "endowed with resources" (to use then-current administrative terminology) and those who, although "unendowed" or forbidden to work, were not "assisted"—created significant divergences. But of course as long as you did not look into details, "there was no poverty." This generally anachronistic image has persisted.

On the morning of June 10, 1944, the head of the Légion's Oradour section, who employed a foreign worker in his home, was visiting his mother-in-law.[74] He was with his son who had come from Bordeaux, where he worked as an "adjunct commissioner" in the Todt Organization.[75] The young man—who had paraded around the village wearing the uniform of that organization, which had been set up to build a concrete Atlantic Wall—is still sometimes identified today by the man in the street as a Milice member. The father and son were busy that day transporting "half a pig" they had gotten from a farmer. Half the "gentleman" (as a fat pig was called) was what the farmer owed the landowner. A dinner was being prepared with the young man's fiancée. They proposed leaving a cut of pork, but the mother-in-law did not need it and took only the blood sausages. Since it was too early in the morning to stay on for lunch, they left. She never saw them again. The father, the son, and the fiancée all died in the massacre.

Changing Opinions and Behavior

The Vichy government worked hard to learn and evaluate the state of public opinion. Despite their often restrained administrative tone, the reports of préfets, sous-préfets, Renseignements généraux [(RG) secret service] commissioners, mail inspectors, and so on provide us with indications that we can compare with impressions from the field.[76]

All in all, Oradour's people lived through these times like people in the Limousin in general, with the same behavior and the same priorities. The "debacle" reinforced their hatred of the German enemy, and the Occupation sharpened it. To the despair of the French administration, which noted the ineptitude of government propaganda, the Germans were held responsible for every problem. The downward spiral seemed impossible to counter. From the middle of 1941, Marshal Pétain's popularity declined precipitously. Laval's return to power only made things worse: the fear of increased collaboration was the cause of it. Laval's declaration hoping for "a German victory in order to eliminate Communism" had disastrous results for him. He no longer had any credibility, even in "circles favorable to the National Revolution." Légion activities declined, to the point where it disappeared from the political scene. The proportion of anticollaborationists kept growing. The people "awaited" Allied victory, as they followed the war in the East and then on other fronts. "Those favoring an Allied victory are still as numerous. Although people continue to criticize England for its failure to aid the Soviets, they place the greatest hope in the power of the United States: as soon as it is ready, the war will end quickly in its favor. The Russians' resistance at Stalingrad is spoken of favorably: the Germans will definitely spend a very hard second winter in Russia."[77]

The long wait gave rise to considerable discouragement and a certain apathy. It did not occur to most people that local action might change matters. The priorities were to find food and to avoid any kind of requisitions or obligatory labor. "Registration and departure for Germany of young men, called to do their Obligatory Labor Service, are the foremost things as far as public opinion is concerned," wrote the sous-préfet at Rochechouart in March 1943. "Police operations carried out by the German authorities are not very likely to calm people down. Arrests made in the widest variety of circles and without any apparent reason render more difficult than ever the job of those who defend the idea of a rapprochement between France and Germany." In short people did what they could to get by; they supported those evading the STO, letting them slip through the nets set by the occupying forces and the Vichy regime. "Opposition was passive but stubborn."[78]

The Resistance and the maquis did not arouse enthusiasm or any special calling. Potential young recruits for forced labor figured they could conceal themselves within the village, "among ourselves." Meanwhile by the summer of 1943 it seemed evident to the government's representatives that "the maquis has acquired a semblance of authority" at the expense of the police and gendarmerie, who were "powerless to prevent or repress the numerous incidents." In November 1943, the sous-préfet wrote: "To my knowledge, no investigation up to now has managed to uncover and arrest the guilty parties. The only successful police operation was one carried out recently by the FTP against a band of armed robbers at Cussac. People have taken note of this and have drawn troubling conclusions, not to mention that the event could reinforce the authority the outlaws have sought to acquire."[79] In December 1943 the "discouragement" and "demoralization" were such that everyone seemed to fall back on his own solution to individual, family, and collective hardships.

During the first half of 1944, people in Oradour were awaiting deliverance by an Anglo-American landing that was slow in coming. Very slow...

There Were No Maquis

All the town residents' accounts have been confirmed by the Vichy administration and the three principal heads of armed Resistance in the département: "There were no maquis; that made us very happy, people would often brag about it."[80] The maquis visited the village several times in 1943 and 1944; they paid for and took with them loads of cigarettes and tobacco, as well as fuel reserves. Of these intrusions we know only of the ones leading to gendarmerie reports. The village of Oradour was a place of business that people passed through; it was too exposed to be of much use to the maquis.

On the other hand they did set up a camp in the hills of Blond, a wooded area some kilometers north. Three other maquis groups were located several dozen kilometers away.[81] The first, under Georges Guingouin's command and the best organized and armed, was east of Limoges on the border between the Corrèze and Creuse départements. To the west of Oradour we find the maquis of Brigueuil and the Confolens region, in the Limousin section of the Charente; and to the southwest that of Oradour-sur-Vayres. These two were FTP maquis groups, which non-Communists joined.

At the time of the Allied landings in Normandy, these four maquis groups were still largely independent. Unified maquis command came about only on August 3, 1944, under the leadership of Georges Guingouin, after his own troops effectively joined the FTP at the end of June 1944. From then on the organization of Resistance forces was strengthened by the arrival of Allied officers from the English and American armed forces, with some French and binational officers among them. Large-scale parachute drops added to the strength of the French Forces of the Interior (FFI). This strength allowed Georges Guingouin to negotiate the liberation of Limoges thanks to the capitulation of the German garrison; it may be the source of the maquis' legendary status in the region. Their renown created a predominant image that made Resistance and maquis synonymous. This image served the interests of the Communist Party and tended to overshadow other forms of Resistance.

The Resistance was multifaceted and took on varying guises. Before the appearance of the maquis in the area, we can note that information networks and movements were being set up there: Combat with Edmond Michelet in Brive and Traversat in Limoges; Libération Sud with Dutreix in Limoges; Franc-Tireur with Bonneaud and Lecomte ... Then the Mouvements unis de la Résistance (MUR) [United Resistance Movements] brought them together; there we find the names of Dumas, Gagnant, Perrin, all those of Libération Sud. They contributed to the strength of the Resistance in Limoges and its outskirts. But the majority of these Resistance members, Socialists or sympathizers, suffered Nazi repression:

Dumas, Dutreix, and Perrin were executed by firing squad, Gagnant died as a deportee.[82] They were absent from the political scene at the Liberation, leaving only the Communist Party, which boasted a leader wreathed in glory, Guingouin, facing Socialist officials (like Betoulle, a former and future mayor of Limoges) whose credibility was diminished by their having voted full powers for Pétain or by their lack of involvement in the Resistance. The Communists triumphed in the 1945 municipal elections in Limoges and (among other towns) Oradour-sur-Glane.[83]

The predominant image—like a rumor—has its origin and its end but conceals a more complex reality: the Socialists' powerful electoral influence in the département of Haute-Vienne, for example. They very quickly took back control of département offices: first the committee of liberation, then the general council. After the Liberation, the shaping of memory of the massacre took place in a context of party conflict. The Communist Party [PCF] had at its command an aura based on the myth of liberation of the French and "Soviet" peoples. Maquis resistance was viewed as the people's implementation of their ideals. At this time the PCF showed greater ability to mobilize than the other political groups: it offered an account that integrated recent history and a glorious past, that of the revolutions of 1789 and 1917, with an agenda, a teleology, that of Soviet communism. But on their side the Socialists still had the benefit of their strong local power before the war.

People in Oradour were not unaware of the maquis nearby. Aimé Renaud: "Four or five days before the Oradour massacre my friend Lesparat, a wheelwright in Oradour-sur-Glane, told me: 'I have a funny feeling: we'd better go to the maquis.'"[84] At first Aimé Renaud and his friend considered staying away from the village as a precaution. Renaud's wife: "Saturday morning, June 10, I overheard a conversation between two residents of the village, this fellow Borie, who escaped, and Lesparat, my husband's friend. Lesparat was asking Borie to get him into the maquis with my husband, saying he didn't feel safe in Oradour. Borie promised him he would look into it right away."[85] Mathieu Borie, a mason who survived the shooting, was one of the maquis "legals" who could be mobilized if need be. The situation at the time was still quite marginal.

The Resistance group in the village of Saint-Victurnien had no known affiliation. What little we know about its operation might make it out to be an independent group. No formal link can be established, but a massacre in Saint-Victurnien on June 27, 1944, claimed the lives of eleven people, two of them villagers. Milice from Limoges patrolled through the village and, claiming to be maquis, ambushed an FTP vehicle. The massacre has still not been explained: no one knows why the Milice came to that place on that day.[86]

Just an Ordinary Village

Oradour was like any other Limousin village; it showed a full range of behavior among its people during the periods of the 1930s, Vichy, and the Occupation, when clandestine dances and movies at the Café Dagoury drew the young people. During the "black years" there were Pétainists, supporters of political collaboration, even one case of "horizontal collaboration."[87] There were Socialists whose pacifism led them to remain passive; inactive Communists cut off from the Party leadership; young men who refused to leave for STO service and others who did finally leave; shopkeepers who "did business" and farmers who made use of the gray market; escaped prisoners of war under the residents' protection; young men who envisioned going into the maquis, and so on. A human "alchemy" that was representative of French society? Prominent citizens "went along" and ordinary people made do until the outcome of an event that was beyond their control and on which they could imagine no effective action at their level. This human group's representativeness (you could almost call it a microcosm) was taken into account later, as the memorial to the tragedy took shape. The absence of involvement by most people would, after the massacre, become proof of their "innocence."

It was an ordinary village also because of the presence of refugees, the gentiles, those beyond suspicion, forgotten, whose birth in Germany would be suspected by no one outside town hall,[88] and those who were seen, because they were too visible in their exile as stateless foreigners. The Jakobovicz family, for example, left Kalisz in Poland in the early 1930s. Aron Jakobovicz arrived in Paris first and was joined there by his wife and children, David and Sarah. They passed through Nazi Germany on their way. David was able to obtain French citizenship, but it would be taken away from him. The German advance put the family to flight. They arrived in Limoges, then settled in a hamlet, La Malaise, between Saint-Victurnien and Oradour. David was married in December 1940 in the attic of the Saint-Victurnien town hall. The family underwent attacks by the Milice. David became a woodcutter. He joined the Resistance, probably sporadically, in a group originating in the Saint-Victurnien soccer team and then in an FTP company. He protected his parents, his wife, and his son as best he could. His sister, Sarah, was sent to safety in the town of Oradour, with a shoemaker, Machefer, who lived across from the fairgrounds. Machefer was a next-door neighbor of the Kanzler family. Joseph Kanzler, born in Budapest in 1893, and his wife, Maria Goldmann, born in Warsaw in 1899, had two daughters, Dora and Simone, born in Strasbourg. With Joseph Bergmann, born in Kokern, Germany, in 1917, they were thought to be Alsatian refugees. Sarah Jakobovicz made friends with the two Kanzler daughters, who were her age. The girls all died in the massacre.

The Population of Oradour in June 1944

According to the 1936 census, the township had 1,574 inhabitants, 330 of them in the village itself, the rest scattered throughout the surrounding hamlets. The 1939 mobilization involved 168 men, of whom 113 returned. The number of refugees constantly varied. From figures available for the end of 1943, we find the presence of 105 French and 50 foreign refugees. These administrative data do not take into account people who were left out of the statistics, either inadvertently or on purpose. If from a total derived from the administration figures we subtract 31 male prisoners still held in Germany and those in the STO (also in Germany), estimated at about 15 by the town, we arrive at a figure of about 1,650 people. This figure is higher than that for the "rationees"; 1,630 people in the township had ration cards. Of course we have to take into account the administration's confusion, counterfeit food cards, double accounts, as well as those who had no cards, perhaps more numerous than we imagine.

The June 1944 population was no longer that of the 1930s. It had been reduced by numerous departures and, at the same time, augmented by the arrival of refugees and "residents" on temporary stays of unspecified length, in hotels or with families. It was complicated by comings and goings, absences and presences—accepted or tolerated at times, unwanted at others.

It was an unstable, constantly shifting population. On Saturday, June 10, almost all the children living in the township had come to the village schools from the hamlets. There were residents who had left town, some early in the week or the day before, still others that same morning. Some of them came back Saturday evening or Sunday morning. Some people had arrived for various reasons the day before, that morning, or that afternoon; some came while the Waffen SS were already in action.

Can this population, with its diverse origins, behaviors, and priorities of concerns, be considered "a unique, distinctive community"?[89] Did the "Oradour community" not appear only after the massacre and the town's destruction?

The village lived a life that was "normal" at the time. The lives of prominent citizens differed from what was normal for "little people"; still more so from the lives of refugees, who did not constitute a homogeneous group. "In Oradour, there was nothing special to point out during those early months of 1944." Could this be possible?[90]

Did the abnormal thing that struck Oradour exempt it from the past that preceeded the massacre?

6 Account of the Massacre

From the heart of the event or just outside, witnesses told about what they had lived through, observed, and heard. But their situation did not afford them an overall view of the tragedy, so they could reconstruct only a fragment of it. Our account is a reconstruction based on documentation conserved primarily in the archives of military justice. We have made use of statements by victims and witnesses that were gathered by investigators of the judicial police in the fourth quarter of 1944, along with cross-references, as concerns the victims; and from then to the end of 1947, for hearings of the accused.[1]

Surprise Attack

In Oradour: right after the lunch break, all were going about their business once more, life was starting up again. Suddenly everything went haywire. Marcel Darthout, age twenty: "Around 1:45 p.m., while I was waiting for the barbershop to open, I saw a column of about five to eight vehicles arrive by the bridge over the Glane." Clément Broussaudier, age twenty-five, was also going to the barbershop: "I arrived a little before two p.m., the barbershop wasn't yet open. Waiting for it to open, I sat down on a bench beside the road under the big oak tree. . . . Around two o'clock I went into the barbershop. I saw by the barber's clock that it was two minutes to two." The oak tree, a "Liberty tree" planted in 1848, would survive the fire. Robert Hébras, age nineteen, was working on rewiring a house: he saw "two armored cars arrive, coming from the direction of the bridge over the Glane, heading up into town. . . . I looked at the time just then, and saw it was two p.m." Armand Senon, age twenty-nine, had been hurt in a soccer game and was laid up in his bedroom with his leg in a cast: "it must have been around 1:45

when I saw two armored cars and a truck coming up into town from the bridge over the Glane." At 2:15 a garage owner, Hubert Desourteaux, age thirty-three, saw "five vehicles, three Ford 4 1/2 ton trucks and two half-tracks with armored sides." Mathieu Borie, a mason, age thirty-four: "The Germans arrived around two o'clock."[2]

None of them had seen the arrival of the Waffen SS column and its short pause on the road from Saint-Victurnien as missions were assigned to the various groups. Yvonne Gaudy lived in the hamlet of Bordes and was going into town: she "saw the officer who seemed to be the head of operations. At that moment he was handing out written orders." SS Sergeant Boos would confirm this: "On arriving at the village, we stopped and orders were handed out."[3]

By the time that the witnesses who survived or who escaped saw the first vehicles and Waffen SS soldiers, these had, several minutes earlier, already begun surrounding the village of Oradour. The inhabitants could not know where the Germans were coming from or why they suddenly appeared in the village.

The Waffen SS soldiers had been surprised by their rapid departure right after lunch, without their packs. They had not been told their destination; only one section head is said to have told them they were "going to search for an officer":

> We left Saint-Junien immediately after lunch, around 1300. I was surprised at the sudden departure and asked one of my comrades why we weren't taking our kits. He answered that we were going to carry out an assignment and told me the maquis had captured an SS captain or commander whose car had been found, and we were going to search for the officer. I climbed into the truck quickly. . . . Other trucks had just left then, and I saw them at Oradour-sur-Glane.
>
> About a kilometer from Oradour the column halted and we got out. Hauptsturmführer Kahn assembled the officers and noncoms and talked to them for about ten minutes. The battalion chief was there during the conversation. His arms were crossed and he didn't say much. It was mainly the company

> chief, Kahn, who did the talking. When the conversation was over—it was meant to explain to the officers and noncoms the operation they were to carry out—we were told to get back into our vehicles.[4]

The column's halt was carried out in sight of the village with no particular precautions, without fear of an ambush.

Surrounding the Village

After the halt not far from the village, the column started up again, only to stop once more when it arrived at the bridge over the Glane. Some soldiers got out and took up a position with their machine guns aimed at the village.

Paul G., a French forced draftee, age eighteen: "On arriving at Oradour, when we were within sight of the first farms, the convoy halted. Half the men were given an order to down from the truck. . . . As soon as half the men in our company had gotten out, we went on toward Oradour, with Major Diekmann and Captain Kahn leading the way. We crossed through the village of Oradour and went to the other road out of town, where Second Lieutenant Barth . . . had us get out, then the vehicles went on. Diekmann and Kahn had already left us, at the center of town. . . . Barth divided us into groups of three. . . . Our mission was to surround the village. The main part of our two 'sections' was sent toward the middle of the village by Barth. . . . He had told us to keep anyone from going into or out of the village and had ordered us to fire on civilians or signal any we saw out of range by shooting in the air. As for the rest, he said that all the residents were to go to the marketplace."[5]

The armored cars and trucks that had gone up and then back down the main street were only one part of the vehicles in the column. Robert Hébras: "when they arrived up in town, they halted and their personnel got out. . . . A little later I noticed that the soldiers had spread out as if for a skirmish and surrounded the area, then made their way into village."[6]

The column had broken up by the bridge at the entrance to town: the encircling maneuver started to the left and right. An identical maneuver was initiated at the other end of the village, the road to Confolens. The positions taken up were signaled by flares. Then the groups divided. Some of the men formed a ring around the village, from which no one could get out anymore, defining the execution perimeter that way. A roundup began, directed systematically toward the fairgrounds, starting with the ring of sentinels and going from the village's edge toward the center. Orders were to shoot on sight. Witnesses heard the first shots.

Despite the weapons aimed at the façades of the houses, the convoy's drive through town did not cause a great deal of concern. People wavered between uncertainty and caution. The barber's customers entered the shop. Yet another drive through did not cause panic, either. Marcel Darthout: "two half-tracks went back where they started from. The few Germans in the vehicles did not look reassuring. They were holding their weapons in their hands ready to fire, and they had stern expressions. We wondered what this show was all about, but still no one seemed to be panicking."[7]

Hubert Desourteaux: "People were curious and came spontaneously out of the buildings to watch the column go by from their doorsteps. This was a rare sight, because people in Oradour didn't get much opportunity to see Germans pass by. The Germans' attitude did not cause any apprehension. At the upper end of the village, to the west, the column did halt, but . . . two half-track trucks came back down to the east end. Seeing this, the people went back in. The druggist and other shopkeepers lowered the metal blinds on their storefronts."[8]

Clément Broussaudier was waiting across from the barbershop: "I counted five or six trucks. Following behind were two or three armored half-tracks . . . ; the men were all armed with either carbines, automatic rifles, or submachine guns. They were pointing their guns toward the houses. . . . The Germans were in camouflage uniforms, and people were impressed by how they were poised ready to fire."[9] That did not stop the barber from leaving to get tobacco. He left his customer in the hands of an assistant, "Joseph, an evacuee from Schiltigheim," who kept on cutting hair despite the comings and goings of the trucks and armored vehicles. At that moment the SS officers, part of the command company of the battalion, and the command platoon of the third company were already at the center of the village. The roundup had begun.

According to Sergeant Boos, who commanded the scouting platoon attached to the second section of the company, the encircling maneuver took place as follows: "The first section went up the main street, leaving one group on the left and another on the right at the west end of town, before going back down to the center; the second section remained at the east end (by the bridge), positioned on the right and the left; the third section rounded the residents up toward the center and the fairgrounds."[10] Other testimony by former SS soldiers and in the trial proceedings lets us conclude that the second section, with the largest number of men, was active in rounding up the residents and moving them toward the center, and fired shots during the operation; whereas the third section, consisting of only two platoons of heavy machine guns, was assigned to guard duty outside town, particularly the four roads converging toward the center.

The way the maneuver unfolded indicates two perimeters and their center. The wider one contained the roundup zone, including fields and hamlets around the village. All the residents found inside this perimeter were herded together at gunpoint and taken to the assembly point. The second perimeter defines the zone of destruction, the area set on fire. Finally, in the center of this system was the fairgrounds, a place set up to watch over those "penned in" there, a "prisoners' camp" with a battery of machine guns. The approaches to the fairgrounds were guarded to prevent anyone from leaving.

The town of Oradour, sealed off and surrounded by a cordon of SS soldiers with weapons pointed at the village, had become an enclosed field. The locking apparatus did not stop entry; it blocked exit. That is how the fate of those caught in the net and taken to the center, never again to leave, was sealed. Some bicyclists rode into town unexpectedly; a member of the town delegation thought he might possibly "go and be of use"; some worried mothers went to look for their children ... All would be caught in the net.

One exception: Yvonne Gaudy, who lived in a hamlet some way from the village, tried to go in. An SS soldier sought to convince her not to cross the line he was guarding—a boundary she obviously was unaware of. Faced with the woman's insistence, a "chief" was called, probably an SS noncom: "I was presented to this chief, who asked me for my papers. I didn't have any and said I came from Les Bordes, a village two kilometers away. He told me to go toward highway 141. I left, but came back with the Lamaud family as far as Puy-Gaillard. There the German in question stopped me and told me not to go any farther, but to go back toward the highway. He even showed me [the way], saying that Les Bordes wouldn't be affected and if I stayed I would be killed."[11] The noncoms and soldiers had precise orders. At that point they knew what the end result of the operation would be. The massacre was programmed.

The nine platoons took their places for an encirclement conducted like a drill; a training maneuver carried out in total calm. Signal flares either indicated to the SS officers that a group had taken up its position or gave a new order. A roundup operation through the fields and yards followed immediately upon the encirclement.

A Roundup without Exceptions

The executioners received an order that the roundup was to be "without exceptions." As the residents were driven from the edges toward the center of town, shots were fired in their direction right from the start. Only the first.

Clément Broussaudier and the Alsatian barber's assistant, Joseph: "After the trucks passed by, we noticed that some people from the village of Oradour who lived in the lower part were coming up toward the center . . . ; we thought it was a search operation. At a certain point a German appeared at the window and held us at bay inside, pointing a submachine gun. Another German came in then and grabbed me by the shoulder to make me stand up. He was followed closely by the first one, with the submachine gun. . . . One of them grabbed me by the arm again and pushed me outside, saying 'Raus.' Seeing that other Germans were bringing people toward the upper part of town, I went along, together with Joseph, the barber's assistant. That's how we came to the fairgrounds."[12]

Hubert Desourteaux, an escaped prisoner of war who had come back home, tried to flee with his employee, a mechanic: "I tried to get away through my yard, which opened onto the meadow on the south side. When I reached the entrance to the meadow I heard Germans running up, firing shots."[13]

Marcel Darthout, coming back to his house, tried to flee "through the yards toward the Glane. . . . When I got to the end of the yard, I saw that the Germans were spread out as if for a skirmish and had surrounded the town; that forced me to go back to the house. A few moments later a German burst into our kitchen. He was holding a rifle in his hands, and he pushed my wife, my mother, and me roughly outside with its barrel. In the street we were joined by neighbors and taken all together to the fairgrounds, where there were already quite a few people from town. Others arrived and little by little the square filled up."[14]

Mathieu Borie: "As they advanced they rounded up all the residents of Oradour, big and little, young and old, to bring them to the fairgrounds. They went into every building along the way, kicking in doors and windows if they had to."[15]

Several young men, finding more or less makeshift hiding places, could watch the various stages of the roundup with evident anxiety. The Beaubreuil brothers—Martial, an escaped prisoner of war, age thirty-two, and Maurice, age twenty-one—were having lunch at their uncle and aunt Mercier's place, one of the town's grocery stores. Martial stated that he saw "a column of seven vehicles with armed Germans in them coming from the direction of Limoges." He had not regularized his status with the occupying authorities. His situation was well known to everyone in the village and protected, "regularized," by public opinion. Maurice could be enrolled in the STO. There was a hiding place at the Mercier's, "accessible through a trapdoor carefully hidden in a corner of the kitchen. I had been in hiding for ten minutes when I heard a soldier call in French: 'Everyone outside.' I heard them rifling through the furniture drawers, too."[16]

Those in hiding saw the others go to the roundup point. Martial Brissaud, age seventeen: "As the Germans were running through the streets of Oradour to round up the inhabitants on the fairgrounds, I hid in the attic and locked the door while my family, which I was never to see again, went off toward the roundup area." Robert Besson, age twenty-six, and Jacques Garraud, age twenty-two, did not obey orders: they saw "the residents of Oradour going toward the fairgrounds escorted by armed SS who, as they went along, had people evacuate the houses. Making their way through the surrounding fields and meadows, other Germans encircled the town and took cover. We hid in a nearby yard . . . and some Germans who had seen us fired a few shots in our direction."[17]

Armand Senon was laid up in bed with his leg in a cast: "My mother came upstairs to see me in my room, to let me know they were rounding up people in the village on the fairgrounds in order to check identity papers. By that time I'd already heard the sounds of the first rifle shots coming from the direction of the bridge over the Glane. One of my aunts, who was visiting us, then urged my father and three uncles who had just arrived to run away. They immediately fled through the rear window, but not far away some of the Germans who had surrounded the village fired bursts of machine-gun fire in their direction. One uncle, a First World War veteran, was wounded then. I heard him washing the blood off. . . . The others, my father and two uncles, headed off toward the fairgrounds for the roundup. A little later some Germans came into our house and made my aunt and my grandmother, who were busy tending to my wounded uncle, leave. They knocked the two women against the staircase bannister."[18]

The perimeter of the roundup of villagers included houses and fields around town. A pencil line drawn on a staff map marked off the death area. Marguerite Rouffanche lived on a farm outside the village: "we saw three Germans armed with submachine guns coming toward our land. . . . They made us get out of the house, shouting 'Raus! Everyone to the marketplace.' We left all together, just as we were, escorted by the Germans. There were six of us including the baby. Along the way we met our neighbors . . . , all of them also escorted. . . . Going up into the village we saw Germans everywhere. They were forcing the people out of their houses, furiously yelling 'Raus! Raus!' People were paralyzed with fear. Everyone was headed toward the fairgrounds; I saw Germans knocking in doors and windows."[19]

To be complete there were roundups in the four village schools: only one child managed to run away. Roger Godfrin, age eight: "I was with all the pupils in the 'Lorraine' class, taking shelter from the bullets in the kindergarten room with my teacher; a German came in and shouted 'Raus!' . . . Realizing that the German was going to take all the children away, I ran off." His sisters, ages eleven and twelve, did not follow him. "I ran very fast and lost one of my sandals as I was leaving the school . . . but didn't try to pick it up because I didn't have time. I stepped on some thorns." Roger remembered: "my mother had told us that day . . . that if we saw Germans coming, we should run off into the woods." In his flight Roger bumped into his father's boss, a refugee woman from Lorraine, and a fourteen-year-old girl he knew. He stopped near this group for a while, then ran on when he saw "two Germans armed with submachine guns." Running behind the houses he reached the woods. Some SS soldiers saw him leave for the woods. "They shouted at me and blew their whistles, but I ran away as fast as I could and they started to run after me. I got to the other bank of the Glane by going through the stream. . . . On the other side I hid behind a tree. So the Germans left me there and went back toward the woods. . . . I saw them fire a flare in my direction. The flare fell near me after flying through the air in a big arc."[20]

Martial Machefer lived in a house on the corner of the main street and the fairgrounds. Seeing the troops, he was afraid he would be captured and taken away: he knew he was under surveillance by the police. He left the village shortly after two p.m. leaving his wife and two children at home. He also left Sarah Jakobovicz, a fifteen-year-old Jewish refugee. In May, Milice men from Limoges had paid several violent "visits" to La Malaise, the village where she lived with her parents. Another Jewish family living in La Barre, which was also on Route 141, had divided up its four children. The eldest, Raymond Engiel, placed on a farm in the hamlet of Dieulidou (in the township of Oradour), was in the village school. Sarah did not go to the roundup area. She was burned to death in the fire. Raymond, born in Nancy in 1933, suffered the fate of the schoolchildren.

Martial Machefer: "I was on the second floor of my house, on the fairgrounds side facing the road, when I saw about five German vehicles come up, at least two of them armored cars. I saw them go through the village with some of the men watching the windows, others the ground floor. A few moments later I saw a group of these vehicles go back down the street with a small number of men. Seeing these suspicious comings and goings in the village, my wife insisted that I leave the house, since I was already being closely watched by the Gestapo. After burning any papers that could harm me, I left the house around 2:10 p.m. and fled by the Saint-Junien road. When I got past the village of Oradour, I met a group of thirty or so Germans who stopped me and asked who I was. I answered: 'I'm a wounded war veteran, out of work, going to help some neighbors.' The Germans demanded my identity papers. I showed them only my wounded veteran's card. They made me take off my shoes, examined my wound, and the one who questioned me gave me back my card and said to me in French, 'Get going.'"[21] Martial Machefer slipped through the net, on Département Road 101, guarded by one or two platoons that were still perhaps waiting for the order to deploy.

The roundup was supposed to be "without exceptions," including children and the sick. Marcel Darthout: "I saw some women in tears while others, holding their babies more bravely in their arms, seemed confident. Many of the women had come with their baby carriages. I recall seeing an old man who had to be propped up and looked as if he had gotten out of bed."[22] But Pierre Giroux—another old man, born in 1867, who was paralyzed—was killed in bed in his home.

Clément Broussaudier: "People kept arriving from all over. At least twenty or so soldiers were lying down behind their automatic weapons and guarding the fairground. . . . Some isolated shots were fired in the surrounding area. The armored cars went back and forth through the village. A half-track going through the fields brought back peasants they had picked up, from time to time. After an hour, the schoolchildren arrived with their teachers. Madame Binet, who was very ill, arrived in her pajamas with a coat over her shoulders."[23]

The SS soldiers received orders to kill runaways as well as people who could not go to the roundup area. A thirty-one-year-old SS soldier, a Frenchman who had been drafted by force, A. L., later indicated that his platoon leader, Sergeant Staeger, "had specified that the sick and the people who couldn't or wouldn't go to the square were to be shot right on the spot."[24]

During the roundup, a motorized unit of the département railway, the "tramway," on a supposed test run and empty, unexpectedly arrived from Limoges with three company employees aboard. One, who was not on duty, was going to a craftsman's shop in Oradour. The "tram" stopped a little before the bridge and blocks had to be put in front of its wheels to keep it from rolling. At the same time a group that had been rounded up on the outskirts of the town walked by, escorted by Waffen SS. An employee named Chalard, who was the "passenger," got off the tram car. Did the Waffen SS order him to join the group making its way toward the village? Did he make a gesture or a move toward his colleagues? He immediately was shot, then finished off, and his body was thrown into the riverbed in full view of the group and his workmates.

We do not know how many people were in the village at the time the Waffen SS arrived or the number rounded up in immediately surrounding houses or fields who were brought to the central square under armed escort. It is certain that all school-age children in the schools except one were taken to the roundup area. It was unthinkable that teachers would abandon their pupils in danger, so not one of them attempted to flee. A good number of inhabitants tried to run away or hide.[25] Some succeeded; others quickly failed and went to the roundup. We know the names of those who succeeded completely and saved their lives. We do not know the names of all those who hid for a while, who were discovered and then executed outside the places designated for the massacre.

A Communist militant who knew he was under surveillance managed to get out of the village. Escaped prisoners of war whose status was not regularized hid. This was also true for young men who were afraid of being called up for the STO. The same exact reaction from Jewish refugees: a Monsieur Lévy from Rennes hid and survived; a Monsieur and Madame Lang from Caudéran survived.[26] Before going with his wife to the roundup, Robert Pinède (mentioned in Chapter 5) hid his three children. Their lives were spared. People had to have experienced fear and had strong motivation not to obey the SS's orders. Some of those in town tried to avoid going to the roundup. Afterward a chain of circumstances, luck or chance, allowed some to escape the massacre.

Waiting on the Fairgrounds: The Demand for Hostages

The executioners, who in a way had brought time to a standstill for their victims by enclosing them in the fairground area, then no longer seemed in a hurry. After the rapid movement of the roundup, a time of waiting began.

Marcel Darthout: "The fairgrounds was guarded by a ring of Germans armed with rifles, and six light machine guns in position with their crews beside them. I had the impression we would be shot at the slightest false move."[27]

Robert Hébras: "The schoolchildren, boys and girls, had already arrived by then. All the schoolchildren stayed with the women and girls on the right side, the men and boys fourteen–fifteen [years] and up on the left side. A half-track came over later, bringing five or six people in the truck."[28]

Marguerite Rouffanche: "We stayed at the fairgrounds for about an hour, with all the people gathered together, men, women, kids, schoolchildren, babies of all ages, three priests. Armed Germans, some lying on the ground behind their automatic weapons and others standing, guarded us on the square. The talk among the groups of people suggested that the Germans might perhaps take some people hostage, and others would be taken to concentration camps. We couldn't imagine what was going to happen. . . . After a while, when everyone had been brought together on the square that way, a German asked for the mayor, Monsieur Desourteaux, through an interpreter. He spoke with him in front of us, but I was too far away so I didn't understand any of the conversation."[29]

Clément Broussaudier: "A German came forward and called forth the mayor, Doctor Desourteaux, in French. He asked him for a list of fifty hostages. The officer had the male residents minus the schoolchildren put in one row, lined up in front of the houses. The mayor left with several Germans almost at once for the town hall. Meanwhile they had us face the wall, and at that point the Germans took the women and children away. . . . The mayor came back alone and got into line with us. He looked very brave but he didn't say anything to us. After a little while the German staff came back, too, and the same officer, who spoke fluent French with a strong accent, asked the mayor if he had chosen the fifty hostages. The mayor answered him: 'I cannot find fault with any of my residents, so I am unable to designate hostages.' The officer answered him with 'you've got weighty responsibilities.' When the mayor again told him he offered himself and, if need be, his closest relatives as hostages, the officer burst out laughing and had us counted off and put in groups of forty or fifty people."[30]

In the East it was common practice to have the mayor designate Communist and Jewish residents and then to take them away as hostages or execute them on the spot. Was Paul Desourteaux, the president of the Special Delegation, taken to the town hall? Did the Waffen SS request that he designate fifty hostages? In Saint-Junien it was forty, according to statements by collaborators. As far as the fairground episode goes, we have only one attestation that is so precise. We cannot know what they demanded of Paul Desourteaux. On the other hand, he definitely did not designate any hostages besides himself and his close family.

Did the executioners really want to take hostages, as the Milice member and the Gestapo collaborator said and the demand made to the mayor confirms, or was this just a trick to calm the fears of the assembled people? We do know for certain that this episode duplicated a procedure common in the East, in similar operations against the "bandits."

As soon as they had been assembled in an enclosed area, the victims were deprived of their space, the village. They were deprived of their time as well. They no longer had a future. The time of the massacre was an "extended present."[31] The survivors and escapees had to reconstruct the time of the massacre in their accounts. They would construct it using a combination of "points," accumulations of "at that point." They would give timetables reconstructed under the pressure of questions: "and before that?" and "after that?" At times such timetables would be very precise, when we think that these were people who either had no watches or, considering the danger and the urgent need to escape, could not memorize the time when they managed to extricate themselves from an inferno. Still others made simultaneous use of several time systems in effect during the occupation: "German" or "Vichy" time, solar time, traditional time ... The Germans had imposed the Berlin time zone, which became, sarcastically, "Vichy time"; farm work was regulated by solar time. The victims reconstructed the time of the massacre so as to reappropriate a temporal sequence for themselves, something their executioners had deprived of them.

Separation

The final seconds, during which the men, standing there guarded by machine guns, saw the women and children leave ... At such an intense moment of separation the consciousness of danger, an anguish not yet shared by all, grew keener. The men who survived would always retain a tragic, wrenching image.

Marcel Darthout: "Around three o'clock an order was given and the young and old men were separated from the women and schoolchildren, the men to the left and the others to the right on the fairgrounds. It was then that I embraced my wife and mother for the last time. I was a long way from suspecting what was in store us."[32]

Marguerite Rouffanche: "After an hour the women and children were separated from the men and taken to the church, while the men stayed where they were. As I left with the women and children, heartrending scenes of farewell were taking place. The Germans put up with or couldn't stop us from embracing our dear ones. It all happened quickly. As we walked to the church, the Germans were guarding us on both sides."[33]

Marcel Darthout: "They almost immediately had us line up by threes along the houses, facing the buildings. Meanwhile, as we learned later, the women and schoolchildren were taken away to the church. I turned my head to watch the column leave, despite the ban. It was a very sad sight. Heartrending cries were uttered by some women or children. You could feel they were anxious for their fathers, husbands, or sons. I saw some women faint. Others picked them up and dragged them along with the column, which was leaving, well guarded by armed Germans."[34]

From the window of his bedroom where he was in hiding, which looked out on the fairgrounds, Armand Senon saw what was going on in the square: "the Germans had them open the doors of the houses on the square, beating on them with their rifle-butts . . . , a little later I heard women and children crying out in the square. That troubled me, so I drew back then from the window so I wouldn't hear or see any more. I thought they were taking hostages. . . . When I didn't hear any more sounds coming from the square, I went back to the window; then I saw that the men were sitting along the edge of the sidewalk on the curb, guarded by Germans who had set up light machine guns. . . . I saw a German officer come from the lower end of the village; he spoke to Monsieur Desourteaux, the doctor and delegate-mayor of the town. I couldn't understand the conversation, which was brief. Almost immediately the men stood up and formed groups; I saw about four of them, with fifty or so men in each one; these were led away one after the other, all guarded by armed Germans."[35]

Already an episode of extreme violence, this separation was a laceration, a tearing apart, as shown by the "heartrending cries." The calm that the SS men needed to pursue their activities was broken. To restore it, further periods of waiting were necessary. A propaganda movie from the Nazi film archives shows a comparable sequence in a village of Eastern Europe. The residents of the village have been rounded up. The men are grouped together, then separated from the women and children, who are then taken away, escorted by soldiers. You can read the terror on their faces. Brief signs are exchanged from a distance. The men watch the women and children leave.[36]

The Men Are Kept Waiting in the Square

After the women and children left, the men who remained at the fairgrounds could sit down: a time of anguish and uncertainty. About half an hour went by before they were led away toward some barns. Meanwhile, the SS inspected the premises; they had a vehicle that was in the way removed from the wine merchant's storehouse. Marcel Darthout: "He [the wine merchant] and his son-in-law left with (two) Germans then and came back quite a while later to rejoin us. Half an hour later, when the interpreter also returned, he had us stand up. That's when the German announced: 'We have been told there are weapons in Oradour, weapons that were left here by terrorists. Do any among you own weapons?' Several residents then declared that they owned rifles of authorized caliber, but this did not interest the Germans at all. The interpreter informed us at this point that we would be taken into barns and meanwhile searches would be carried out in the village. 'We'll search the houses.' The residents said to each other, then: 'They can go ahead and search, there isn't anything.' They immediately counted us off by groups and led us off, my group into Laudy's barn. On the way there I was shoved violently."[37]

SS Sergeant Boos would confirm this: "Kahn had the interpreter tell the people they shouldn't be afraid, they were going to search through the houses and look for weapons and ammunition. After this speech, Kahn had the men taken away to various barns that he had reconnoitered himself with Barth and Diekmann."[38]

From the start of the operation no identity papers had been checked. Uneasily, some men had tried to show theirs. They thought these were in order; might there not be some mistake concerning them? The Waffen SS men pushed them back roughly without looking at the papers held out to them.

The maneuver to surround the village of Oradour began a little before 2 p.m. A standing guard had been set in place to prevent anyone from leaving the village; a wider perimeter, one or two kilometers from the center of town, was subject to a systematic roundup; but beyond this nothing. The residents were neither assaulted nor disturbed.

The roundup was violent, with things broken, doors and windows smashed in; there were shots, wounded and dead people. Nevertheless not all those in the group under pressure felt anxiety and fear. Indeed, what was there to fear for these people, who had lived in the village for so long, who thought without feeling the slightest doubt that "their papers were in order"? But the escaped prisoners, the young men who might be picked up for forced labor in Germany, those on file for political reasons, and most especially the French and foreign refugees, some of them Jews, who were never fully in order with the Vichy police and occupation forces—what might they feel under this threat of imminent danger?

For the people who arrived first, the wait on the fairgrounds must have lasted close to two hours, with the Waffen SS inspiring swings from fear to confidence. The request for hostages may have been a test imposed on them, but in the aftermath it seems to have been forgotten and unimportant. The demand concerning the arms caches seems to have been formulated as if there were a need to "calm things down" and reassure people before the measures that followed were put into effect.

Identical sequences of events can be observed in other massacres that occurred around the same time, for example the one perpetrated by the Hermann Goering division in Italy in Civitella della Chiana, a Tuscan village near Arezzo, on June 29, 1944.

Execution of the Men in Enclosed Areas

Darthout: "When we got to the barn, I carefully made my way to the back of the building . . .; since the barn was strewn with carts, the Germans had us take them out. While we were crowded together, they neatly swept the area outside the door, then set up two machine guns there. There were six Germans in all guarding us. Two of them were lying down, loading their machine guns; another one, with a rifle or automatic rifle, was sucking on a lump of sugar he took from his pocket; when one of my neighbors tried to sit down on a pile of hay the Germans ordered him to stand up."[39]

SS Sergeant Boos: "Kahn called the group leaders together and told us that by order of the battalion leader these men were to be executed right away. Kahn would give the signal to open fire with a submachine gun burst. We didn't get any other explanation. Then I went back to my group and passed the order on. Kahn was five meters away from me. He gave the signal and we opened fire. For my part, I didn't shoot. Kahn came up and said to give the coup de grâce to anyone who was still moving. He gave me the order personally and I carried it out on six or seven men. . . . The order was executed, and as far as I know other platoons did the same thing to other Frenchmen in other barns. I did not take part in the executions in person, limiting myself to passing on the signal to fire to the platoon, but I did kill the wounded lying on the ground with shots to the head. The execution had lasted only a few minutes. Then I received Töpfer and Kahn's order to cover the bodies with pieces of wood and to pour oil over them."[40]

Marcel Darthout and Robert Hébras said they waited for about ten minutes in the barn, where they were packed in with forty or so men and boys: "We heard the sound of an explosion from outside, followed by a burst of automatic weapons fire. Immediately at a brief command the six Germans discharged their weapons at us. On the first burst I was wounded by two bullets in my calves. I collapsed when I got two other bullets in my thighs. In a few seconds I was covered with dead bodies, and the machine guns kept firing their bursts. I heard the wounded moaning: it wasn't cries, but muffled gasps. I was there under the wounded, suffocating, flattened and covered with the blood flowing from my comrades in misfortune. Once the gun bursts stopped, the Germans came over to finish off a few of us from close up. I heard them cock their rifles. I expected to get the coup de grâce but the Germans had left the barn without spotting me, covering us first with hay, straw, and other things. I got the impression that they had trodden on the corpses next to me as they were covering us with straw. As they left they were laughing among themselves."[41]

A French SS soldier from annexed Alsace, B. was in the platoon commanded by SS Sergeant Boos and took part in the shooting: "in a barn in the middle of town not far from the church; the Frenchmen were lined up in the barn and we positioned ourselves on the sidewalk opposite them; the barn doors were open. The signal to open fire was a pistol shot by Kahn. Immediately upon that, Boos ordered us to fire on the Frenchmen and we did. We were armed with submachine guns, automatic rifles, machine guns, and rifles; Boos had a submachine gun. He was the first one to fire."[42]

A forced draftee, Jean-Pierre E. was eighteen in June 1944. He was put in a platoon of the first section of the third company, commanded by SS Sergeant Lauber: "We went to a garage located on the main street. It had about thirty civilians in it, boys and men of all ages. The entrance was guarded by machine guns and Kahn himself was standing at that entrance. The machine gun crews had taken up their positions on the road and were prone behind their automatic weapons. The civilians tried to discuss things, brandishing identity papers that they tried desperately to show to Kahn, and they crowded around him begging him not to fire at them. Kahn seemed implacable and he pushed them back into the garage, finally stepping aside and ordering the men to fire. Immediately the machine guns chattered and the civilians collapsed on one another. I figure a hundred shots were fired at them. No one could escape from that garage, and anyone who still showed signs of life was shot dead or finished off with submachine guns fired by noncoms Maurer and Boos; the two Unterscharführers [platoon leaders] had rushed into the garage right off, turned the corpses over with their boots, and discharged their submachine guns point-blank at the dying. They hadn't been ordered to do it. The battalion head wasn't present at the massacre. Kahn immediately gave an order to go get straw from a barn. I formed a chain to pass the bales of straw into the garage."[43]

Darthout: "Once the footsteps had left the barn, I tried to change position since I was suffocating under the weight. I touched my neighbor's hand. We exchanged a few words in an undertone. It was Monsieur Aliotti. He told me his two legs were broken. Another man had just gotten loose and he told us that the Germans had really gone. In the distance we could hear a radio playing. I heard someone speaking German, soon followed by some music. The door to our barn was closed. My neighbor, Aliotti, must have been suffering terribly. He called out to his wife, his children, then he said 'Good bye!' As for me, I felt my legs growing stiff. After about fifteen minutes the Germans . . . set fire to the hay and straw covering us; they had even put firewood on top of us. The fire spread pretty quickly and I started to feel the flames licking at my hair. As I tried to protect my head with my hands, I could feel that they were being attacked by the flames, too. My clothes also started to burn; so, feeling the fire on my shoulders, I yelled to my comrades to escape with me even if we got shot. When I got loose I expected a bullet to finish me off, but I saw to my utter surprise that the Germans had left. There were five of us survivors in the back of the barn; all the others must have been burning up in that inferno—some of them still alive. Borie, one of the survivors, quickly widened a hole in the wall there, four meters above the ground. One after the other we all crawled through the opening, with my comrades helping me to manage it. We concealed ourselves in the straw."[44]

The SS officers had chosen the places and assigned the platoons, which it seems logical belonged to the first two sections of the company, if we take the duty assignments into account. At the trial hearing in 1953, the presiding military judge indicated the names of the platoon leaders who ordered the firing:

— the Poutaraud Garage: SS Sergeant Baïer, first section;
— the Denis Storehouse: SS Sergeant Lauber, first section;
— the Desourteaux Garage: SS Sergeant Boos, second section (Boos commanded the company's scouting platoon);
— the Laudy Barn: SS Sergeant Staeger, second section;
— the Milord Barn: SS Sergeant Genari or SS Sergeant Kabbeck, second section;
— the Bouchoule Barn: X. This might be either the platoon commanded by SS Sergeant Tscheyge of the first section or the platoon in the second section commanded by SS Adjutant Lenz. Perhaps the latter, who was present at Oradour, had been stripped of his command as he claimed at the trial. This was a common disciplinary punishment against SS noncommissioned officers who had low marks from their superiors. The names of the noncoms, which we have reason to recall here, match with the list of the company's men mentioned earlier.

Three successive orders were given by the company commander, who called the group leaders together each time. The first one ordered the shooting, signaled by a single pistol shot for all the different places. The second one told the SS noncommissioned officers to finish off the wounded, although it is possible some of them may have anticipated this order. The third was the order to put combustible materials and products on the bodies and set them on fire.

Until the very last moment, the final second before the guns were fired, the people, who had become hostages awaiting execution, did not imagine the gravity of their situation. Survivors' testimony shows that they did not believe death was imminent. They could not and did not believe it. The victims' surprise must have been total. The Waffen SS's maneuver had succeeded: the execution took place in peace and quiet, without disturbance or panic.

Pillaging, Arson, and Butchery in the Streets

The executions were carried out by platoons with two machine guns, leaving four or five men per platoon available to carry out a systematic search of the village residences and shops. Pillaging could begin as soon as the village had been emptied of its inhabitants. Pillaging was followed by burning. While the SS soldiers in SS Sergeant Boos's platoon brought inflammable materials for the bodies into the barns, "the whole platoon of the company leader searched the houses and carried out the things that were meant for the officers. Among them there were some objects of value, but . . . only the officers profited from the pillaging. . . . After the executions the first section dispersed to set fire to the village."[45]

After straw was strewn over the bodies, SS soldier Jean-Pierre E.: "[I] didn't see how they set the fire, because Lauber took me away with his group toward a small property located about 300 meters from the garage, in a yard surrounded by a wall opposite the railroad station shed. He went into the house, where he found several boxes of matches, which he handed out to us. We searched through the entire house, some men broke open the desk drawers, others the wardrobes, and I'm certain that several of us committed thefts . . . ; in one desk drawer there were bundles of banknotes that one of the German SS men was going to steal, but Lauber came in just then and stopped him. . . . Two of my comrades carried some things out of the building, one a lighter, the other a coin collection. Without delay Lauber had us set fire to the garage in the yard, attached to the wall along the road; in the garage were a motorcycle and a car. We poured the gasoline we found there and set it on fire. . . . meanwhile, flames were already shooting up in the village, where houses had been set on fire. Shots were ringing out from all directions."[46] This description matches the property of Doctor Paul Desourteaux.

One of the Beaubreuil brothers, who were still hiding inside the Merciers' grocery: "I . . . heard them ransacking the furniture in the house. I clearly made out the sounds of a hammer and a saw, . . . an explosion coming from the church, followed by a big burst of machine-gun fire from all corners of the village. Around 5:15 p.m. my aunt's young maid . . . came back into the house; she ran through it, crying 'Oh my God! oh my God!' She went into the yard where a woman shouted to her, 'My poor girl! My poor girl! It's horrible!' All was calm until 5:30 p.m. Then two Germans came into the house and went all the way up to the attic; they came back down two or three minutes later. Their departure was followed by a loud crackling noise that sounded like a fire to me. The air was becoming unbreathable. I managed to get out of my hiding place with great difficulty after I got across the floor, which was on fire."[47]

The residents whose reaction was to hide were driven out by fire and forced to move. For some the risk turned out to be deadly. There were a few exceptions: Hubert Desourteaux stayed in his hiding place; Armand Senon left his burning house, dragging himself along with his leg in a cast. The Pinède children, two girls and a boy, were discovered by a Waffen SS man under a stairwell, and he chased them toward the meadows. But for others more numerous, it meant death. The body of Poutaraud, the mechanic, was found machine-gunned next to a fence near the cemetery; at least one body, perhaps several, were thrown into the bakery's ember pit; some bodies were flung into a well; Foussat the miller, a member of the Special Delegation, was machine-gunned as he tried to enter the village; the body of a département railway employee had been thrown into the river at the beginning of the roundup.

Before leaving the bedroom where he was hiding, Armand Senon, trembling with fear, saw the spur-of-the-moment execution of a group of people he did not know: "I saw seven or eight men escorted by Germans arrive at the fairgrounds. They must have been strangers passing through the village area; some of them had bicycles. I didn't recognize any of them. The Germans held them for a while until a leader arrived and without checking any of their identity papers gave instructions to the soldiers. The latter, who had automatic weapons, made them line their bicycles up in front of the wall of the building, and a German emptied his weapon at them from ten meters away. I saw the butcher, standing in front of the hostages. He swept the row with his fire. The men fell down immediately. . . . He turned his weapon down toward the ground and continued emptying it at the civilians; the dust rose from the ground."[48]

Later on, Armand Senon would recognize among the victims of this slaughter the body of Albert Mirablon, who was born in 1909 in the United States. Mirablon's mother, Anna Chaleix, was born in Oradour in 1885 and died in the massacre; she had emigrated early in the century with her sister, Maria. They had found husbands among the European immigrants in New Jersey and returned home as widows. Albert Mirablon had two main interests: bicycle riding and photography. He had joined the Libération Sud movement as soon as it was started by Armand Dutreix in Limoges in 1941. He had come to visit his mother in Oradour this June 10 on his way to or from a mission in Saint-Junien, where he had been sent by the head of his unit.[49]

SS soldier Paul G. was on guard duty or leading a cleanup operation: "From over by the cemetery, where we were guarding the gates, I heard machine guns chattering. . . . Right after I heard the shooting I saw flames rise in the village. . . . When we had left Saint-Junien, Untersturmführer Barth walked along the convoy and told us: 'Today you're going to see blood flow.' . . . A man and a woman were hiding, with a girl of about sixteen, in this meadow with a hedge around it. The three of them were lying flat on their stomachs. A Russian-born corporal . . . went up to the group and shot the three of them point-blank. The woman was wounded in the chest. She got up and started to shriek, clutching her arms around her waist. Then I personally finished her off with a point-blank rifle shot. Officer Barth, drawn over by the shots, came up and had the bodies of the three victims thrown over the hedge."[50] On Barth's order the bodies were thrown into the fire.

B. and L. indicate that two (or three?) women were murdered by SS Sergeant Boos. B: "two women came to look for their children, who were locked up in the church. Boos called them over, then took them into a shed and we heard two revolver shots . . . ; he had just killed the two women." L.: "In my presence, he (Boos) killed two girls around twenty-two and eighteen years old, plus a woman forty or forty-five. The three people in question had come out of a house facing the church on the day in question when the church was on fire. Without asking any questions at all, he pushed them into a shed . . . and killed them with his submachine gun. Seeing that, I asked him if he hadn't killed enough people already, and he answered: 'Shut up or I'll shoot you, too.' I let the matter drop." SS soldier Paul G. stated that Pakowski, a Waffen SS soldier in the command platoon of the company, "told us he had just clubbed a young woman and her baby that he had found in the toilets near the church to death with his rifle butt." This was probably the young woman with a baby who tried to follow Mme Rouffanche in her escape.[51]

The Waffen SS pillaged and then set fires. SS soldier Jean-Pierre E.: "Barth entered the grocery store I was in with a few comrades and told me to start a fire. To make me do it he threatened me with his revolver, and so then I started a fire with my comrades inside that house, by setting everything that was inflammable on fire with matches."[52] The pillaging was carried on mainly inside the village and in the nearby hamlets. Its area corresponded to that of the fire. The hamlets within the roundup's perimeter but outside the destruction were less thoroughly pillaged. The Waffen SS helped themselves to money and jewelry in the houses that had been emptied of their inhabitants.

When it came to transportable materials (fabrics, for example) or objects, the fruits of the pillaging were for the SS organization ("for the officers," as Boos said). From the June 1941 invasion in the East onward, the Wehrmacht had been ordered to live off the production and reserves of the occupied territories, as the 1940 armistice also specified for French territory, though by means of a daily indemnity ... With the pillaging of food products and cattle, the SS troops once again felt the reflexes of their campaigns in Eastern Europe. The thefts committed individually by Waffen SS men (musical instruments, bicycles) were of a "ludic," "playful" nature, part of the men's "release" after the massacre. Some of the stolen objects quickly were broken and for the most part were abandoned, particularly the bicycles.

Fire followed the pillaging, except for the buildings occupied by the Waffen SS during the operation. These were set on fire when they left that night or the next morning. The village was set on fire systematically, and multiple points of arson were needed. To clear themselves of any responsibility, the executioners would provide only minimal and "euphemistic" information. The motorman of the test "tram" who was turned back in the afternoon reported the preparation of incendiary supplies made partly from materials found on the spot and the placement of drums in front of the houses.[53] The use of incendiary ammunition was also reported; incendiary cartridges or explosives were certainly distributed among the cartridge belts used in the machine guns. Ammunition of this sort could be shot from the carbines that the troops were supplied with; some platoons in the company were equipped with grenade launchers that fired incendiary as well as other types of grenades.

The Massacre in the Church

This was a massacre within a massacre. About 350 women and children were packed into the church, an ideal enclosed space for a mass execution. This Waffen SS action took place at the same time as the pillaging and lighting of the fires. There was only a single survivor who would testify to what she had lived through, having managed to get out of the building. For what happened afterward we must turn to Waffen SS accounts.

Marguerite Rouffanche: "Germans guarded us on all sides on our way to the church. We remained in the church for an hour and a half. We awaited anxiously the fate in store for us. Hardly anyone spoke anymore. I was together again with my two daughters and the little seven-month-old boy. I saw my five-year-old niece fall asleep . . . ; Germans would appear from time to time to see what was going on in the church. All the doors had been shut and no Germans were guarding us inside. The entire nave was filled. I was in the center and I couldn't see what was happening near the door. After an hour and a half the Germans opened the door and started to evacuate the church on that side. Some women and children went outside. Just then two Germans, both about thirty years old, pushed their way through the women and children and set a box about two and a half feet long down in front of the altar. The box must have been heavy, since it took two to carry it; it was full of white strings sticking out of the wrapping. I saw the box not far away from me and I saw the two Germans open it. It was when they opened it that I saw it had those white strings. Immediately after that the Germans went out without saying a word or appearing to be concerned about us. So then I thought they were going to blow up the church and us with it. Meanwhile everyone remained calm, though. A few moments later there was a little detonation from the box, and right away black, acrid, stinging smoke came from it, filling up the entire church. The smoke was suffocating and the women and children started to scream and shout. Everyone was in a panic and trying to get away. We had all the schoolchildren with us, including the thirteen- and fourteen-year-old boys.

"I headed with my two daughters and the women near me for the sacristy, to find shelter from the suffocating smoke. Since the shouting kept up and the screaming got louder, that probably ended up by annoying the Germans. So then they rained a hail of bullets through the sacristy windows. Beside me, my youngest daughter was killed by the bullets slicing through her carotid artery. So I played dead; I lay down on the floor. A moment later some Germans came into the sacristy and fired machine guns from the door. The victims uttered loud screams at that point. Luckily I wasn't wounded and I didn't budge from where I was. Right after they unleashed the hail of bullets, the Germans came into the church and set up a pile of wood, bringing in straw, firewood, throwing church benches and chairs on top to make a fire. When I saw the flames I left the sacristy and took shelter behind the altar. I noticed the stool used for services there and got up on it to reach one of the windows, the one on the left, and threw myself out of it. . . . A woman next to me, . . . the mother of a little seven-month-old baby, followed me through the window. She passed her child to me, but I couldn't grab it in time, and, hearing bullets rattling around me, I got up and went to hide in the garden. . . . I was machine-gunned and struck by five bullets in my legs and shoulder."[54]

Waffen SS soldier L.: "I had heard Hauptsturmführer Kahn say that the church which the women and children had been shut up in was to be destroyed by explosives. The explosion hadn't brought the church down as the Germans had hoped, and the women and children inside were massacred by machine-gun fire and pineapple grenades thrown through the main door into the church. . . . When the people were machine-gunned enough inside the church, we all had to bring in wood and straw, which were then set on fire. If I had refused to take part in carrying out that order I would have been executed on the spot."[55]

The same SS soldier: "I saw some noncommissioned officers, in particular the one named Boos, throw at least half a dozen stick-handle grenades inside the building, from which you could hear cries and shouting. It gave off an acrid, bluish smoke, and that made me think they had tried to dynamite it. Then the noncoms went inside the church to wipe out everything with machine guns. I learned later that a woman had tried to throw herself out a church window, but she had been shot dead by an SS man. Myself, I had been ordered to position myself opposite the church down on the road, to make sure no one escaped, because some women had tried to escape through the church windows. I didn't see anyone else try to flee, but I did notice a trail of blood by the wall under a church window."[56]

SS soldier Jean-Pierre E.: "Lauber, an SS sergeant, led us into the church square, and we had to run to get away from the thick smoke all around us and filling the streets, since everything was burning already. Along the way I saw that a garage where they had executed a group of residents was on fire. Battalion Leader Diekmann was in the church square when we arrived. He was standing there with his arms crossed. Kahn was directing operations in the same square. From inside the building you could hear women and children yelling and screaming. Some SS men were busy carrying bundles of firewood and straw into the building, and during the operation I saw two Unterscharführers, SS Sergeants Maurer and Boos, go into the church and shoot bursts of submachine-gun fire, while other SS men threw hand grenades into the building, definitely to finish the people off. . . . At the end we were assembled in the street facing the church to witness its destruction. I saw noncommissioned officer Boos come and give Captain Kahn an explosive charge. Kahn went into the church accompanied by a few armed SS men. There was an immediate explosion and within just a few moments the entire inside of the building was in flames, with smoke coming through the church windows.

"I didn't really see how the explosive charge was prepared since I was pretty far away from where it happened. Battalion Leader Diekmann had us stand at attention on the road during the operation. . . . As they set fire to the church you could still hear cries inside, although less than at first, which proves that when they set it on fire people were still alive or dying. . . . In the square beside the church the body of a child about a year old lay under a plow. . . . Later I asked a German SS man . . . whether there had been any Alsatians in the church. . . . The German informed me that there was an Alsatian woman in the church who asked to speak to Captain Kahn, but he refused to see her, saying no one should survive so there wouldn't be any witnesses."[57]

SS soldier B.: "Kahn had us assemble so as to get us away from danger while the church blew up; we took shelter. . . . The explosion was so powerful that SS soldier Gnug was thrown against a wall and wounded near the church. The church didn't come down. I didn't know what was happening, when Kahn came to get the head of my group, Boos, and ordered him to take the wounded man to the hospital in Limoges. . . . Just as there was the explosion in the church, I heard women and children crying out. When I returned they told me that, since the church hadn't been brought down by the explosion, the SS spread straw and set fire to it."[58]

From the same man: "Boos told us we should take shelter because the church was going to be blown up, it had been mined by a noncom from the third company. . . . When he blew up the church he was wounded by a fragment. I accompanied the wounded man to the hospital in Limoges and when I got back the village was on fire."[59]

SS soldier Paul G. also gave the name of the noncom who set the charges in the church: "They had tried to blow up the church using explosives, but the operation was unsuccessful because the charges weren't powerful enough, and Gnug was seriously wounded in the head then and evacuated. I happened to be with that noncom during July–August at the military hospital in Dijon where he was treated. His head was split open. . . . He was close to insane and had become unapproachable."[60] From several interviews in 1947, ex-Sergeant Boos would make it possible to reconstruct the sequence of events: "Adjutant Gnug blew up the church where the women and children were."[61]

Boos in May 1947: "Töpfer was in position with a group of men (near the church). He told me to take shelter because they were going to blow something up. Five minutes later there was a pretty violent explosion. I heard the detonation, and they came to get me ten minutes later. Kahn told me to go with two men and take Gnug, who had been wounded, to the hospital in Limoges. Gnug was wounded over the forehead; he was in a coma. I found out that when the explosion took place he didn't run away fast enough. . . . I took Gnug to Limoges in an armored car, accompanied by Lange, who was going to take a report to regimental headquarters."[62] SS Lieutenant Lange was the battalion commander's adjutant.

Boos: "The company adjutant, Gnug, blew up the church where the women and children were. . . . I remember SS Sergeant Picha, the company munitions expert, who took part in the affair of the church. During the explosion in the church a stone fell on SS Adjutant Gnug's head, and Kahn ordered me to take him to the hospital in Limoges. Kahn chose me for the job because he knew I was a medic."[63]

An explosive charge was prepared. It cannot be determined whether it was dynamite or mines, two types of munitions that the SS company had, or some special compound of the munitions expert's. Placing and setting off the charge was the job of the company pyrotechnics specialist, SS Adjutant Gnug, the head of the command platoon. He was wounded by a flying stone and taken to the hospital. Numerous accounts agree on that.

The destruction of the church vault was a failure. Did the rest of the massacre result from an order, or from initiatives by SS noncoms? Most likely the combination of an order and individual initiatives: the accounts of those who carried it out describe something like "battlefield frenzy," when men let loose all their violence, with their commanders' authorization. But here there was no battle.

The women and children were machine-gunned inside the church, into which grenades had been thrown: "I saw Sergeant Genari, the leader of the command group of the third section, breaking statues with his gun butt and ripping out confessional doors."[64] The profanation included physical involvement by the Waffen SS, and involvement in the violence required profanation.

Placing the woodpile in the nave and under the sacristy, the Waffen SS soldiers brought straw and firewood that the residents had set aside in June, in reserve for the following winter. They also set fire to the roof timbers over the vault. "The entire company was near the church . . . ; we saw the church crumble. We stayed there until the church roof collapsed."[65] The SS troops, many of them very young and put in the position of spectators, saw what they were supposed to learn how to do, following the example of the SS noncoms who were seasoned killers after their campaigns on the Eastern front.

SS Lieutenant Lange, Major Diekmann's adjutant, made the roundtrip to Limoges with Boos's vehicle, which carried the wounded man. He took a report to the Der Führer regiment's headquarters. Later statements by SS officers Weidinger and Werner—mentioning the SS colonel's surprise and the reproaches he was said to have made right away to the battalion commander when the latter stopped by regimental headquarters—were part of a "window-dressing" campaign surrounding the massacre.[66] Propaganda orchestrated by the SS authorities in Limoges was meant to implicate the Resistance in the massacre, to make it bear responsibility.

The Survivors' Flight

Six survivors of the shooting managed to get out of Laudy's barn and hide in nearby lean-tos, until the advancing fire drove them out. Robert Hébras: "Everything was burning all around us. Darthout, who was wounded so we had to drag him, . . . was thirsty; I gave him some water that was there for the chickens and he drank it. About two hours later, towards five in the afternoon, we fled in the direction of the cemetery. There were still some Germans, but they didn't catch sight of us, because there was smoke everywhere covering our retreat. We left Darthout concealed in a corner and I ran off, along with Borie."[67] (The approximate hour of the flight is given here in solar time.)

Mathieu Borie: "We managed to get out and run away across the fields by going from one building to another up to the edge of town. It was around seven o'clock when we got past the roadblocks. . . . The whole town was ablaze by then."[68] One of the six survivors died while fleeing.

Clément Broussaudier: "We hid in a rabbit hutch. I stayed with Roby in the hiding place for two and a half hours. When the hutch caught fire we were forced to leave. We jumped over a wall and arrived in the area of the fairgrounds, but shots were still crackling from various directions, so we decided to run as fast as possible across the square toward the cemetery. That must have been around 7:45. . . . We didn't see anyone, so since we could see that all of Oradour was in flames, we fled across the fields.[69]

Darthout stayed behind: "Everything around us was burning. We heard the buildings' roof timbers crashing down around us. The streets and the square were . . . black with smoke. First the roof of the barn collapsed nearby, then our hutch caught fire. But I was in a lot of pain and wondering how I would be able to get away. . . . The fire spread quickly . . . , we had to get away. We didn't see any Germans in the vicinity so my companions left me, running for their lives across the fairgrounds. I followed after them but I was too weak, so I collapsed in the middle of the square. Because of the risk of recapture by the Germans, I went on crawling along on the ground. . . . In a yard beside a burning house I found some towels that I used to bandage my wounds temporarily. When I felt a little stronger I went and hid in some bushes."[70]

Marcel Darthout stayed in hiding a few yards away from a friend, Armand Senon, who had fled from his burning house. Frightened out of their wits, they sensed each other's presence nearby but could do nothing. Armand Senon: "Some Germans grazed by me, so to speak, passing by the bushes, but they didn't see me. . . . I saw a head with red hair not far from me, that scared me. I thought I would be discovered." Marcel Darthout: "He was huddled in the bushes and I hadn't noticed him. Around about five o'clock (solar time), I heard a woman's piercing scream. I started to cry, thinking of my family." Darthout recognized some Limousin voices and called to them. After Darthout left, Armand Senon remained in the bushes until morning.[71]

No one else would escape from the shootings. Five survivors escaped from Laudy's barn. No witnesses would ever provide an account of the executions in the Bouchoule barn or the Milord barn, the Desourteaux garage or the Poutaraud garage, or Denis's wine storehouse.

The Horrifying Discovery of the Town on Fire

That evening, travelers returning or passing through Oradour were horrified to discover the village enveloped in flames. The first was a railway engineer named Jean Pallier, who was riding in a truck with some other men, on business. Although by order of the military command all traffic had been forbidden in the former free zone since June 9, the day before, he had authorization to arrange a detour through Oradour to visit his wife and children, who had taken refuge there. Once he completed his business, he left Limoges around six p.m. and arrived in Oradour after passing through a checkpoint about four kilometers away.

Jean Pallier wrote an account of what he found: "At the top of a hill we could see the village, which was just a mass of flames. . . . About 300 meters from the town we were stopped under the threat of an automatic rifle by a squadron of five or six German soldiers. We were told to get out of the car quickly and put up our hands, then we were briefly searched to check whether we were carrying weapons. I took advantage of the opportunity to explain in German . . . that I had been authorized by a German officer to go as far as Oradour. A bicycle courier left then for Oradour to get the necessary instructions from the command post. He came back about twenty minutes later saying we should stay where we were. The département electric train connecting Limoges with Saint-Junien and Bussière-Poitevine by way of Oradour arrived at that point."[72]

The evening "tram" left Limoges around six p.m., despite the afternoon's dramatic incident involving a test train that had been sent back and the death of a département railway employee. Three kilometers from Oradour, a young man warned that "some Germans were shooting hostages and burning houses. . . . The driver continued on his way nonetheless, as far as Puy-Gaillard, where he was stopped by the Germans."[73]

The travelers who lived in Oradour or were going there were ordered to get out of the cars. The Waffen SS checked the identities of those remaining in the "tram" and sent them back toward Limoges. The people who had gotten out waited for orders to be given for their situation. The railway engineer sent his companions back to Limoges with the vehicle and had to join the group of Oradour inhabitants.

Monsieur Pallier: "It was around eight at night. As we made our way across the fields we saw that a ring of armed troops completely surrounded the village. We underwent further questioning at the command post. There were five or six men and eight or ten women. Since the detachment's leader wasn't there the questioning was done by a noncommissioned officer, who then let us know that we had to wait for the commanding officer. While we were in the command post the soldiers guarding us, all of them Germans, kept fooling around with the women and showing the sort of cheerfulness that you have after a pleasant outing. None of the men was drunk. Around ten p.m., the German soldiers' attitude suddenly changed. The commanding officer had just arrived. I was told to line up with the other men along a wall, as if we were going to be shot. Another identity check was carried out. All of us were men who had come to see their families, and none of us lived in Oradour. Was that the reason? Or was it because it was late and the officer was in a hurry to get back? Whatever it may have been, we were told to get away from the village quickly. As we left, the noncom who had carried out the last identity check, and who spoke proper French, said to us: "You can consider yourselves lucky."[74]

At the end of the afternoon, when the village was burning, the Waffen SS set up a command post outside the perimeter of destruction at the Masset farm, where the passengers of the evening "tram" were taken.

One of the Waffen SS men, Paul G., confirmed Jean Pallier's account: "When the church roof collapsed, Captain Kahn had us assemble . . . just outside the village near a farm, where the officers had had some chickens prepared. I saw twenty or twenty-five civilians arrive. . . . After half an hour Captain Kahn came, examined the civilians' papers rapidly, and sent them away. Not far from there was Unterscharführer Lauber (an SS sergeant, the leader of the second platoon of the first section), who started gesticulating and shouted that these people ought to be killed."[75]

In the evening the Waffen SS's actions changed. The massacre was over. During the operation the SS officers refused to look at the papers held out to them by people who thought they could show proof there was nothing against them and their papers were in order. That evening the SS captain rapidly, almost absent-mindedly and as a formality, examined documents identical to the ones that had been held out to him in the afternoon. Then he dismissed their holders. It was time to leave.

One group of SS troops remained in the village, however. They set up a camp at the northeast end in a dry-goods store that had previously been pillaged. There may have been some carousing. Empty bottles were found at the spot. After the executions, wine and liquor were handed out. In the evening, once the operation was over, the slaughterers were jovial: they joked with the women who had been made to get off the département train. Jean Pallier noted the soldiers' satisfaction after "work." Mission accomplished.

Some of the Troops Leave

Since the action was considered over, there were departures at nine p.m. and some time around 10:30. One section remained to provide overnight guard for the village.

SS Sergeant Boos, following the round-trip to Limoges: "I returned to Oradour with Lange. When I got back to Oradour, it must have been eight or nine at night, the whole village was on fire. I found my men in a vehicle at the edge of the village on the road that goes by the church. They were just waiting for me to return before leaving. We went and slept in a little village where we stayed for two days."[76] They went to the camp set up in Nieul, a few kilometers away.

Justin Darthout, a farmer living in La-Barre-de-Veyrac on the Saint-Junien to Nieul road, saw a column of about twelve vehicles go by in the early afternoon: "That same evening toward seven (solar time, that is, nine p.m.) we saw a German motorcyclist. He stopped at the intersection of the Limoges-Saint-Junien and La Barre-Nieul roads and wrote in chalk on a wall '3 K 3/1 H,' followed by an arrow indicating the direction from La Barre to Nieul. . . . Almost immediately a column of at least twenty automobiles [arrived]. In that German column I noted several sedans. In one of them two civilians were sitting in the front seat. . . . Amid the military trucks was a car belonging to M. Dupic, a cloth merchant in Oradour. . . . There was the wine merchant's small truck. . . . A German was playing the accordion on one of the trucks. He was perched atop the vehicle, which was heavily loaded. There were sacks and bundles."[77]

The Waffen SS column left Oradour with a larger number of vehicles than it had arrived with, which matches the division SS general's order to requisition as many vehicles as possible. It may be supposed that the large number of vehicles left behind were not in working order or ran on charcoal gas. The pillaging carried out by the military command and the SS organization in France was notorious.

The presence of civilians in a sedan seems surprising. No witnesses mentioned it, either in or outside town. They might have been SS plainclothes policemen or the Milice team assigned to follow the activities of the SS battalion. An SS police assistant named Hubsh stated: "I know that Second Lieutenant Kleist, with Patry, Simon, and Meyer, must have been part of the detachment that committed the massacre."[78]

Patry would deny it. He put forth two contradictory versions of his schedule. On his return from the expedition to Saillat he supposedly came back to Saint-Junien, where he noted Diekmann's appearance around six p.m. Then he said he left for Nieul, where he spent the night. But he would also assert that he returned to Limoges on the evening of June 10. Intelligence coming to the SS police center that evening, probably brought by Waffen SS Lieutenant Lange, may have been the reason for the SS policemen's trip to Oradour-sur-Glane. Did Patry then accompany a certain SS lieutenant named Wyckers of the SD, the SS intelligence and security service? Patry provided a third version when he told people in a Limoges café that he was in Oradour at the time of the massacre. He offered as "proof" the fact that he tried to save the daughter of "his friend Joseph." (This could have been German-born Joseph Bergmann, who had arrived in Oradour-sur-Glane with the Alsatian evacuees.)

It cannot be ruled out that a French SS assistant may have been in Oradour during the afternoon or, more likely, the evening. He would not have been identifiable by his uniform. The role of the "plainclothes" Milice members has not been entirely clarified. They were with the Waffen SS of Battalion 1, Der Führer, from Saturday, June 10, until the time they left for Poitiers on Monday, June 12. It is not impossible that this squad of Milice men passed through

Oradour before going to the Waffen SS camp at Nieul. The Milice could have been in the convoy that left Oradour in the evening. Although the presence of collaborators in Oradour cannot be ruled out, there is no documentary evidence of any direct participation in the massacre and pillaging.

Night in the Devastated Town

A Waffen SS column left Oradour between nine and ten p.m. One unit of the troops stayed where they were; we can say nothing more precisely except that it was not the second section, who relieved them on Sunday morning. The men who stayed provided a nighttime guard for the burning town.

Under cover of darkness and the smoke from the fire, some escapees left the village. But others were there all night and the following morning. Madame Rouffanche remained hidden in a garden: "I fell down between the rows of peas and stayed there until Sunday, June 11, around four or five p.m. The next day, Sunday, I heard Germans in the town. I had also heard them part of Saturday night, June 10, but I wasn't aware of them anymore toward morning."[79]

Armand Senon also spent the night and following morning in the bushes, unable to move: "During the night I saw a searchlight near me, shining in the direction of the département tram and the post office, both toward the upper part of town. The light went on only from time to time. . . . At daybreak I didn't see it anymore—it seemed to me it gave off a pale blue light. Two men, two Germans, came by around six or seven o'clock Sunday morning to take it away."[80]

After managing to leave the inferno in the Laudy barn despite his wounds, Marcel Darthout gathered up his strength again and went to hide in the same bushes as his friend Senon. He did not see him: "I was in the bushes about fifty meters from the cemetery, until night fell. Just then I heard people walking in the cemetery. They were speaking Limousin patois. That gave me confidence, so I called for help . . . and explained the atrocities the Germans had just been committing. We went . . . and spent the night in a wheat field. . . . I can't tell you how much pain, both physical and psychological, I endured during that night lit up by the reddish glow of the fire and, from time to time, searchlight beams combing the sky."[81]

Hubert Desourteaux remained in his hiding place for part of the night: "For several hours I watched the town burning, all alone. Around nine at night I heard a woman cry out near me and then a round of automatic-weapons fire." A little before midnight he left his hiding place and came upon his mechanic and his wife. He did not hear any more gun shots after eleven p.m. The three of them decided to flee across the fields around two in the morning.[82]

Martial Beaubreuil was hiding in a sewage pipe with his brother. They remained there until around two a.m. Sunday morning. "Until ten p.m. I heard isolated shots and a few bursts of automatic weapons fire here and there." He also heard the sound of an explosion but was not able to tell where.[83]

Jean Pallier headed for the hamlet of Les Bordes and was taken in for the night. There he learned "that the Germans had arrived around two in the afternoon, searched through that house, and ordered them to prepare a hot meal for their officer, as hearty as possible. The woman of the house had been informed from the start that the Germans' mission was to burn down Oradour because a highly decorated command officer had been the victim of an attack a few kilometers from there. She also told us that a mason had been killed during the afternoon, no children had come back to the hamlet from school, and the worried mothers who had gone off toward town at the time of the fire had not come back either. We spent the night in terrible consternation."[84]

Searching for the Missing

So the people that railway engineer Pallier met in the unscathed hamlet of Les Bordes, two kilometers from town, were all plunged into "terrible consternation." But they could not begin their searches until dawn.

Pallier: "The next day at sunrise five or six men, including myself, went off toward town in hope of getting news of the missing. An indescribable sight awaited us. The house that was still being used as a headquarters the night before had burned to the ground. Around it you could see a lot of empty cartridges, and bicycles, most of them damaged, in a pile. A little farther on we entered the town itself and walked through its entire length. All the buildings, including the church, the schools, the town hall, the post office, the house my family lived in, were nothing but smoking ruins. Only two houses had been spared: one on the road into the town toward Les Bordes, and the other one at the other end, toward La Fauvette.

"Altogether we saw only three charred bodies in front of a butcher's shop and the body of a woman, not burned but killed by a bullet in the back of the neck.

"We continued along the La Fauvette road as far as the first farm that hadn't been destroyed, to learn whether they had seen women and children go by. Unfortunately, no one had seen a thing.

"So then we walked back toward town, intending to check out another road, the one going to Saint-Junien via Le Masférat and Dieulidou. But right at the first houses we bumped into a German patrol, in which I recognized a few soldiers from the unit that had stopped us a few kilometers from Oradour the day before. After they checked our papers again and I told them who I was, the noncom leading the patrol ordered us to get out of there right away if we didn't want him to give an order to shoot. He also asked us where we were coming from, and I'm certain he would have massacred us if he had found out we had gone through town.

"So we went back to Les Bordes, taking an indirect route around Oradour. When we arrived, rumor had it that the women and children had been gathered together at Le Masférat. As we were about to leave we saw an old man, over eighty years old, on the road from Oradour. He had escaped the massacre by hiding. . . . The day before he had heard shooting throughout the afternoon from his hiding place, and he had been there during the fire. He assured us no Germans were left in town.

"To avoid the morning's detour we decided to go through Oradour again. There we met some men who, like us, were trying to get news of their families. They told us they had found several mass graves. But since we were in more of a hurry to find our wives and children, we lost no time taking the road toward Le Masférat. We were disappointed again when we got there.

"Deeply troubled, we went back to Oradour, where the number of men searching the ruins had grown considerably since we last went through. That is when I came to the mass graves that had already been uncovered. The sight was horrifying.

"In the middle of a pile of rubble you could see charred human skeletons emerging, especially pelvic bones. In an outbuilding on the village doctor's property I found the charred corpse of a child with only the torso and thighs remaining. The head and legs had disappeared. I saw several mass graves: one beside the junction of the Saint-Junien and La Fauvette roads, another in the village garage, a third in a barn located next to the Chêne Vert [Green Oak] café. Although the skeletons were three-quarters burned, the number of victims appeared to be very high.

"As I walked around the town I was able to note that the three corpses I'd seen at sunrise that morning had disappeared and the two houses that had been spared had burned down. . . . That was when I learned, at five that afternoon, that they had just discovered corpses of the women and children in the church.

"There are no words to describe a horror like that. Although the roof timbers of the church and the bell tower were completely burned, the vaults of the nave had held up against the fire. Most of the bodies were completely charred. But some of them still had human shape, though they were so badly burnt that only ashes remained. In the sacristy two little twelve- or thirteen-year-old boys were clinging together, united in a last burst of horror. In the confessional a little boy was sitting with his head leaning forward. In a baby carriage were the remains of an eight- or ten-month-old baby.

"I couldn't bear any more, and walked back like a drunken man."

Jean Pallier went away and left Oradour. His text, dated June 23, 1944, and written right after the tragedy, was the account of a man who had some scientific education. He distinguished consistently between what he had seen, what he had heard secondhand, and what he hypothesized. The writer did not identify an SS unit, he indicated "the Germans." He searched in vain for his wife and children, first in the hamlets and then in the ruins.

Although Pallier's text was published by two clandestine Resistance newspapers, it appears to have been intended for the Vichy government, as we can suppose from a typewritten note added at the end on the copy kept in the military justice archives: "Monsieur Pallier was given assurances that this report reached the head of the Laval government." Jean Pallier was not interrogated during the police investigations or called as a witness at the trial. He had left France to work in Indochina.

The sous-préfet of Rochechouart, Monsieur de Chamboran, went to Oradour-sur-Glane on the evening of Sunday, June 11. He reported to the préfet: "Some German troops stationed (a euphemism!) in Oradour-sur-Glane from Saturday, June 10 around two p.m. to Sunday, June 11. The district seat and the village of Puy-Gaillard were totally destroyed. The people of the town and that village were machine-gunned.

"Since I was totally cut off from communications in any direction from Friday, June 9 to Sunday, June 11, I learned of this event only once telephone contact with Limoges was restored, through a phone call from the deputy préfet on Sunday, June 11, around five p.m.

"After stopping for a few minutes in Saint-Junien to give the mayor's office instructions to organize immediate relief services, I went to Oradour-sur-Glane, where I found only smoking rubble once I got there, around seven p.m., and realized that no immediate aid could be given."[85]

The sous-préfet does not mention in his report that he evacuated a wounded man in his official vehicle. He took Marcel Darthout, who had survived the execution in the Laudy barn, to the hospital at Saint-Junien. He left the sous-préfecture of Rochechouart in July under pressure from the Resistance and was not examined during the investigations or by the court.

Corpses Desecrated

"Not satisfied with killing, the murderers mutilated the corpses and killed the dead for a second time."[86]

SS Sergeant Boos: "The next day I was sent by Töpfer with the entire second section and the section's platoon leader to bury the corpses that had been burnt in the meantime, and on Töpfer's orders I personally cleared out the church. I wore gloves for the job. I took the corpses and remains, carried them out of the church, and put them in a grave that had been dug for that purpose. During this work a line of sentries was in position . . . and shot at civilians who approached from the edge of the forest. When the job was done, we left."[87]

At dawn on Sunday, June 11, the second section of the third company returned to the scene of the massacre. The section consisted of fifty-eight men, SS noncoms and troops. From six a.m. until the end of the morning, it was busy with this job. A ring of sentries had been put in place surrounding the town. When these troops departed, the "job" had not been finished, if we are to believe SS Sergeant Boos himself: "On the morning of June 12, the entire second section went back to bury the bodies. I was one of them; we had been ordered not to shoot anymore." An SS soldier in the platoon commanded by Boos confirmed this: "The next morning we came back to bury the dead, on Kahn's orders; I was in the church to carry out the corpses; how many I can't say, they were so badly burned, corpses of women and children. We buried them behind the church and when it was all done we left."[88]

The Waffen SS were not thinking of "health" considerations; they would have had the job done by others. The Nazis' practice in Eastern Europe, mass incineration and common graves, was to prevent anyone from identifying the dead. The disappearance of the bodies—or the fact that they were rendered unrecognizable—resulted in an enduring bar to the mourning process. Only fifty-two bodies could be identified before burial. It took a long time for the number of victims to be determined—until a decision of the civil court at Rochechouart in December 1946, two and a half years after the event, set the list of victims at 642. Before this figure was legally recognized and used in the indictment at the 1953 trial, two other decisions had set the number of dead at 635 on December 31, 1944, then at 637 in December 1945. In all, 590 of the victims were never "recognized."

Silence Concerning Acts of Sexual Violence

The accounts were silent concerning acts of sexual violence. In the police investigations, the men accused of the massacre were not going to bring up aggravated acts of violence. The witnesses were silent in public and broached the subject only in private.

However: "On Sunday, around three in the afternoon, I saw the appalling sight of the church, where charred bodies were piled a meter and a half deep where they had fallen on the floor, especially near a little exit door of the church. One woman whom I couldn't identify, with no visible wound, or traces of burning and her lower part stripped bare and her genitals clearly evident, was set on top of the charred bodies. In my opinion this woman must have been brought there dead after the fire. I had a definite impression when I saw her that the woman had been raped."[89]

This account was confirmed by four people who entered the church on the afternoon of Sunday, June 11. They saw this corpse among the charred bodies, "not burned" like the others. Jean Hyvernaud: "The body of a woman who could have been identified by her family was lying on its back, with the clothing completely burned." René Hyvernaud: "A few meters from the main entrance, inside the church, I saw the body of a completely naked woman." Tarnaud, "In the middle of the church there was the body of a woman." This "realistic" presence of a woman's body amid the piles of charred, dismembered bodies came up again several times. Arthur Sénamaud:

"There was smoking rubble, whole or cut-up bodies, the charred body, probably of a woman, lying on its back with the arms and legs spread out." The witnesses seemed to recoil from this additional horror, amid so many others, as if it was the hardest to tell about. Again Arthur Sénamaud: "I wondered whether the Germans hadn't used the Dupic house—a cloth merchant's that served as an overnight bivouac and wasn't burned down until Sunday morning—to spend the night and perhaps to commit immoral acts or engage in orgies."[90]

The woman's body could only have been brought to that place on Sunday morning and thrown on top of the ashes and charred corpses. Some Waffen SS troops spent the night there and did a "cleanup" of the area on Sunday and Monday, June 11–12. It is certain that they moved bodies, as several accounts already quoted have indicated.

Rape, a family secret, especially in a rural society not immune from acts of sexual violence, for a long time imposed a taboo of silence. "Nothing must be said about it."[91] In the name of "family honor," public opinion would not let it be openly admitted.[92] The disgrace of the stain incurred overshadowed the rapist's crime. Families lived with their loss and the knowledge of the crime after the rapists had gone. We have noted a conspiracy of silence over these so-called immoral acts of violence, spoken of only rarely and in private conversations. The taboo, which applied to any public mention of the rape, marked off the boundary between perception of the sacred and its violation. Here an unspeakable private violence comes to light amid the mass of all the other "public" horrors of this tragedy. One senses that this insurmountable duality between the public and the private would emerge as one of the incentives for constructing memory of the massacre for the victims' families.

The trial indictment was silent about rape. The hearings did not cite these acts of violence as aggravating counts against the accused. The rape was impossible to speak of, but it still haunts people's memories.

The Waffen SS Troops after the Massacre

Between June 9 and June 10, as we have seen, other units of the Das Reich division went to Marsoulas and Saillat-Chassenon. Around Limoges that same day, June 10, the stationmaster at Saint-Denis-des-Murs was killed under circumstances that remain unclear. In Salon-la-Tour, Waffen SS troops captured Violette Szabo, who had dual British and French citizenship. An officer of the SOE who had parachuted down near Sussac on the night of June 6, she was sent to Ravensbrück and later executed.[93] An SS unit pillaged Ambazac. The next day, June 11, dead bodies were seen around Limoges, in Nantiat, Saint-Priest-Taurion, Saint-Jouvent, and Saint-Bonnet-de-Bellac. Battalion 1 went to Chaptelat and burned the château of Morcheval, where they thought they might find Resistance members; at least one person was killed. Returning to camp, the troops "rested." Their fare was considerably improved by the pillage from Oradour. The SS soldiers would remember eating a good deal of meat for several days. On Monday morning, June 12, the battalion left Nieul and joined the column. The Milice men went back to Limoges.

Some tanks and artillery were loaded onto trains at the Perigueux station. On June 14 some elements arrived in Normandy and were sent toward Caumont on June 20. At the end of June around 4,500 of the Waffen SS troops stuck in the Toulouse area headed toward the front, passing once again through the Limousin to go into action in Normandy. Some "remnants" of the SS division, about 5,000 men lacking means of transportation, did not leave their camps until the retreat that began on August 18. They left for the Rhône valley then with the command staff of army group G under Blaskowitz and the German forces in the Toulouse area.

In Normandy the SS division engaged the enemy at Avranches and again at Mortain, then retreated via Rouen as far as Malmédy, passing through Amiens and Arras. They were following their 1940 route in reverse. They were withdrawn from the front, in very bad shape, in late September. Diekmann, the Battalion 1 leader, disappeared. He was allegedly killed at the end of June and buried hastily without military honors. Even though several depositions agreed, his disappearance would become the subject of speculation: Had he really died? Was he hiding somewhere? Kahn replaced him for only a short time as battalion commander: a wound took him out of the picture. He would turn up much later in Hamburg, where he lived after the war despite two judgments in absentia in France. Lammerding was wounded and resigned his command in July. He then joined Himmler's staff. He, too, would turn up later, oblivious to the three death sentences pronounced in absentia by French military justice. Second Lieutenant Barth vanished from sight in 1945. He inexplicably turned up again in the early 1980s in the German Democratic Republic, where the authorities found and tried him. He was sentenced to life in prison by an East Berlin court in 1983, but he was granted a pardon and a pension for war wounds after the reunification of Germany. Stadler, the SS colonel of the Der Führer regiment, lived on peacefully in Austria despite a death sentence imposed in absentia—for crimes other than the one at Oradour.

At the end of the war, part of the division that was in the Dresden area was captured by Soviet forces. Remnants of the Der Führer regiment were scattered around in the final campaigns, not far from Mauthausen in Austria, where the "prestigious" Waffen SS regiment had paraded in 1938.

Otto Weidinger went through the battle of the Ardennes and then the fighting on German territory. He held out until the end and surrendered with the remnants of his regiment to an American unit only on May 9, 1945. Proud of having been a Waffen SS soldier, in retirement he considered himself a "professional soldier," defeated perhaps but "unblemished." He was convinced he had remained faithful to a political "ideal." Weidinger always considered himself a professional soldier, innocent of any crime; he did not understand why he had been imprisoned "for so long" in France. It is true that French military justice authorities cleared him of charges. His activity in Limoges from June 9 to June 12, 1944, was of no interest to the court that had indicted him for "conspiracy to commit a crime."[94] Returning to civilian life he became the "official" historian of the Das Reich division: five volumes were published in Canada, in both German and English. In a sanitized vision of the war, with no mention of acts of violence or massacres, he talks of the heroism of his "comrades." After all, the struggle against Communism continued through the Cold War.

Weidinger also published a pamphlet about the massacres at Tulle and Oradour. In it he proposed reconciling the Germans and the French after these "regrettable affairs," by accusing Resistance members (which for him meant Communists) as being their cause. Depiction of the "bandits," who had to be segregated, remained a constant of Nazi imagery. Distributing this brochure—which the negationists revel in—has been outlawed in France.

Under cover of decorated veterans' associations, Weidinger presided over the association of the Das Reich division's veterans and continued to show off his Iron Cross until he died in 1990 (he was able to rejoice in the fall of the Berlin wall).[95] In 1986, recalling a triumphal reception he received in his hometown after being awarded the most prestigious Nazi military decoration in May 1944, he wrote: "That is how Germany then honored the recipients of its knight's cross."[96] Weidinger would end his days peacefully in Würzburg.

7 The Victims

Jean Pallier went off from Oradour "like a drunken man," and spent no more time looking for the corpses of his wife and children. He left them there in the ruins. The anguish of those who were searching through those ruins is hard for us to imagine. They were aware—and had no other hope than to receive confirmation—of their misfortune. There was nothing left to do but to bury the dead. But first, since they could not even identify them, they had at least to count them. That would be a long, hard task. Organizing family funeral services proved impossible. In June and September of 1944, and again in March 1945, public demonstrations in their honor—from both sides of the Liberation—replaced private ceremonies. Messages of sympathy were sent to the people. But the identity of those expressing them gave a specific content to the messages according to circumstances, and this symbolic accompaniment of the victims conferred status upon them.

Counting the Dead

Overwhelmed, weakened by the occupying forces and by power struggles, the civil authorities of Limoges lacked any means of intervening. The regional préfet learned the day after the massacre "through the rumor mill . . . that the town of Oradour-sur-Glane [had] been razed in an operation by German troops." The mayor of the nearby town of Saint-Victurnien informed the Vichy-appointed préfet of the département. The rumor mill spread the news through Limoges, whose residents would long remember a reddish glow in the West.[1]

Confined to his office, the regional préfet was a passive witness to events. The director of Maintien de l'ordre had been placed under arrest by the regional head of the Milice (at this time, Vaugelas). The préfet had to ask the German authorities for a pass in order to go anywhere. The telephone worked only sporadically. The first administrator to arrive at the site in Oradour, late in the afternoon on Sunday June 11, a day after, was the sous-préfet of Rochechouart. The regional préfet did not get authorization to go there until June 13. In the interim he had received a visit from the préfet of Tulle, who informed him of the massacre of hostages that had taken place in Tulle on June 9. They went together to see the German general in command of liaison headquarters in Limoges. It seemed to them he was just finding out what had occurred.

The regional préfet's report dated June 14, 1944, indicated that he could not "assess the exact number of victims . . . ; it might be set at approximately 800 to 1,000 dead." This information came from a report that same day from the Renseignements généraux, which had itself been informed by the Red Cross in Saint-Junien: "The number of victims may have exceeded 1,000." Apparently this unbelievable figure was immediately lowered by the government. A *samizdat* [underground press release] dated June 15, 1944, citing a source in the préfet's office set the number of victims at between 750 and 800. Resistance leaflets distributed in June and July revised the estimate upward to between 1,000 and 1,200.[2] An RG report signed on July 4, 1944, by a commissioner named Massiéra gives a figure of "at least 800 people."[3] The two "official" publications of 1945 repeated these estimates: "The number of victims of the massacre must have been around 850";[4] as for that of the Comité du souvenir [Memorial Committee], it noted: "The number of dead in Oradour cannot be precisely estimated."[5] However, the authors who published the list established for population statistics by the mayor of Oradour's office indicated that the Vichy-named mayor of the town had cited the names of 634 victims. An undated document reproducing this list was appended to the judicial police report of December 23, 1944.[6]

In August 1945 the regional delegate of the Service de recherche des crimes de guerre ennemis [Enemy War Crimes Investigative Service] used a figure of 650 dead in Oradour, a number representing 20 percent of the total (3,045) of those killed by Nazi occupying forces in the Limousin.[7] Uncertainties stem from population movement and a large proportion of refugees who may in certain cases have wished to avoid checkpoints.

The list of victims was to be the subject of several decisions by the civil court of Rochechouart. The last one, in January 1947, set the list at 642 deaths. This figure—of "legally recognized deaths"—was used for the indictment in the 1953 trial.

The killing methods, the breakdowns in the administration (which was not able to send competent judicial officials), and the pressing health situation, which necessitated burying the corpses, did not permit identification of bodies—most of them badly charred. Members of Civil Defense emergency teams, Red Cross volunteers, road workers, scouts, and seminarians from Limoges worked to remove corpses from the mass graves and to try and put them back together on window shutters used as makeshift stretchers before burying them in communal graves. In and around the town they found bodies strewn in houses, wells, meadows, and hedges.

Some people took surreptitious photographs. They set the charred and dismembered bodies down on film in order to "make death public."[8] Could photographs—more than the accounts of those who struggled under horrible conditions amid pestilential odors—later substantiate the incredible atrocities endured by the victims? They tell us about the tortures these people went through, but their suffering is left to the imagination. The charred and dismembered bodies nonetheless were extensively photographed, as if to immortalize them, to display the bodies and the mass graves for posterity.

Only fifty-two bodies were identified and granted death certificates. The relatives of the others had to settle for a "List of Names of the Massacre Victims Officially Classified as Missing": 584 names. Indeed, the compiler of the list was uncertain as to birthplaces and residences and at times merely gave the last known address, which may well have been only temporary. Household servants went nameless: "Monsieur Picat's maid" is number 439 on the list.

Since the town hall had burned down, no archives were left. The chairman of the Special Delegation and the last elected mayor (Beau) were dead. The town clerk had been drafted into forced labor in Germany. Département services were in disarray. Appeals were printed in the local press after the Liberation. No one was able to say precisely who was in the town during the early afternoon of June 10, 1944, who was taken to the fairgrounds, who arrived unexpectedly in town or tried to enter it for some reason or other during the afternoon. In November 1944 a newly appointed mayor of the town was able to draw up descriptive cards for 634 people who had died. He reckoned that some families had not been able to report disappearances or were still uncertain. The number of these unidentified missing people must not have been more than 100 or so, according to the Vichy mayor: "And so we find a total of about 700 or so people massacred."[9] Six months after the event, there remained considerable uncertainty.

The Escapees

It is impossible to determine how many people who hid inside the town or fled on the troops' arrival escaped the killing. A document from the gendarmes' post in Saint-Junien gives the names of thirty-seven escapees: six survivors of the massacre (one woman from the church and five men from the shootings), nineteen who hid inside the town and survived, twelve "tramway" passengers.[10] This list is incomplete, but it has one great quality: it draws attention to the names of refugees who would not appear and who would not show up in the trial. This documentation—police investigations and trial hearings—enables us to discover another fifteen or so people. They had fled on the troops' arrival and had hidden inside the town (eight of them), or else they were on the evening "tram." At least forty-five people who faced massacre in various circumstances were spared.

We know of people hiding in the village who managed to leave it amid the flames. How many tried to save themselves this way and failed?

Many executions took place in the streets, houses, yards, and fields throughout the afternoon and early evening. Bodies were moved and hastily buried by the Waffen SS troops on Sunday and Monday morning. The men looking for their children in the village on Sunday morning saw corpses that by evening had disappeared.

The Waffen SS counted victims according to where they were executed: several statements indicate such an account. One German archive, taken from the Der Führer regiment's war diary and certified as an exact copy by an officer of the Limoges liaison headquarters, indicates the number of "enemy dead" for the two days, June 10–11, as 548.[11] We know that one, perhaps two, were killed on Sunday, June 11, at the château of Morcheval; the others were in Oradour. The difference between this number and the one stated officially (that is, a difference of around 100) gives some indication of the number of victims in addition to those rounded up on the fairgrounds. About 540 people may have been assembled there, then distributed among the places of execution: 180 men over fourteen years old executed in sheds and garages—six groups of about 30 each, according to witnesses—then 360 women, girls, and children under fourteen massacred in the church.

About one hundred people, at least, who were inside or near the town did not go to the prescribed roundup spot. We must add the thirty or so others who entered the trap during the afternoon and could not get out again, whose arrival added to the number of victims. Not everyone obeyed. The overall atmosphere of submissiveness evident from the statements of some of those who escaped must be reconsidered: some, a good number, tried to save themselves. A small minority, less than 5 percent of the total number of victims, managed to do so.

Nevertheless, since the number of dead represented almost twice the number of village residents (330 by the 1936 census), and because all the schoolchildren died but one, an impression was created that all the residents perished: "Since the populace was totally annihilated . . ." as the authors of the official book wrote in the last quarter of 1944.[12] This idea has spread through people's memory of the place and, for example, has been taken up in the dictionary entries that lower the number of escapees.

Burying the Dead

At the end of 1944, before the return of the prisoners of war and STO recruits, 1,093 lived in the thirty-eight hamlets of the township.[13]

Not only the size but also the uncertainty of the number of dead—and the fact that all families in the hamlets were affected by the death of 147 school-age children, plus 62 children under the age of six—may explain the formation and persistence over time of a notion that became prevalent. The Oradour community would dedicate to the children the first commemorative monument after the tragedy, near the new school in the temporary village of huts.[14]

Two lists of those who died can be seen at the site. One list is on three sides of the Tomb of the Martyrs; the other is inside the state monument, on the walls of what was intended as a crypt to contain the victims' ashes. Both lists give the names in alphabetical order by family.[15] But the list in the crypt, plunged in shadow, includes the victims' ages; the names of the youngest children are spattered with greyish spots where the stone has been brushed by thousands of visitors' fingers. Can this gesture, of pity or perhaps naïve piety, be likened to the beneficent touching of the relics of "holy innocents"?

As much as the material act of burial, we must also consider what was said: the personalities and social positions of those who spoke, the forms of discourse and words used, each of them a determinative factor in the formation of memorials and the process of mourning.

About fifty bodies were identified. Some families went ahead with burial in their vaults in the town cemetery: ceremonies were out of the question. Most family funeral services were held after the Liberation.

But for the bodies that proved impossible to identify there was no other solution than a quick burial in the communal grave. And then there were the ashes. People realized very quickly that it would be impossible, unthinkable, to part with the heaps of ashes and scattered bones. These were the final traces of those whose death had not been formally certified. "No body, no death!" What should be done with these final remains? They were gathered together, first in piles, and then put into "boxes," coffins for those who would not have one, and were kept in a temporary chapel. The fate of the ashes would be at the heart of a clash that occurred after the trial verdict and the amnesty in 1953, which set the Oradour community against the authorities. The result was the rejection of the state monument and the construction of a private monument: the Tomb of the Martyrs.

Seminarians from the large seminary in Limoges undertook to move and deposit the bodies—more often than not fragments of bodies—in graves dug by road workers. Although it was a difficult task, the seminarians carried out this "pious labor" with their usual dignity. It was normal enough for them to recite prayers for the dead over the open graves in an impromptu ceremony, after an exhausting day.[16] This homage embraced the dead in the rites of the Roman Catholic Church, which the victims had not all shared in before and which some of them would have rejected. This spontaneous ceremony of prayer could not help but ignore the opinions and status of the non-Catholic agnostics (a great majority of the people) and of the Jews and the Protestants among the refugees. The Catholic Church had lost two priests and one seminarian ("three cassocks," as the bishop wrote), and a place of worship. Since the situation strengthened its concern for control over reverence for the deceased (as has remained the case until recently), the Catholic Church would play a dominant role in an area where it showed little presence before the tragedy.

The first public speeches after the massacre were given by clerics in Limoges, the département's administrative seat, and thus not even in the destroyed village. On June 13, 1944, the regional préfet received authorization to go to Oradour. He was accompanied by the bishop, Monsignor Rastouil, who gave an account of this visit: "We arrived in Oradour-sur-Glane, which I knew well, having often passed through it, always enlivened by the housewives' comings and goings, the artisans' labor, herds of sheep, yoked pairs of oxen, fishers on their way toward the Glane, and, at certain times, the noise of children."[17]

The setting, a "peaceful" representation of the village's past, was thus established as if it were seen from above: it was a "well-known" village. The image of the town was set. Then the visitors discovered the horrifying devastation: "Today it was a place of the dead! A vision of horror! The road going up into town, lined with ruins. There to the left on its knoll the old church with its burnt roof, its walls and vault still standing, though, in its Limousin granite."[18]

Stirred by this vision, the prelate gave a speech during a public ceremony in his cathedral on June 16. In his homily the bishop issued what was both a declaration—what everyone knew, but the press and radio did not mention—and a judgment, a condemnation, in which religious authority took a stand before the civil authorities did: "Last Saturday, June 10, 1944, the town of Oradour-sur-Glane in Haute-Vienne was the scene of atrocities that have never had their equal on French soil, either in 1914–1918 or in 1939–1944, and that we condemn in the simple name of natural morality; we declare that, since they are incapable of harm, it is never permissible to kill innocents."[19]

On Sunday, June 18, the pastor of the Reformed church, Albert Chaudier, gave his customary sermon at Sunday services.[20] The biblical verse he chose to base his sermon on was a text from Jeremiah, 46:5: "The horror is everywhere," which can also be rendered as "The terror is all around them."[21] The pastor addressed the audience: "You cannot expect your pastor, in the presence of such events, to keep a silence that in the eyes of God would be one of the gravest condemnations of his ministry." The Protestants of Limoges were more influential than their numbers might suggest, and the regional préfet may have been among those present that Sunday. Marc Freund-Valade, the regional préfet in Limoges since September 1943, was born in 1899 in Schiltigheim, where the Alsatian refugees in Oradour had come from.[22] He was the son of a Protestant pastor in Strasbourg, and a parishioner of Albert Chaudier. The events recalled to the faithful by the pastor were known to the préfet: "A week ago, a small, peaceful town, among the most irreproachable in its conduct for these past two years, during which our common ordeal has left

France scarred, was destroyed in a few hours and burnt to the ground; its residents and all those who happened to be there at the time perished under conditions whose horror exceeds the normal resources of language and did not spare old men, women, children, even newborn babies. In less than half a day, this calm village was turned into a vast grave."[23] The theme of horror—linked with that of the inhabitants' irreproachability, of calm, of the slowness of an unchanging rural world—would be common to depictions of the massacre.

On June 21, the civil and religious authorities organized an official day of mourning in Limoges: "French flags at half-mast on public buildings, cafés and moviehouses closed, mass in the cathedral," and funeral ceremonies in the cemetery at Oradour. These events had been authorized by the German general. The préfecture staff in uniform, the "mayor" and the president of the Limoges chapter of the Légion, the bishop and the pastor, all took part in "funeral ceremonies for the victims of Oradour-sur-Glane." Indeed, it was thought that the remains of most of the victims had been discovered and buried by the first-aid teams, according to an RG report, which indicated that 300 people were in attendance. Three "celebrants" spoke publicly: Bishop Louis Rastouil, Albert Chaudier, Marc Freund-Valade.[24] The bishop sang absolution, the pastor improvised a prayer, and the préfet gave a brief speech generally inspired by the pastor's sermon. The speech was published widely, partly thanks to the préfet's own efforts but also partly independently, since Resistance fighters reproduced it in leaflets that the Renseignements généraux were more than a little surprised to find.[25]

The Process of Memorialization

The speech by the Vichy préfet seems, at least formally, to have laid the foundation for the memory of the massacre.

The ideas of a "pilgrimage of unspeakable sorrow" and a "sacred town wall" were expressed from the start. Those responsible for the crime were stigmatized without being specifically designated. The events were "contrary to French and German law." The massacre was said to be contrary to "conscience." "The sack of Oradour and the massacre of its residents are revolting to the conscience, which is gripped with horror." The allusion to Chaudier's sermon is evident. "The French language does not have words strong enough to characterize this act; . . . Farewell, residents of Oradour-sur-Glane, who died in unspeakable torture." The speech ends with a promise: "We swear on your graves that we will not stop at any effort to prevent others from enduring your fate in the future. This will be our cause: that your martyrdom may serve to save the living." The "never again" was formulated; and "martyrdom" justified a call for "pilgrimage." Finally, nevertheless, the préfet set Oradour in the context of Vichy France, of discipline, calm, and "great, silent . . . sorrows," thus uniting all in "the immense pity of France."[26]

The préfet declared himself to be "representing the head of state and the government of France" without naming them.[27] Circumstances did not permit it anymore. He nonetheless set the tragedy of Oradour within that of Vichy France, which, saying it was outside the course of events, claimed to be outside the war. This "exteriority" would come up again as a fundamental element in local memory, like the "peaceful" character of the village, which the préfet affirmed in his June 15, 1944, report to the government, in order to express the "incomprehensibility" of the massacre. The residents could not be suspected of some broad compromise with the maquis, with which they were shown to be unconnected. In a manner admitting no doubt, this certainty led to qualifying the victims as "innocent" because they were not "engaged."[28] In a more insidious manner, this allowed the préfet to relieve Vichy of any responsibility.[29] Furthermore, Oradour became emblematic of the regime that, undergoing external events, presented itself as a victim. Measured by these "great, silent sorrows," the martyrdom of Oradour became that of Vichy.

The first words pronounced at Oradour expressed the speakers' emotions. They were also intended to "mend" the temporal continuity of a community ripped open by tragedy. Coming from a blend of patriotic and religious culture, far from regional cultural forms, the concepts of martyrdom and pilgrimage were not a part of local culture. But from this point on, they would be seen as essential elements in the collective memory of Oradour.

The choice of the notion of "martyr" to characterize the victims was one proposed by the civil and religious authorities as early as June 1944, but it also formed a link with the victims of "engagement": martyrs of the Resistance. The victims of the massacre were martyred and considered innocent because they were not "engaged."[30] Is a martyr not an "engaged" witness? On the other hand, is there a category of victim that could be termed "guilty"? And according to what criteria: "engagement," or birth? The concept of martyr seems to transcend, at the same time as it reinforces, the concept of victim.

Victims are generally plunged into the anonymity of misfortune, whereas martyrs attain a form of individual sublimity, a visibility. People remember their names in invoking them. Use of the term *martyr* stems from a desire for distinction, a distinction accorded from June 1944 onward by the regional préfet and the bishop, and confirmed at the Liberation by the new préfet, Jean Chaintron—a Communist Resistance fighter—and General de Gaulle. Would the Catholic Church make the victims of Oradour into martyrs, or witnesses, of the twentieth century? The question was put before the competent Vatican body. To question the correctness of the term verged on sacrilege.

The ceremony of farewell to the dead on June 21, 1944, brought everyone together in a common spirit of compassion. It embraced the victims, most of them unidentified, in a single identity: of having perished on that day, in that place. By doing so, it unwittingly perpetuated the acts of the Waffen SS, who had stripped the dead of their individual past by "massification" in a collective massacre. The personal stories, "family narratives," nationalities, religions, commitments, and so on, that constituted the thread of past lives disappeared in the "all-embracing" homage by civil and religious authorities. The victims no longer had a story, only a status. They became representative of the great, silent sorrows of France.

Postcard postmark dated 1913. The presence of the rails to the right of the car and electric cables of the département railway, which was completed in 1911, indicates the period of this anonymous shot. (Private collection.)

The "Grande Rue" or Main Street, officially called "Rue Emile Desourteaux." Judging by the sidewalk in front of the Beau-Desourteaux grocery store, the picture must have been taken during the twenties. Photo by Beau, no date. (Private collection.)

Postcard, reproduced from an earlier one, reissued by the National Association of Families of Martyrs in 1945, postmarked 1946. The stamp, placed at the left so as not to interfere with the picture, shows the massacre in the church in accordance with publications of that period; it reproduces the cover picture of a brochure published in 1944 by a Resistance organization, the FTP *(Francs-Tireurs et Partisans* "Snipers [Irregulars] and Partisans"*)*. A 2-franc surtax was added to benefit the Association of the "disaster victims." (Private collection.)

Ruins of the church and the covered marketplace. (Anonymous; no date — probably September 1944 because of the presence of a tricolor flag and the absence of the plaque placed behind the crucifix in October.) (Private collection.)

Interior of the Oradour church, after the collapse of the vault of the nave. (Anonymous; no date) (BDIC)

Town of Oradour, the fairgrounds: flag-raising ceremony of the Foreign Workers Group *(Groupement de travailleurs étrangers)* (GTE no. 643). The participants are foreign refugees: Spanish Republicans and Jews of several nationalities, led by officials of the French State ("l'Etat français," the Vichy regime). (Anonymous; no date—Spring 1942?) (Private collection.)

Ruins near the fairgrounds: two years later, the same buildings as in the photo above. (Anonymous; no date—Summer 1944?) (Private collection.)

The charred and dismembered bodies, here laid out on shutters, were photographed to make "death public." These pictures were used by the authors of the earliest publications and at times on postcards. Anonymous photo, probably taken around June 15, 1944. (Private collection.)

Anonymous photo probably taken in the days immediately following the massacre. (AD Haute-Vienne, Fonds Jean d'Albis.)

Funeral of Sarah Jakobovicz, organized by the UREJF (*Union de résistance et d'entraide des Juifs de France,* "Union for Resistance and Mutual Aid of the Jews of France") of Limoges. A catafalque was set up on the fairgrounds in the ruins of Oradour, the coffin covered by a tricolor flag, and FTP soldiers formed an honor guard; David Jakobovicz is to the left of the coffin. Anonymous photo, September 21, 1944. (CDJC [*Centre de documentation juive contemporaine,* "Center for Jewish Contemporary Documentation"], Paris, Fonds List-Pakin.)

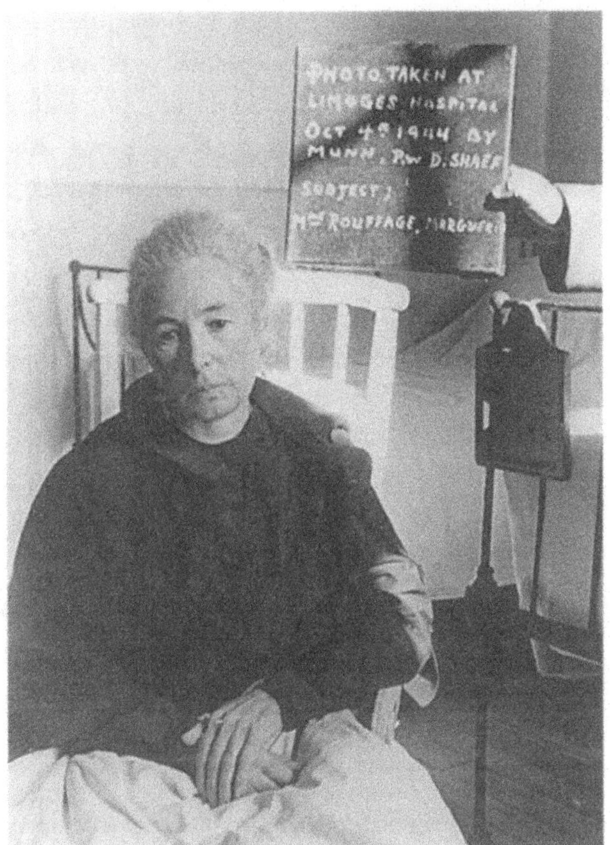

Marguerite Rouffanche, the sole survivor from the church, in a photo dated October 4, 1944. This snapshot was taken by someone who was attached to SHAEF, the Supreme Headquaters Allied Expeditionary Forces—the Allied high command during World War II prior to the defeat of Germany. (Private collection.)

Il ne faut pas confondre la barbarie nazie et l'allemagne.-

Il faut lire Börne, Buchner, Heine en France.. pour distinguer entre l'allemagne immortelle et ses maîtres d'un jour. Et surtout il faut témoigner des noms d'aujourd'hui qui sont l'espoir et l'hymne de l'avenir: Thomas Mann, Bert Brecht, Heinrich Mann, Anna Seghers, Lion Feuchtwanger, Willi Bredel, Emile Ludwig, Egon Erwin Kish, Erich Maria Remarque, Ludwig Renn, Franz Werfel, Musil..

Il y a tout ce qui passe en eux du grand peuple muselé et qui trouve pour s'exprimer leurs paroles ardentes, leur talent, leur colère.

Tout ce qui est vraiment français en France devrait connaître aimer et défendre cette allemagne de l'exil.

Excerpt from the diary of Denise Bardet, a schoolteacher in Oradour (Private collection): "We must not confuse the Nazis' barbarity with Germany...

"We must read [Karl Ludwig] Börne, [Georg] B[ü]chner, [Heinrich] Heine in France... to distinguish between immortal Germany and her masters of the day. And especially, we must speak up for the names of today that are the hope and a hymn for the future: Thomas Mann, Bert[olt] Brecht, Heinrich Mann, Anna Seghers, Lion Feuchtwanger, Willi Bredel, Emil Ludwig, Egon Erwin Kish, Erich Maria Remarque, Ludwig Renn, Franz Werfel, [Robert] Musil...

"There is everything that has been passed on to them from a great, silenced people and that finds expression in their burning words, their talent, their anger.

"Everything that is truly French in France should know, love, and defend this Germany in exile."

General de Gaulle—without of course alluding to it—would confirm the speech by the Vichy préfet. As president of the provisional government he came to Oradour in March 1945 and set the massacre within the nation's history: "Oradour is a symbol of what happened to the fatherland itself."[31] The tragedy of Oradour took on a meaning then that it had not had in the Vichy speech: it brought to an end a tragic period of national history that had opened with the defeat and was usurped by the illegitimate Vichy regime. A parenthesis was closed; the future lay in reconstructing the country, relying "first of all on ourselves." Since the meaning of national recognition was evolving, it was no longer just a matter of the despair of "victimization," but of new prospects. Nonetheless the form of recognition remained the same: in the future, the victims of Oradour would represent all of the "unengaged" people.

A few months apart, then, two national authorities, although antithetical in their irreconcilable opposition, could show a recognition, identical in form but with contrary implications. For the nation, regenerated by the Liberation, all victims of the conflict were thus reunited, whatever their "engagement" or "nonengagement." This union in a single martyrology did away with past rifts: General de Gaulle was seeking to unite the people while lessening the influence of the Resistance fighters within France. The status sketched out a few months earlier was thus confirmed: in the eyes of the nation, the victims of the massacre were martyrs.

In 1945 other sites in France might have warranted a similar proclamation.[32] Chronologically, the process of memorializing the massacre at Oradour was the first.

The memory of the survivors was built not only on the loss of the dead but also on forgetting who they may have been. Among the survivors, some sought to reconstitute family stories, which they told as they walked through the ruins.[33] This account was a smoothed-over story, dominated by trivial anecdotes. Rough patches and, generally, troublesome memories were more or less unconsciously eliminated. Memory selected and highlighted certain events, neglecting the context of the times and, more particularly, those things that aroused guilt feelings. This intellectual operation, part of the grieving process, was not possible for the refugees, who were only passing through. They had no story in Oradour to which they might attach any feeling of belonging. These "other" victims, who were not "from here," were admitted among the "martyrs" and thus into the memory of the massacre, but their story would remain unappreciated. They had a different story, linked to other lands. Political conflicts—which, euphemistically, became "trivialities," "stupid details"—would also remain unknown to the public because they were overshadowed by local memory: those who favored Vichy versus those opposed to collaboration with the regime.

Martyr status, equality in death, canceled out any membership in Marshal Pétain's Legion or in a Resistance movement that had existed prior to the massacre. Recognitions of the victims, first by a representative of the Vichy regime, then by the symbol of Free France, succeeded each other with no apparent contradiction. Both bespoke the same idea: the compassion and unity of all in misfortune.

The consensus of a standardized representation can be seen even in the vocabulary that was used to try and characterize the massacre. "The horror goes beyond the normal resources of language" for the pastor; the préfet could not find "words in the French language for unspeakable torture." The three known Resistance leaflets also repeat the term *unspeakable:* "unspeakable savagery" (MUR), "unspeakable terror" (FN-FFI-FTPF), "unspeakable atrocities" (a Communist-inspired tract entitled "Katyn-Limousin").[34] The massacre fell under the category of the unspeakable, absolute evil, the unpardonable. All referred to the "peaceful" character of this "pleasant village, the little town whose tile roofs were reflected in clear waters" (the MUR), to signify the victims' innocence. But whereas the bishop employed the concept of "innocent," it was the pastor alone, at this point, who used that of "martyr."[35] It would not reappear until later, in the title of the National Association of Martyrs' Families, and in January 1945 in the dedication of the MLN book: "To the martyrs of Oradour-sur-Glane, to the families in mourning, to the 'Black Book' of German atrocities, to the entire world, confident in its faith and its rights."[36]

Adopting the term *martyrs* for the Oradour victims meant lending a connotation of heroism to death. The heroicizing of the victims as martyrs placed them in a different perspective than in a bombing or an accident. The speeches before and after the Liberation incorporated the victims of Oradour into the "mystical body" of the fatherland as participants in a sacrifice carried out for it.[37]

Inevitably, this consensual image was contradicted by the reality. It was challenged by the presence of the refugees, in particular the stateless ones who had chosen France as a new fatherland and whom it had not protected. Only Albert Chaudier, in his sermon, made one discreet allusion to "those who were there for a while or for the longer term."[38]

An examination of the list of victims shows that a quarter of them were not from the town, and not even from the département of Haute-Vienne. Limiting ourselves to statistics relating to 635 names and taking into account the document's inaccuracies, it turns out that at least 117 victims had come from areas of France other than the Limousin and its neighboring départements, and about 30 had been born abroad: in Spain, Italy, Poland, Germany, and Hungary. We are considering separately the case of Albert Mirablon, who was born in the United States and was a genuine Resistance fighter.

The daily *Centre libre,* in its issue no. 25, dated September 20, 1944, announced for the next day "the funeral of Mademoiselle Sarah Jakobowicz, who died at the age of sixteen, burned alive in Oradour." A statement from the Union juive de résistance et d'entraide [Jewish Union for Resistance and Mutual Aid], which co-sponsored the ceremony with the family, specified: "Mademoiselle Jakobowicz died a victim of torture during the terrible crime of Oradour; her remains were gathered up by her brother, a soldier of the FTP, who dug a makeshift grave for her with his own hands while the Germans were still present." The ceremony would take place first in Oradour, then in Limoges, on the fairgrounds in each place, before burial in the Louyat cemetery in Limoges, where a symbolic, truncated column rises over the grave.

The same daily paper gave an account of the funeral on September 22. Six hundred people came from Oradour; 800 were counted in front of the house to which the charred body of the young girl had been taken by her brother. A catafalque was raised, surrounded by an armed honor guard with Sarah's brother among them. Wreaths were laid in the name of the military units honoring her: the FTP from the Marceau barracks in Limoges, a company named for "Julien Zerman," and the UREJ (also known as the UJRE). Speeches were given by a priest named Ehrard, Rabbi Deutsch (the grand rabbi of Bischheim in the Bas-Rhin département of Alsace, who was a refugee in Limoges and a chaplain in the camps), and "a representative of the UREJ, which had organized the ceremony." In Limoges, where the ceremony continued, the officials were primarily military (Commander "Fredo"), representatives of Jewish organizations (the Organization of Jewish Combatants, the Union of Jewish Youth, and the UREJ), and Communists.

And so the name of Julien Zerman, emblematic of the Communist Resistance, appeared in Oradour. Julien Zerman, a brilliant young intellectual, lived in the tenth arrondissement of Paris. As a student at the École supérieure textile de Lyon [Lyons School of Textiles], he played a role in founding the Union de la jeunesse juive de France [Union of Jewish Youth of France]; he went to the national front in 1941 and founded Jeune Combat in 1942. He organized protection groups of the National Front (a clandestine Communist Party organization) and was killed in Grenoble on December 16, 1943.[39] He was both a hero and a martyr of the Communist and Jewish Resistance. Those who pronounced his name in Oradour did so conspicuously, to make a statement that had not previously been made: the homage to the dead of Oradour associated with it two elements that had been absent from the ceremony on the preceding June 21, the Jewish and the Resistance victims, as a band on one wreath indicated.

The ceremony on September 21, 1944, with its shifting locations was orchestrated by its organizers. The UREJ made a film (or had one made), which we have seen. Numerous photographs show the size of the crowd. More than just the funeral of a member of the Jewish community, this was a mass demonstration through which the Communist Jewish[40] organization tried to prove to other Jewish organizations that it was representative. After the fiasco of the UGIF, which they denounced (if not fought), they asserted their claim to represent the Jewish community as a whole during a period of regrouping. It made sense that the UGIF was absent from the ceremony: linked to the Vichy regime, it no longer existed.

Of the three ceremonies in Oradour, in June and September 1944, only two have become part of people's memory. Sarah's funeral, organized by the UREJ, has been forgotten. The selection between what is memorable and what is forgettable occurred once a certain reading of the tragedy was put in place.

The Oradour community could not name the Jews as victims of the massacre. That would mean admitting a distinction among the martyrs and would open a fissure in the discourse. Although some were recognized and identified as Spanish or from Lorraine, as the plaques on the Tomb of the Martyrs and the Association's monument or lists published in its internal bulletin remind us, other victims, of foreign or French origin, are shrouded in anonymity. Just like those who were identified by their origins, these people had experienced the racist violence of the Nazis and sought to take precautions against it. Despite the foresight and precautions they marshaled to save themselves, in Oradour they were caught up in what they were fleeing. The identity they had hoped to preserve was not maintained for them.

Commemorating

The customs of mourning mingle private gestures of family intimacy with public demonstrations of the community's attachment to the dead.

The grieving mothers' visits to their dead children would end only with their own deaths. In an expression of unending sorrow, some of these mothers went to the cemetery every day. They never strayed far away from it. The story of their suffering has yet to be written; they were the high point of the community's mourning: those who did not leave off mourning and that it never left. At a time when outward signs of mourning were declining, that of the mourning mothers of Oradour took on the shape of an exception, inspiring respect and distance in those not directly involved. They were looked on with pity and admiration for their steadfastness: their lives were lived for their dead.[41]

The link with the dead shows as well in the annual commemoration ceremonies. Every June 10, a procession led by the president of the National Association of Martyrs' Families and the mayor leaves the city hall in the new town and makes the various stops on a route that has become fixed and unchanging. The procession passes by the places of suffering, the ruins, as if to measure the reality of the event: it is like a demonstration. This processional ritual bears a marked resemblance to religious processions in the Limousin.[42] It starts at the end of mass, now said in the new church.

For a long time the commemoration-day mass was celebrated in front of the ruins of the former church. This practice, instituted by the bishop in 1945, no longer conforms to the post-council doctrine of the Catholic Church. Did the priests serving Oradour in the late 1990s, who resided in Saint-Junien by then, feel that the commemorative mass should no longer take this form, which had turned into a tradition? Did they want to distance themselves in order to avoid having the ceremony used by others? Would the preeminence of the mass, the repetition of Christ's sacrifice, be watered down, as it were, in commemorating the martyrs? The representatives of the Oradour community rejected the possibility of discontinuing it, which would have altered the commemoration schedule. They asked the clergy to keep the mass preceding the procession even if, as they conceded, fewer people would be there for it.

Département parliamentary representatives from all parties, the préfet and the sous-préfet in uniform, local officials, representatives of state administrations and of various groups, the consular corps, religious organizations—all take their place behind the standard-bearers of delegations from patriotic associations: veterans, deportees, and Resistance fighters. The schoolchildren and teachers, with classes canceled on this day, mingle in among the standard-bearers and authorities. A large number of other people attending the event follow them. This is an unalterable marching order throughout the entire procession.

The route leads first to the school complex, where a minute's silence is observed at the children's monument after a representative of the Association has laid a wreath. This ritual is repeated several times along the way. It may have a variant, however, at the second stop, the monument to the town's dead: a plaque near the church. There the mayor may take the opportunity to speak a few words about recent massacres, exhorting those present to vigilance. This is an innovation in the ceremony's program.

The procession then goes to the church in the former village where the ceremony is repeated inside. Then a stop is made at the shed from which the only survivors of the shooting escaped. Wreaths are also laid at the other execution places. Finally—and avoiding the state monument, which it merely walks by—the procession arrives at the Tomb of the Martyrs. The ceremony culminates there and comes to an end.

The standard-bearers are standing around the platform. The authorities and delegations present are invited to come lay their wreaths. The Association, as the "host power" in its place of commemoration, lays its wreath last, after the local authorities and representative of the state. The ceremony continues with the playing of taps by the bugler of an honor guard. A minute of silence is requested of those present by a representative of the Association, who then invites the bishop of the diocese to say the Lord's Prayer. This (only the bishop is invited to speak) ends the ceremony. Apart from this, the commemoration is wordless, silent.[43]

The veterans' and Resistance associations all take part in the commemorations of Oradour. But the National Association of Martyrs' Families is not represented at Resistance commemorations, except for those of its members who take part out of personal commitment.

Nor does the Association take part in the celebration organized every July, at Mont Gargan in Haute-Vienne, in memory of the main heroic action of the Resistance in the Limousin. The Liberation was a "non-event" for Oradour, where joy was unthinkable. From that point of view Oradour is an exception.

The silent ceremony initiated by the Association in 1948 was a reaction to "too many speeches" in demonstrations organized by the Communist Party that year and the ones following. Although the first three commemorations did not raise any problems, the Cold War era brought about dual ceremonies and competition between the Association and the town government. The ceremonies of the Communist town government gave speakers an opportunity to denounce government policies: the beginnings of German rearmament and the spread of wars of decolonization date from this period. For the Association, political speeches perverted the meaning of the commemoration by diverting attention from exclusive homage to the dead.

From 1953 onward—with the Communist town government eliminated and the court's verdict rejected, since the amnesty for the forced draftees was felt to be an affront to the memory of the dead—there was only one ceremony. The tradition of silent commemorations was strengthened and became unalterable. Since the authorities and local elected officials were excluded from organizing the commemoration ceremonies, to which they were no longer invited, their participation henceforth became not merely a mark of the compassion owed the victims but also a demonstration of allegiance to the Oradour community. On June 10, 1994, the fiftieth anniversary, President Mitterand gave a speech.[44] He spoke within the precinct of the historical monument, in the part of town that was state property, and ended his visit by reflecting in silence at the Tomb of the Martyrs. A head of state's public recognition, that of the government or its representatives, was being addressed to a private community, in a private place. The authorities were accepting a specific protocol that mingled public and private forms and that was determined outside their jurisdiction.

The martyrs lent to the Oradour community, as guardians of their memory, an essential legitimacy and, consequently, authority both over that place and over discourse. The silent ceremony showed there was nothing to say—by implication, nothing else, more, or different—than what had already been said. But did this silence not convey ambiguities? It was "deafening," it emphasized a deficiency, a serious failure that weighed on the community's memory: justice had been judged defective. On one hand, this silence meant that the community was asking that nothing be added to its story, but on the other hand might this not be, in a perverse way, unwittingly to continue the act of annihilation?[45] Silence is saying something that the silent community deems it does not have to make explicit; it does not mean "nothing."

What other symbolic form than a mute ceremony could be more suitable for the celebration of a misfortune? How should a "negative" event be commemorated? Only silence enables an unfortunate community to unite in its suffering, which it considers unappreciated. But does this silent manifestation not also express the continued existence of the national community's debt toward those whose calling it is to represent the victims?

The old Oradour, profoundly unchristian, seems not to have had a cult of the dead. The June 1944 massacre opened a gaping wound in the populace; a community that did not exist before the massacre was formed in and by the cult of its dead. The martyrs' memory became a bond for the families in mourning and a glue that united the community bearing it.

Through symbolism put into action, the commemorations justify and serve the immediate concerns of the Oradour community. Memory of the massacre once could be included in political debates: it thus became a "living memory." The retreat toward a memory cut off from politics removed it from the present and brought the community back into itself exclusively—the "among ourselves" of Limousin culture.

Mourning may engender respect; at the same time, it creates a distancing, an isolation, of the mourners. But in Oradour the solitude is deliberate, even though presented as being imposed by circumstances. The ritual of the commemorations, by their withdrawal inward and detachment from the surrounding world, demonstrates a specificity and thus a difference that obviates all comparisons and, consequently, all discourse. The commemorations could only be mute once justice had been called for. Might not this absence of justice—whose discourse could not be heard since a mockery was made of it by the amnesty—be what makes Oradour such a unique case? The silence of the commemorations, answering that of justice, affirms by proclaiming to the entire world that "this story is not ended." The debt has not been paid.

8 Conflicting Accounts

Without a historical account, it is impossible to get inside the event known as "the massacre." This is the only intermediary that would enable reconstructing its evolution and passing it on. But a narrative tells a story; it formalizes things: it takes its place within the general narrative pattern of massacres, a stable form with unvarying elements. Witnesses stray from their subjective experience in telling the story; they objectify it. Passing it on necessitates this distancing. An account sets forth facts that, linked together and placed in order, create a meaning, which the person telling the story gives to them. It puts into words the cause or causes of the event, tying the anecdotal elements together into a whole. Memory and imagination enter into the organizing of these links. Whoever hears the account discovers in one impulse both the facts and the meaning attached to them. But the account belongs to the person bearing witness: he is what he is telling as he recounts what he has experienced; he stakes his credibility on his very existence as a witness who stands as proof. Control of the story is fundamentally at stake. The witness finds himself confronted by other accounts that either confirm or attack him. Distortions due to cultural images or to ideologies are possible. Some are explicit and willful: true "instrumentalizations," they can, according to the circumstances or intentions of those who propose them, misrepresent the meaning.[1] Sometimes they even seek to deny what happened.

The Accounts Given by the Perpetrators

A denial was set in motion by the SS men in the division and those in the Limoges police, contemporary with the massacre.[2] The SS invented their justification for the massacre even before they carried it out. It can be seen in the terse comments made to the troops by the Waffen SS officers on their departure from Saint-Junien: "to look for a missing officer," or, "it's going to heat up," or, "we'll see what these Alsatians can do." These indications suggest a confrontation with the "bands." The aim was to make the operation acceptable to those who were to carry it out. The real motivation for the action, set out in Lammerding's notes, was concealed from the participants. The need for the massacre was incorporated into propaganda against the "bands."

The SS issued two versions to justify the massacre.

The first explained the presence of a "band" within the town, indeed inside the church: supposedly the fighting that took place caused the massacre and the fire; the destruction of the village was unintentional. On June 13, 1944, the person in charge of German military censorship in Limoges issued a communiqué: "Using around 500 reliable people as spokesmen, we are issuing the following version concerning the events in Oradour. The local women and children had been assembled in the church to ensure their safety. Terrorists had installed an explosives and ammunition storehouse under the church; it caught fire during the fighting and set off an explosion that destroyed the church."[3] On June 19, this version was repeated to the local press.[4] According to an officer from Goebbels's ministry, "it was not by chance that the German troops went over there." Pierre Poitevin reported on this meeting held for the representatives of French censorship and newspaper directors.

The second version was based on the searches following the capture of Kämpfe, the commander of DF Battalion 3, northeast of Limoges during the evening of June 9. SS officer Gerlach, also captured on June 9, supposedly returned to Limoges on the morning of June 10. He was said to have alleged "Oradour" as the place of his mishap.

The SS might have mixed the two explanations together. But they did not. The military censorship made no mention of searches for a missing commander. On the other hand, at a hearing before the military prosecuting judge of Bordeaux in March 1949, Weidinger made no mention of any fighting in Oradour upon the arrival of the Waffen SS. He mentioned only the search for the commander.[5] The chronology of the meetings (see Chapter 4), along with the topography of the area involved in the search, invalidates the SS's justifications. These would nevertheless feed rumors as to "probable" causes, confirming that there were unspoken things in the enigma surrounding the massacre, and would later feed the negationists' arguments.

Gleiniger, the Wehrmacht general commanding 586th headquarters in Limoges, seems not to have been informed about the activities of the Waffen SS troops "passing through." That is what the regional préfet observed when he came to deliver a protest to him. This was not an unusual situation: the general did not exercise operational command but merely administrative and economic responsibility for the territory. He had no authority over the local SS police command. We have found no trace of a meeting, even for the sake of protocol, between the SS officers and those from liaison headquarters (for whom they had scant consideration). Their mutual distrust seems genuine: this was the time when Wehrmacht officers, particularly those in the Paris command, were preparing the plot against Hitler that took place on July 20, 1944. Without necessarily positing any link between Paris and Limoges, it is evident that a divergence of views existed between traditionalist officers, who deemed the war to be lost, and the convinced Nazis, who meant to pursue it and extend the violence.

Gleiniger asked the regional préfet to see him. They met after the préfet's visit to Oradour. He "came to tell me how he felt, as a man deeply distressed. . . . Gripped by the most violent emotion that a human being can show, the general told me the following when I said that the Oradour-sur-Glane massacre dishonored the German army: 'Yes, I feel this dishonor myself, because the misdeed is a crime against the German people; I shall spare no effort until I have had the severest punishment administered according to the laws of humanity.'" The exchange probably took place without an interpreter: the préfet does not indicate the presence of a third party, something he was in the habit of noting in his reports; he was bilingual and gave his own translation of the German general's remarks.[6]

General Gleiniger sent two reports to his superior, General von Brodowsky, in Clermont-Ferrand. The first one, dated June 12, showed it was only the French authorities who had informed him of the massacres at Tulle and Oradour. The second one, dated June 20, must have been hard to write: we have both a handwritten draft and a typed one with extensive corrections, as well as the report itself. In it the German general copied out an excerpt from the Der Führer regiment's war diary tersely indicating "548 enemy dead" for the Oradour operation. "The First SS Rgt. DF assembled on June 10, 1944, at 13:30 hours to go to Oradour and surrounded the town. After the town was searched, it was destroyed by fire. Munitions were stored in practically every house." General Gleiniger confirmed the propaganda campaign by military censorship. He noted that "hatred for the Germans has grown considerably among the people, even in circles that had not been unfavorable to us up to now." Finally, he asked that a speedy investigation be carried out. We have found a report by a "mission of inspection to the town of Oradour-sur-Glane" dated July 21, 1944.[7] A telegram on June 24 from Clermont-Ferrand had ordered them "to do nothing further."

Hauser, the highest military officer in the Waffen SS at the war's end, would declare before the Nuremberg tribunal that he first heard the name Oradour as a captive. Before that he had never heard of either Lidice or Oradour.[8]

The negationists have adopted the SS version in order to try and turn the responsibility around. They treat the victims' and the SS accounts differently. They grant those of the SS an unwavering trust, whereas they seek out and believe they find contradictions in those of the victims, according to a method of their own devising.[9] The negationist accounts go back to those of the SS: they do not deny the reality of the massacre, but they justify it by citing specific, clearly delimited, localized activities of the Resistance. Resistance members and Spanish and Jewish refugees are said to have had hidden weapons and ammunition and are therefore responsible for the massacre. The negationist account is remarkably inconsistent: it incorporates significant variants. Were ammunition deposits located in "every house"? That would explain the fire. Only in the church? The destruction and the death of the women and children would be due to the presence of Resistance fighters who had hidden in it and thus provoked the carnage in trying to break out! Responsibility for the massacre was attributed to the Resistance. One proponent of negationism has even written that these Resistance fighters came back during the night following the massacre to wipe out their tracks: an impossible feat in a town guarded by Waffen SS troops.[10]

Sometimes the militant negationist waves a document from the archives as irrefutable proof of what he says; but he is unable to provide the document's origin and recipient.[11]

In taking the Oradour massacre as their target, the negationists are not aiming at the victims. They are inclined to "honor" them, once their accounts have been stripped of value. This distinction—clearly perverse at this point—allows them to attack the memory of the Resistance fighters. The ultimate aim of negationism becomes clear: to rehabilitate historically and politically the far right, the heir of Vichy, the only French political force not to have been compromised—corrupted?—by the thought and action of the Resistance. History imbued with negationist ideology cleanses of "Vichyist" disgrace and Nazi contemptibility those who today can no longer refer to the accomplishments and "positive" aspects of Pétain's and Hitler's governments.

The SS account, adopted by negationist ideologues, attributed responsibility for the massacre to the Resistance. It referred to maquis actions with so many variants as to discredit it. The mention of fighting in Oradour was a fiction. At times it was embroidered with the effects of Nazi imagination concerning the "Germanic" warrior's hair-raising fear of women: either the virile fighting woman, armed, wearing a helmet, or the wild witch dancing on corpses.[12]

Fed by a Manichaean and vindictive ideology, the negationists' imagination repeats that of the SS. Beyond their verbosity and mendacity, the negationists' remarks seek to reestablish the Waffen SS's honor by destroying that of the Resistance. For them, as in the past, the Resistance is to be segregated and "excluded from the populace."

What is implied is the universal, deliberate segregation of the Resistance from the French people. It is beneath the surface, but active nonetheless, sustained by the negationists' accusations, which catch the Resistance fighters in a perverse trap by reversing the roles: it is up to those who are segregated to prove they were neither responsible nor guilty.

The Instrumentalization of Oradour

The préfet of the Vichy government, General de Gaulle, and the Communist Party all stepped in—as we have seen—to give the massacre a meaning. The governments of the Fourth Republic, in turn, would confirm Oradour's uniqueness.

Oradour transcended the rifts of the Liberation. Pierre Paquet, an architect with the Bâtiments de France and inspector with the Monuments historiques, who was appointed in July 1944 by the Délégation générale à l'Equipement national [General Commission for National Facilities] as the sole architect in charge of operations[13] for the reconstruction as well as the historical buildings, would be appointed to that post by the new government at the end of the year.[14] An official chosen by Vichy, who had worked throughout the entire Occupation, was [thus] given responsibility for preserving the "testimony to German barbarity," restoring their ravaged inheritance to the victims or to their rightful heirs, and taking charge of reconstruction.

As we have already shown, preservation of the former village site and the reconstruction were decided upon by the provisional government.[15] But both had been contemplated before the Liberation. This chronology explains how quickly the first steps were taken to preserve the town. Doctor Pierre Masfrand, a Rochechouart physician, was appointed curator of the ruins by the département préfet on September 21, 1944.[16] An official Committee of Memory was formed on the initiative of the commissioner of the Republic with the backing of the Minister of the Interior, Adrien Tixier, a Socialist and member of the Free French Resistance who settled in Bellac, a sous-préfecture of northern Haute-Vienne. The new sous-préfet of Rochechouart, Guy Pauchou, that sous-préfecture's former chief secretary, was entrusted with the committee chair.

This "Active Committee for Preservation of the Ruins and Creation of a Shrine at Oradour-sur-Glane" met for the first time on October 21, 1944. In addition to the sous-préfet and the "curator of the ruins," it included the mayors of Confolens (Charente) and Oradour, two representatives of ministries (those of Health and Historical Monuments), representatives of Resistance movements (the Mouvement de libération nationale and the Front national), two liberation committee chairs (Rochechouart and Confolens), three representatives of the Catholic Church (the parish priest, a representative from the diocesan charitable organizations, and one from the religious art commission), and three representatives of the "disaster victims," who were thus in a minority. The site's future was slipping out of its residents' hands.

So that Oradour would take the lead in the competition for wartime "martyrdom," a race got under way among the local memorial committees, but also between them and the national authorities. The memory of horror—they would ensure that it did not happen again—put an end to the Vichy period and the shameful acts of collaboration. It did not much matter that those charged with patriotic vigilance within the official Committee of Memory had not been in the Resistance, except marginally. Devotion to the cause of Oradour became a stamp of respectability. People forgot that the "Never again" had been formulated first by a Vichy préfet and that another official of this same government had been put in charge of developing the symbolism of the martyr site.

Why preserve the ruins of Oradour? The chair of the Memorial Committee explained it at the first meeting: "Beyond the slightest doubt, the savage butchery at Oradour-sur-Glane constitutes the most monstrous crime in our history. The ruins of what only yesterday was a charming little town eloquently symbolize the Germans' terrible barbarity, and it is our duty to ensure their preservation so they may serve as a lesson to future generations." The curator of the ruins then presented plans for turning the site into a museum and for a memorial museum. They had to act quickly to preserve the church ruins, which were "threatened with imminent destruction." The département architect was asked to undertake "as soon as possible the most urgent task of consolidation." As he also made clear: "It will be our responsibility to present some of the houses in the condition they were found in right after the fire." Since visitors were expected, guards were needed to ensure security, prevent the disappearance of relics, and give "any useful explanations." There was provision for an ossuary crowned with a monument. As for the memorial museum, it would contain objects found in the ruins. "Reverently preserved and exhibited . . . they will summon up in the visitors' minds the most notable episodes of this monstrous tragedy."[17]

Finally, the committee was troubled to see "literature that ought to be controlled flourishing here, there, and everywhere. The truth is often distorted, and the aims pursued are not always disinterested." It was decided to appoint a "censorship commission" from among the committee's members, charged with halting abuses and making sure that accounts published about Oradour-sur-Glane "do not turn to fiction." The issue of controlling the story was there right from the very start.[18]

Postcards of the ruins were published "for the benefit of the victims," but many initiatives slipped from the committee's grasp. Ceremonies were organized in a disorderly fashion: benefit concerts, the publication of a song, plans for a commemorative monument by a foreign sculptor, Apel. les Fenosa, commissioned by the Front national.[19]

The writing of the official booklet is relevant here.[20] Understanding of the site as a museum has to be accompanied by understanding of this account. Published in the summer of 1945, it was competing with other publications that had appeared over the previous months and with the efforts of the police, who now had at their disposal more detailed and trustworthy information concerning the massacre's perpetrators. This did not keep the official committee's book from being recommended for its "great documentary value," and its authors from being praised for "serving France and the martyrs of Oradour-sur-Glane."[21] Forewords by the commissioner of the

Republic and the préfet gave their backing to this work. An "official history" thus took control of the tragedy. The German people, not the Nazis and Nazism, were condemned. The conclusion, that "the Germans are distinguished from other peoples by a frenzied taste for torture, death, and blood" (p. 143), echoes the commissioner of the Republic's foreword: "Oradour, a symbol of the barbarity of the people among whom the killers were recruited" (p. 12). At the time the "official" book appeared, its authors were unaware of what the police already knew, that French forced draftees and French collaborators were also implicated in the massacre. The book thus reflected the ideological objectives of the times. Its continuing distribution showed that the survivors accepted these objectives. Recognizing a unique quality for Oradour's case distinguished its victims from other victims; the debt owed them was given an uncommon value.

Then the administrations of the Fourth Republic entered into competitive bidding with the Communist Party, each striving to prove itself a better defender of the Oradour martyrs' memory. The victims were given incomparable symbolic status. They could consider themselves as possessing a moral power equivalent to the concern of which they were the object.[22]

Unanimity was the watchword until the President of the Republic, Vincent Auriol, laid the first stone for the new town on June 10, 1947. But cracks began to appear once the Communist ministers were ousted from government. The law of September 15, 1948, was voted in unanimously by Parliament, however.[23]

As early as June, however, the municipal government of Oradour, supported by the Communist Party, organized its own commemoration. The government delegated a state secretary to bestow the first decoration—the Croix de Guerre—on the town. The following year, while legal proceedings against those responsible for the massacre were at a standstill and work on reconstruction was delayed, Socialist Minister Paul Ramadier came bringing the Croix de Chevalier de la Légion d'Honneur [Cross of a Knight of the Legion of Honor], which had been awarded to the martyrs.[24] The municipality rejected it and organized a campaign against the government. Local Socialists could neither follow the Communist Party in this defamation campaign nor refuse to receive the minister and his decoration. Therefore the National Association of Martyrs' Families, chaired by a Socialist sympathizer, agreed to receive the Legion of Honor.

The ceremony on June 10, 1949, was silent. The minister pinned the medal on a cushion carried by two children. The text accompanying the Legion of Honor stated that Oradour-sur-Glane was "the theater of a tragedy unique in its horror in the annals of war." Two days later, the Communist Party replied with a ceremony organized with the Centre national des écrivains [National Writers' Center], the Mouvement de la paix [Movement for Peace], and *Lettres françaises*, the emblematic cultural weekly directed by Louis Aragon that grew out of the Resistance.[25] The "pilgrimage to Oradour," organized by the Communist Party two months after the signing of the North Atlantic Treaty on April 4, 1949, turned into a defense and illustration of the "peace policies" of the USSR.[26] During the next three years (notably in 1950, when Paul Eluard attended), the Communist Party would use the anniversary of the massacre and the ruins as a rostrum.[27] These ceremonies, like the National Association of Martyrs' Families and national and local authorities' silent commemorations, would then be attended by large crowds. It is certainly possible that numerous participants attended both of them.

The Communist Party would make consistent use of the name of Oradour throughout the early years of the Cold War. The "Message of the Survivors of Oradour-sur-Glane to Marshal Stalin on the Occasion of his Seventieth Birthday,"[28] along with the inscription of the name at the center of an imposing memorial erected by East Germany on a hill above Weimar at Buchenwald, shows that the name of Oradour had become a symbol.

The Inaudible Account of Justice

The longer it was taking to be done, the more justice was expected. Some, supported by the Communist Party, insisted that the "butchers of Oradour" be judged right at the scene of their crime.

The legal proceedings, which could not start until after the Liberation, seemed endless.[29] Two major difficulties hindered the action of the courts. The first one was purely legalistic: the August 28, 1944, decree of the provisional government of the Republic, which dealt with the punishment of war crimes committed on French territory by enemy military forces, had not anticipated the participation of Frenchmen in those crimes. The courts of justice alone were competent to judge these. The second difficulty arose from the status imposed on West Germany by the Allies. Waffen SS officers, those principally responsible for the massacre, were thereby beyond the reach of French justice.

The Cold War further complicated the situation: former SS men could be recycled in the struggle against Communism. The Communist Party was indefatigable in its denunciations of these inconsistencies. It linked them to the rearmament of West Germany, which had become an ally of the North Atlantic Treaty powers.

Without the Das Reich division chiefs, French justice had only minor figures at its disposal: noncommissioned officers and SS troops. But out of twenty-one defendants who could appear before the military tribunal, fourteen were Frenchmen from annexed Alsace, thirteen of them forced draftees.

The political situation of the forced draftees was not settled immediately after the war, as the August 1944 decree would have permitted. The military authority for the Limoges area, Colonel Rousselier ("Rivier" in the Resistance), had decided in February 1945 that, by virtue of this decree, former Waffen SS members of the Das Reich division who were forced draftees did not have to be handed over to military justice, since their enlistment made them victims of a war crime.[30] Eventually this decision was held not to constitute a valid precedent.

On January 30, 1945, the Garde des Sceaux ordered the cases to be separated, which forced the tribunals to conduct separate proceedings for German defendants and for French nationals involved with enemies or foreigners in war crimes cases.[31] The Oradour "affair"—a crime committed by enemy soldiers—should be conducted by military justice. Accordingly, on November 25, 1944, the prosecuting judge of the Limoges court of justice turned his proceedings over to the military tribunal of Bordeaux. Frenchmen accused of collaboration crimes, however, were to be brought before a court of justice.

The legal confusion was obvious. One member of the Waffen SS troops, who admitted participating in the massacre, was found in early September 1945 in Strasbourg, where he was a postal employee. Arrested by the military governor of the city, he was handed over to the Limoges court of justice, although it had relinquished the Oradour cases. The man admitted the acts he was accused of: he had killed a woman and taken part in the town's destruction. He appeared at the court of justice hearing on March 12, 1946, presided over by an appeals court counsellor who had been in office during the Occupation. Several cases were heard that day, and the trial was "dispatched" swiftly: witnesses who had escaped the massacre recognized the accused as being a young adolescent refugee from Alsace. He might possibly have guided the killers at the crime scene. The five jurors unanimously answered yes to the six questions determining the verdict. The Alsatian lawyer's defense plea was not able to keep an "Oradour butcher" from being condemned to death by a working-class jury.

But on March 22, 1946, the appeals court of Limoges quashed the verdict. The accused was a minor at the time of the events and was wearing an enemy uniform. His case therefore fell under military justice. The civil court passed the accused along like a hot potato to the Bordeaux military tribunal conducting the "Oradour affair" trial. The military judge also recused himself and on October 10, 1946, wrote a long report to his superiors summarizing the legal situation and requesting instructions.[32] The attorney general's office and the minister were hesitant. The president of the Oradour Association lost patience and wrote to the prosecuting judge: "Was Oradour due to the revenge of some Alsatians who claimed to have been received badly during their forced stay in Oradour and swore when they left that 'Oradour would burn, and the people with it?'" Rumors were rife, fed by political conflicts; hatred was simmering. A police investigation showed that the accused had never been to Oradour before June 10, 1944, which the escapees refused to accept.

To avoid problems in the Limousin, the legal authorities shifted the trial venue to the Toulouse civil jurisdiction, hoping that the "question of competence [would be] settled once and for all."[33] But the Toulouse district attorney, who made no attempt to hide the pressure being put on him by the Alsatian deputies, found no satisfactory solution. He therefore proposed that the defendant be amnestied by decree. The government thus found itself faced with a "double incompetency" of both civil and military justice.[34] It hoped to find a "judicial miracle." This was an emergency law voted on with odd indifference that established collective responsibility and took effect retroactively. An unreasonable legal exception satisfied the consciences of people who were calling for the punishment of those accused of a unique crime. It did not matter if the law was unique!

Who was to be judged? German prisoners of war? Weidinger, the former Waffen SS colonel being held in Bordeaux? Charged with "conspiracy," he was interrogated as a witness only in the Oradour affair before being acquitted in 1951. Frenchmen? In April 1947 a sergeant named Boos was found in a prisoner-of-war camp in Great Britain. So he could be tried. For the forced draftees, the dilemma seemed to be solved on August 1, 1948, by a nonsuit judgment exempting them from prosecution—until the emergency law reinstituted the proceedings. As for former Waffen SS officers Lammerding, Stadler, Kahn, and Barth, they were beyond the reach of justice. In any case, the indictment did not include the names of the first two.

The indictment file was declared shut by the military judge on October 22, 1949, without including the cases of SS Sergeant Boos and the defendant being held in Limoges. The proceedings relating to them were added at the hearing. The absent defendants, all Germans, were called "fugitives."

On January 12, 1953, three years after the fact-finding inquest wound down, the trial of the "Oradour killers" opened before the Bordeaux military tribunal; it ended the following February 11.[35] This court did not allow for inclusion of private parties. The victims' families, who had just laid wreaths at the war monument in Bordeaux, could be heard only as witnesses, without lawyers representing them.

The national and the regional press were on hand.[36] National radio sent its most celebrated commentator, Frédéric Pottecher, who reported on the hearings every evening on the radio. The military tribunal was held near the city limits at Les Barrières, in a setting that Armand Gatti, the special envoy from the *Parisien libéré* and a well-known reporter, described as "an abandoned Turkish bath, tricked out with tricolor flags and neon lights . . .; they installed loudspeakers, but, after an unsuccessful test, these were abandoned and from now on will play only a decorative role in the proceedings . . .; three large maps and four charts are hanging on the walls: the Limousin, Oradour before and after, the movements of the 'Das Reich' division before, during, and after June 10."[37] In *Libération,* a newspaper close to the Communist Party, Madeleine Jacob reported being shocked at the courtroom, where the area set aside for the public was scanty, although the main hall of the court of assizes was not in use; in this she saw an order from Paris seeking to minimize the trial.

From the opening of the discussions, the forced draftees' "Alsatian defense" emphasized the implausibility of the proceedings: "We do not want to answer for a crime that others committed on our soil. We do not understand how Alsatian forced draftees can be judged alongside their Nazi tormentors." The tone was set. The presiding judge of the tribunal, Nussy Saint-Saëns, tried vainly to point out that his intention was to put Nazism on trial. In the eyes of the Communist press, he was lacking in firmness toward the lawyers who, to the victims' families' deep indignation, made countless preliminary motions: "Aren't you ashamed! These people killed our children, and you defend them!" Madeleine Jacob reported them as saying.

The indictment was not devoid of ambiguities: it used the term *Alsatian* to designate the nationality of the French defendants. Thus this trial would be about an Alsace whose defense took up a good portion of the discussion.

The presiding judge of the tribunal examined the defendants often by setting forth the answers contained in the files. Out of apathy or as a strategy, the defendants, except for two of them, were not very talkative. The judge questioned the massacre victims and witnesses, often breaking into their accounts. Then he would let the defense witnesses, authorities, and elected figures speak without interruption. While the trial was on, Parliament modified the law, repealing the basic points of the text that sent French forced draftees before the tribunal. To rule on an exceptional case, there was nothing left but the penal code.

Lieutenant-Colonel Gardon, the government commissioner, made his closing speech for the prosecution at the hearings on February 4–5, 1953; he set forth the "account of justice."[38] Despite the limitations of the prosecution file—in particular, the absence of the archives of SS troops and of the chain of command—and the proceedings' oral nature, this account made some excellent points. It set the massacre in a series of criminal acts that were recalled within the local context. The speech was put together by cross-referencing the witnesses' and the defendants' accounts. The executioners' methods were spotlighted. The Nazis' notion of a "partisan" was defined, using references borrowed from the Nuremberg trials. However, the closing statement did not answer the victims' question: Why did "the Germans" come to Oradour? The judge could only assert the basic point in the context of the trial: that all the defendants had "shared in the crime."

The verdict was pronounced on the night of February 12, 1953: two death sentences, for Boos and a German adjutant; sentences to forced labor and prison sentences for the other defendants. One German defendant who was able to prove he had not been present in Oradour was acquitted. All the absent defendants were condemned to death in absentia. The Bordeaux military tribunal, which pronounced sentences against conscientious objectors, now was condemning failure to disobey. This anomaly was noted by reserve officers, who were indignant that the military institution itself could subvert the principle of obedience. For their part some Protestant Reformed pastors, notably in Montbéliard, revived the debate over conscientious objection, which in their eyes was justified by the war in Indochina and by the military repression of colonized peoples.

The verdict was intensely disappointing. For the victims it was too little; for the Alsatians far too much. It satisfied no one—quite the contrary.

Anger was rumbling in Alsace.[39] The war memorial in Strasbourg was draped in black crêpe. That region, which had undergone annexation by the Nazis, once again considered itself the victim of aggression by a central power that recognized neither its special status nor its past suffering. It went into mourning. Elected officials shut down city halls. The parliamentary representative of Haut-Rhin, Bourgeois, an ex-forced draftee who had escaped and joined the French army, told *Paris Presse* on February 17, 1953: "We are afraid that people from beyond the Vosges don't really understand what an insult this trial is to our patriotic spirit. . . . We cannot accept their being convicted. The first ones to feel offended are the Resistance members." The elected officials of the Haut-Rhin protested as a group "the lack of understanding of which the forced draftees were victims" and demanded that the government "immediately suspend execution of the sentences." The association of Haut-Rhin mayors declared: "We cannot accept. All Alsace declares itself in solidarity with its thirteen sons unjustly condemned in Bordeaux and the 130,000 forced draftees." The conservative parties of Alsace, reflecting majority public opinion, transformed the forced draftees into "unfortunate victims," thus eliminating the regional influence of the Communist Party for a long time.[40]

Amnesty, the Memory of the Forced Draftees

The government's perplexity matched the confusion created by the Bordeaux verdict. Vincent Auriol, the President of the Republic, was in favor of pardoning the accused. General de Gaulle understood the irritated grief of Alsace. "In this grave affair, what must above all be avoided is for France, after losing so many of its children murdered by the enemy in the tragedy at Oradour, to let a bitter wound be dealt to national unity as well."[41]

The government prepared an amnesty bill, but it was a parliamentary proposal that the deputies and senators from Alsace stayed out of when it came under discussion in the assemblies. The first article of the text submitted to the National Assembly attempted an unlikely reconciliation: "The victims of the attack [?] on Oradour-sur-Glane will be granted a national order citation." This odd blunder preceded the main point: "Full and entire amnesty is granted to Frenchmen drafted by force into the German army for any act characterized as a crime or offense committed during a criminal action carried out by the unit to which they were assigned." The message was clear: beyond the thirteen convicted men, the amnesty was aimed at the 130,000 forced draftees. Prime Minister René Mayer made the object of the amnesty clear to the Senate: "It is to maintain national unity. . . . We are thinking of the country's misfortunes and we want to prevent it from experiencing others."[42]

When Alsace's plea had been heard and granted, there was widespread anger in Oradour. Demonstrations were held in Limoges and at the ruins. The Limousin went through the same kind of turmoil that Alsace had experienced a few days earlier. Aimé Faugeras, the mayor, gave back the Croix de Guerre he had received in 1948. The National Association of Martyrs' Families formally returned to the préfecture its 1949 Legion of Honor, along with another symbol: the plaque laid by General de Gaulle at the victims' tombs. Even partial erasure of the unsatisfactory verdict was an insult, an offense to the martyrs' memory.

Amnesty, a magical way to manage crises politically, requires that the sin be forgotten. It not only erases any trace of a conviction, it theoretically forbids any memory of it. But how was an event whose repercussions were so enormous not to be recalled?

The amnestied prisoners left Bordeaux during the night of February 22, 1953. Driven to Saverne in five RG Citroën sedans, they were greeted by the president of the "Against Our Will" Association: "Here you are in Alsace. We refused to let you become victims. But we do not consider you to be heroes. . . . Try to be forgotten."[43] But was that possible?

Back again in their sanctuary, the amnestied prisoners hoped they would be forgotten. "I ask only for silence. . . . I am happy." The press accommodatingly photographed them at home. For the delegates at the "Against Our Will" meeting on February 23, 1953, at the Café du Grand Pêcheur in Strasbourg, they had been "cleared."

In Oradour, the National Association of Martyrs' Families fought back with the only weapons it had. It decided to post the names of the amnestied prisoners along with their respective convictions and the names of those who voted for amnesty. The government authorities did not try to stop this. Then the Association decided to take control of the commemorations and build its own Tomb of the Martyrs, spurning the monument erected by the government. Finally, thanks to municipal elections, it gained power in the town. Thus it took control of its territory and the symbols of its mourning. Since the effects of the amnesty only intensified those of the massacre, "the executioners" were considered in fact to have been cleared.[44] The account of justice therefore no longer had any credibility. Henceforth, it was useless to the victims.

Conversely, the amnesty created a new legitimacy in Alsace: it confirmed its victim status and consequent lack of guilt. For Alsatian public opinion, it was obvious that Parliament would never have adopted such a measure in favor of criminals. The amnesty law—approved by all the political groups except the Communist Party, the CGT, and Socialist politicians from the Limousin, who could not do otherwise—constituted a "reparation." In April 1954, the Ministry of Finance dropped the collection of court fees, defining its conception of amnesty: "It results in dismissal of criminal charges, legal proceedings, and sentences and so it is as if these crimes had never been committed."[45] Boos and the German adjutant were pardoned and set free in the early 1960s.

Oradour's Account, a Collective Memory?

The accounts of the witnesses who survived the massacre, who lived through the tragedy right in the town, were oral ones. To them may be added the accounts of all those on the fringes who followed its events. Then those from the earliest people to have seen its effects: parents looking for their children and loved ones. Then some of those who were "foreign" to the massacre, Resistance fighters who came for news, like Marc Bernard, who immediately published the earliest study.[46] Like the rescue workers in the emergency crews, they noted the extent of the disaster. We have already cited these accounts.

Mutual influence of the oral and the written marked the appearance and the shaping of individual accounts. When the investigating commissioner interviewed the witnesses during the last quarter of 1944, the beginnings of a community account could start to take form under the influence of the curator of the ruins and the guides who greeted visitors and informed them about the story of the massacre. An oral account from within the ruins was circulated at the same time as several published accounts. The written accounts reproduced the oral one, which in turn was fed by the written ones.

The Oradour community, which came together when the National Association of Martyrs' Families took control of the town government in 1953, did not foster the writing of its history from within itself. It received the texts it disposed of as signs of gratitude, as gifts. By distributing these texts to visitors to the ruins, the community drew from them the necessary resources to ensure its financial independence. The community was seeking recognition and justice. It received recognition and it called for justice, even though some would have preferred vengeance. For the verdict to be preceded by an account was of little importance. The community was not asking for an account of its story: its members had lived through it and felt they alone could pass it down.

The status of the written account was secondary at this point when compared to the oral account, which brought together and combined those of the witnesses. A block of individual accounts had become the equivalent of a "grand account" relating "the events of Oradour." This account was no longer identified with any one particular witness but belonged to the community, which projected it outward. Reflecting the anonymity of those who died in the massacre, it too was anonymous. It was passed down to new generations within the families, which punctuated it with the commemorations. It was also passed on to visitors to the ruins by guides chosen by the administration from among the members of the Association. Benefiting from such double legitimacy, this "grand account" did not have to be verified by a scientific body; it created a community of victims, which imposed specific rules connected with mourning: life in Oradour was not like that anywhere else. The memory of the dead, of the past, and of its tragedy overshadowed the activities of the present.

In Oradour the dead were present. They were its sacred portion. They exercised a decisive influence over the living, as if the community had taken for itself Barrès's formula (but reversing its terms) of a union of the living with the dead.[47] The community required that those born into it be aware of their duty toward the dead.

The existence of a "grand account" through which the victims' group gave itself the position of narrator precluded any individual expression. Anyone who took the initiative of publishing his own account found himself excluded from the community: this was the case with Robert Hébras in 1993.[48] The contents of the individual account mattered less than its mere existence. The legitimacy of the person speaking about Oradour was immediately put into question unless he was speaking for Oradour, like the authors of the "official book."

The collective memory formulated by the community's account filtered out all other memories. It was an instrument of power. The Oradour community was its account.

The predominance of the myth over other accounts matched the emotion felt by visitors to the ruins. An enduring basis for the renown of the site and the name of Oradour was ensured by the union of a basically sentimental and emotional perception of the ruins—as desired by the Memorial Committee's leaders and their museum—with the account that had been controlled in this way.

Why?

The historical account did not satisfy anyone's expectations. The problem with it lay not only in access to documentary sources: compared to the emotional charge of the ruins and the force of the myth, the accuracy of a historical account is fragile. Even worse, it can be treated as if it were just another rumor. The risk is that it may seem merely an intellectual construct; the myth, on the other hand, is perceived not as myth but as something representing reality.

The Oradour massacre did not have any one single cause. Its origins can be explained by multiple strands of causes, whose conjunction was at times fortuitous, but which can be teased out. The Oradour victims were not due to destiny, to fate. Their death was the result of a culture of violence, an institutionalized practice of brutality, a particular context of war, but also a combination of circumstances. None of these elements can be considered in isolation. In the main body of our work we have attempted to show what constituted these elements.

What remains unanswered is the victims' question, Why? Why did the Waffen SS come to Oradour in particular? This Why? is still the subject of critical and scientific discussion.

One concrete answer can be found in the SS troops' path. On June 10, 1944, they moved from one billet to another. In the evening, the main part of Battalion 1 regrouped in Nieul, northwest of Oradour on a possible route from Saint-Junien and Rochechouart, where the entire battalion was still stationed in the morning. We have been able to follow the vagaries of this regrouping, including the unit that went to Saillat, and the detachment of this unit that detoured via Aixe-sur-Vienne. The company that massacred Oradour arrived at the billet in the evening, along with the "services" that had requisitioned trucks in Saint-Junien. Such a random path may be considered to constitute an adequate explanation, especially since the terrorizing strike was meant to be perceived by the victims as having no precise origin.

But an answer that gets to the heart of the matter can be found in SS General Lammerding's notes, expressed straightforwardly and without euphemisms: "Counter-propaganda and segregation [of the Resistance] starting right now, denouncing the terrorists as Communist troublemakers, actions with the objective of setting the populace against the terrorists."[49] Segregation of their opponents reflected a frequent practice of the Nazis and the Waffen SS. A brutal operation, a basically arbitrary decision apparently taken at random, was meant to arouse a sense of exclusion. The aim was to have those excluded bear the responsibility for the terror, to make them guilty of it in the eyes of the people, as if they were faithless and lawless bandits. Because the poisons secreted and spread by this practice have endured, it was a tremendously effective method.

Why Oradour, since there were no maquis? We must now offer our own interpretation, based on an observation: The Waffen SS and the residents of Oradour, like most French people, did not share the same idea of the Resistance fighter.

The Waffen SS were looking for "bandits." They did not necessarily go after the maquis, however. Before their arrival in the Tulle and Limoges area, starting June 8, 1944, they had carried out raids around Figeac. They did not aim their activities directly at the maquis but went into towns and villages and terrorized the general population. They sought out those they called "partisans," that is to say, for them, "Judeo-Bolsheviks." And if they could not kill or capture them, they segregated them. The maquis were not attacked in the Eymoutiers or Oradour-sur-Vayres zones, where the Waffen SS might well have carried out combing operations. On the other hand, the SS did go into places where they thought they could find "partisans": Nexon, Saillat, Aix-sur-Vienne and . . . Oradour-sur-Glane. Was the segregation operation not aimed at places where the Nazis imagined they were acting against Communists and Jews? The SS general's notes indicate this obsession with "a Communist government." The description of the Saillat operation, although it seems spotty, is testimony to an enduring obsession with the image of "Communist bandits."

One important element is missing: we do not know what hostages the Waffen SS may have asked the "mayor," Paul Desourteaux, for. We know for certain only that they made such a demand and that it was not satisfied. It is possible this was just part of a show aimed at calming the people assembled on the fairgrounds and getting them to play their part. But it was a common practice in Eastern Europe, where the Nazis called on a village head to identify and point out Communists and Jews, whom they executed immediately or deported. Furthermore, the SS police in Limoges, at a time when they had increased their pressure on area Jews, took part in setting up the "brutal operation." We know that an SS officer of the Gestapo was accompanied by French auxiliaries and Milice members, including an inspector for Jewish Questions. Reports by the police and sous-préfet as well as denunciations suggested real and/or imaginary activity by Communists and Jews in Oradour.

The residents of Oradour, like most French people, knew nothing about the Nazis' retaliatory practices aimed at Communists and Jews in Eastern Europe. The Nazis' image of the "bandit-partisan" was incomprehensible. For them, the Resistance fighter could only be portrayed with the features of the maquisard. The residents were unaware, say, of the clandestine Resistance activity of Albert Mirablon, the amateur photographer and bank employee who was born in the United States; they would remain unaware of it even after the war was over. After the liberation of Limoges, the "maquis capital," and of the entire Limousin without direct intervention by Allied troops, this image achieved the status of the dominant one. The arrival of the Waffen SS in Oradour could have been only a misunderstanding, a mistaken objective, or an act of "gratuitous barbarity."

The practice of arbitrary, systematic, and discriminatory violence against Communist and Jewish "bandits," designated as partisans and absolute enemies, was a constant of the Nazis' war in the East. During the first half of 1944, the progress of the war on Soviet territory, the growing likelihood of a new front opening in the West, and the increasing strength of the Resistance forces in France, all resulted in the transferal of combat methods. This change was emphasized by the arrival of troops, including some Waffen SS, who had gone through the moral universe of the war's brutalization. These units, withdrawn from the eastern front and undergoing reorganization, with their raw, ill-trained troops, took part in the struggle against the "bands" by combing zones where they terrorized the populace in order to segregate the "partisans."

In early June 1944, two days after the Allied landing in Normandy, a combat group of the Waffen SS Das Reich division was sent into "the area of Tulle and Limoges," where the Resistance was seen to be active, to carry out such combing operations. The Waffen SS combat group restored order in Tulle and elsewhere. It made use of bloody repression as it went along. There were encounters with the Resistance and there were Waffen SS losses.

At the time he received the order to proceed to the front that had opened in Normandy, the SS general decided on the principle of a "brutal operation" of arbitrary retaliation, to punish the populace by terrorizing it and to segregate the "bandits." This operation, as in many other cases, was prepared in conjunction with local SS police and Milice. It was carried out by a unit going from one billet to another. The search for Communist and Jewish partisan "bandits" brought this unit, under a battalion commander, to Oradour-sur-Glane. The denial of any massacre came immediately after execution of the operation. For the victims, the "gratuitous barbarity" was incomprehensible. That was the aim sought by the Nazis for effective segregation.

Afterward, events unfolded differently from what the Nazis had foreseen. The war was more or less won by the advance of the Soviet forces. The Allied forces' push caused the Wehrmacht to retreat from southwestern France starting on August 18, 1944. The French Forces of the Interior were able to liberate the territories in which they had gained supremacy.

Oradour entered French history through the speeches that gave meaning to the massacre. "The pilgrimage of France's great, silent grief," in the Vichy version, and "The symbol of France's suffering under the Occupation and collaboration," in the provisional government of the Republic's version, created the conditions of possibility for the renown of the site, with its "ruins bearing witness to German barbarity." This renown was broadened by the militancy of the Communist Party and the intervention of other political currents that did not want to miss out on the fallout. The media's takeover of the ruins at Oradour, whose massacre was considered "the most monstrous of war crimes," helped intensify its renown. This takeover reached its climax with the 1953 trial. But if the Oradour massacre seems to be the only one of its kind in Western Europe, it nevertheless echoed innumerable collective massacres by the Nazis in Eastern Europe, which the authors of the literature published up to that point could not imagine.

The symbolism of Oradour enabled the French people, the majority of whom were not involved in the conflict, to find their place once again in this new direction of the Republic. The amnesty restoring to the national community those French former forced draftees from Alsace who had fought, under constraint, in the Nazi army came at the expense of the Oradour community. Out of justifiable pride, the Oradour community then decided to reject the instrumentalization of its tragedy by others for their own purposes; it turned in on itself, among its own, on the soil where the dead were buried. Oradour continues to deal by itself with the debt owed it in the name of its dead, without reference to the national gratitude from which it benefited earlier. It maintains the practice of silent commemorations, accompanied by haughty vigilance over an oral account that it insists on controlling.

Despite all the tokens of gratitude, the debt has not been canceled, since no one among those either directly or indirectly responsible for the massacre, including the former forced draftees, has ever asked the victims for pardon. No sign has come to Oradour from Germany like the one that [Roman] Herzog, the President of Germany, made toward the victims of Guernica. In the absence of any request for pardon, the victims have wrapped themselves in the motto "neither forgive nor forget" that still inspires them today. They have not had an opportunity either to accept or to reject a pardon that alone might put an end to their mourning.

And so the story of the Oradour massacre is not finished. Might not such an ending offer an opportunity for the victims themselves to go beyond forgetfulness and imagine the possibility of passing on, not a debt, but the ideal of memory that has become history?

9 Souviens-toi—Remember

Signs on the ground greet visitors to the ruins with these words, "Souviens-toi—Remember."[1] The text is painted on wooden boards that long hung on the road signs at the entrance to the village. Another sign nearby asks for silence. The signs are a part of the site. They are not left over from the museum of the ruins set up by the Memorial Committee, which installed plaques engraved in stone on the church and at scenes of the massacre. Neither are they from the administration in charge of preservation, which put up silk-screened plastic signs. These are independent, clearly tolerated by the administration, which would never have allowed itself such "lowly" materials, particularly set out this way on the ground. The signs are old and look as if they have always been there. When the Centre de la Mémoire first opened and a new route became the required entrance for visitors, the signs appeared along this new pathway. An unknown hand had moved them to that place to ensure the permanence of the greeting and, of course, of the message addressed to visitors. The new materials could not replace the old request. The signs represent a living memory.

If the sign requesting silence means that this site is a graveyard, the sign requesting remembrance conveys, by the grammatical form of the present tense, an imperative that is self-evident and requires no further explanation beyond itself. This sign tells of a wounded, unhealed memory. It gives an order that the victims be remembered. By keeping it unrepayable, the sign maintains a debt that is held in reserve. More than the changes in the tour of the ruins, the presence of the signs reminds us how absolute is the imperative of remembrance: the "duty of remembrance" existed in Oradour long before its widespread use in political speeches, the media, and academic circles.

"Never more!" says the raven in the poem.[2] The first to say "Never more" in Oradour was a Vichy préfet: could he have been "an ominous bird of yore"? Did the memory of Oradour "come to a stop," as Sarah Farmer so rightly put it, because it was not fulfilled?[3]

On the one hand, those responsible for the massacre, whatever their degree of responsibility, have not really been brought to trial. As we know, not one of them has expressed a wish for the victims to pardon them. These people, obviously, have refused to accept the debt of their past.

On the other hand, did the instrumentalizations of the massacre's memory—and then the rejection of those instrumentalizations by the Oradour community—not result in the creation of a "memory screen." A screen of the victims as a group, which promotes a myth as an "official" discourse while at the same time adhering to a strategy of indebtedness? Can this posture as victims, closed up tight within the repetitive, silent commemoration of their misfortune, lead eventually to a civic or moral program? Oradour, a symbol of massacres, is not exempt from the forgetfulness of "the others." The silence of the commemorations has stilled the voices of time. The authorities who appeared in Oradour during the postwar period avoided any comparison with the colonial massacres for which they themselves bore responsibility.[4] At one and the same time, France could acknowledge the exemplariness of a symbol and still massacre colonized peoples demanding independence.

Afterword

Oradour-sur-Glane, July 16, 1999

OPENING CEREMONY

Dense fog has shrouded the countryside of the Glane River Valley since daybreak.[1] Usually that is a sign of sunny weather to come; but early this morning it is a bit troubling to all the people in charge of final preparations for the event, greeting guests, and security. Will the President's plane arrive on time? A bulletin arrives that it will be a little late. Jacques Chirac will be coming to Oradour to inaugurate the Centre de la Mémoire d'Oradour.[2] "On the morning of June 10, the sky was cloudy, a little overcast; afterwards..." as one of the last survivors of the massacre remembers.

Of the event—the massacre itself—there remains a tangible scar: the ruins of the "martyr village," destroyed on June 10, 1944, by a Waffen SS unit. These ruins have been preserved by the services of the state and classified as a historical monument.

Close by the ruins, other elements surround them like so many heaped-up signs: a new town, constructed between 1947 and 1953; a crypt known as the state monument, which since 1974 has been turned into a reliquary shrine; a monument of the National Association of Martyrs' Families called the Tomb of the Martyrs; a sculpture by Fenosa, *To the Martyrs of Oradour*. The new facilities, designated as the Centre de la Mémoire d'Oradour, are designed to receive and inform visitors. Oradour is a "realm of memory." It is a reference term, as well.

Unlike other names that are symbolic of the history of twentieth-century wars in France (Verdun, Drancy), the name of Oradour does not just represent a realm of memory.[3] An Oradour now signifies the massacre of a defenseless civilian population by military force. The proper noun has become a common noun. After World War II was over, when other massacres were learned of, the name Oradour became a term of reference for them. "There were Oradours they were discovering," as Pierre Nora wrote in his historical evocation of the year 1945.[4]

Wars of decolonization, international crises, and conflicts within states would give rise to many an Oradour. Powerlessness or indignation at repeated collective murders would lead to the reference being constantly invoked.[5] This exemplary character is what justifies the presence of the President of the Republic at the ceremony. Following in the footsteps of Vincent Auriol, Charles de Gaulle, and François Mitterand, Jacques Chirac is the fourth President of the Republic to come to Oradour in a little over fifty years.

Little by little, the mist clears and gives way to sunshine. A fine day for the public, and for the guests, who include members of parliament and local officials from the Haute-Vienne département and the Limousin, as well as some from the rest of France. They represent the entire political spectrum, except the far right. The presence of the Front national (that is, of Le Pen), the heirs to Vichy and spokesmen for the former Nazis, is inconceivable. Aside from this, Oradour transcends political divisions.

The President begins his visit in the ruins—that is how the local people refer to the former village. There he is greeted by the Oradour community:[6] the board of the National Association of Martyrs' Families (abbreviated locally to "the Families" or "the Association") and the municipal council. Then he walks through the streets of the village, accompanied by the president of the Association (a survivor of the massacre), the mayor of the town,[7] the Minister of Culture and Communication (Catherine Trautmann, who is a representative of Alsace), and parliament members for the département. This visit has been labeled "private," so like all visitors he stops at the church in which almost four hundred women and children perished, then in front of the barns and garages where almost two hundred men were shot. He passes by the state monument—the shrine where a few charred objects are preserved—without entering; then he meditates in silence before laying a wreath on the Tomb of the

Martyrs, erected by the Association in the town cemetery, outside the area designated for the historical monument. The President of the Republic is respecting a formality that has been set and accepted for several decades, followed by ordinary and celebrated visitors alike, such as members of the préfecture administration on the day they take office in the département. This formality was stipulated by local authorities within the walls of a state monument and sanctions an exception to normal procedure. Then, preceded by a group of children, the President walks to the Centre de la Mémoire.

The facilities are presented to him rapidly, with the permanent exhibit, following a strict schedule. Since I have been in charge of historical research and organizing this exhibit, I am the one to discuss it. The visit is interrupted halfway through by the Elysée chief of staff, so the temporary exhibit is omitted.[8] The guests and public are awaiting the President on the square, where he unveils an inaugural plaque and delivers a speech.

Presidential security has cordoned off the area, set up a platform with the ruins looming like a stage set in the background, and provided a public address system for the presidential speech, for which TF-1 has secured exclusive rights.[9] The one o'clock afternoon news schedule must be met. The President of the Republic expresses his sympathy for the victims and their families: "Oradour, deeply scarred, with its wounds still gaping, makes us all search our consciences." Then he takes up the general question of massacres and their ongoing existence, citing examples from the events of recent years, among them the massacres of Sabra and Shatilah in Lebanon, Kibuye in Rwanda, Srebrenica in Bosnia, a village in Kosovo. What do these names have in common? Victims, to be sure, but also those responsible and guilty: "Every martyr reminds us that barbarity is common to all countries and all times." Might barbarity be a constant of human nature? Might this example of barbarity explain all massacres? Should we perhaps seek the causes of these tragedies elsewhere, for example in the political circumstances from which they originate? Might the massacres be part of fallible human nature, or might they be produced by a culture of violence?[10]

The President asserts his conviction that a code of ethics will let us go beyond these tragedies: "The twenty-first century, learning from the lessons of the past, will be the century of ethics. I hope so and believe so."[11] Vigilance in the defense of the Rights of Man will let us halt the repetition of massacres. That is how "temples of memory, which show what humans can invent when they fall prey to fanaticism, denial of the Other, and the forces of hatred and death," may be of use. After he finishes his speech and signs the visitors' book, the President enjoys the mutual pleasure of mixing with the crowd.

For both the President and the parliamentary representatives of the département, who have been responsible for its creation, the opening ceremony of the Centre de la Mémoire d'Oradour is a public relations operation. The Haute-Vienne département, in the Limousin, is a bastion of the Socialist and Communist left. The département had not generated much enthusiasm among members of its Socialist majority for [conservative] Jacques Chirac—elected in 1995 over [Socialist] Lionel Jospin, who became premier after the dissolution [of Parliament] and early legislative elections of 1997—to come and open the regional council's facility. For the Oradour community, which from the very beginning rejected any outside presence, especially a potential German one, only the President of the Republic had the requisite authority to open the new facility. If the Premier wanted to accompany the head of state, he would of course be welcome. But he will not be coming.

It was the office of the President that set the date for July 16.[12] This was non-negotiable. In the chronology of Vichy France under Nazi occupation, the allusion is significant: it is the anniversary of the roundup of Jews on July 16, 1942, in Paris, the so-called Vel' d'Hiv' roundup, "the symbol of Vichy's complicity in genocide."[13] It was also the day chosen to commemorate the victims of the Shoah.[14] This coincidence, or any possible confusion of symbolisms, has no effect on the ceremony at Oradour: not one of the speeches refers to it.

On this day the Premier and his wife, philosopher Sylviane Agacinski, are on a private family visit to the camp at Auschwitz. The national and the international press will compare the activities of the two heads of the executive branch at Auschwitz and Oradour, two names often associated together to symbolize the horrors of Nazism.

Remembrance of the massacre became part of conflicting political strategies as early as June 1944. The opening of the Centre de la Mémoire d'Oradour fifty-five years after the tragedy brings no exception to the practice of political exploitation. As the ceremony progresses, it bears witness to the permanence of mourning in Oradour, where the wound has not healed, through the specific and precise constraints to which it has been subjected. And so people speak generally of the "massacre of Oradour," where the word *of* bespeaks a strong meaning contained in the grammatical form: the proper noun becomes the complement of the common noun. A "massacre"—before it signifies a putting to death, or the quarry of a hunt—connotes "butchery," and massacring is the act of ferociously killing one or more defenseless victims; the complement thus indicates localization as much as it does possession. The terms *Oradour* and *massacre* are inextricably bound together. By identifying the event with its place, the association of the two nouns expresses the specificity of the victims' misfortune and the recognition due them. In the village, the older people speak of the Oradour "affair" as something that cut down lives and interrupted the continuity of time.

In August 1964,[15] the poet Paul Celan visited the ruins of Oradour.[16] Born in Buchovina, Romania, he spent the greater part of his life in France, in Paris. His poetic works were written in German. We do not know what his reaction was following this visit, accompanied by his wife, Gisèle de Lestrange, an artist and engraver, and Peter Szondi, a university professor of philology, an "importer" of the authors cited by Denise Bardet, the young French schoolteacher who died in the Oradour massacre.[17] They were traveling from Normandy to the Dordogne, the opposite direction from that taken by the Waffen SS division after the massacre. I can imagine the French artist, the German intellectual, and the Jewish émigré poet from Eastern Europe walking through the ruins, stopping to read the signs. There was no one to tell them about a schoolmistress who, in this place, loved German literature; nor of Albert, the Resistance fighter and photographer who was born in the United States; Robert, the Sephardic Jew born in Bayonne, France; the two Josephs, one born in Budapest and the other in Kokern, Germany; Sarah, born in Kalisz... They knew there had been young and old people, men, women, children; and murderers who spoke... German.

One of Celan's poems, written in Vienna in 1945, is entitled *Todesfuge (Deathfugue).* A poem written for those whose faces the poet did not see:

dann habt ihr ein Grab in den Wolken da liegt man nicht eng

[you have a grave in the clouds, there people don't lie crowded together]

Glossary of Abbreviations and Foreign Terms

AD	Archives départementales [Département Archives]
AJM	Archives de la justice militaire [Archives of Military Justice]
AN	Archives nationales
AS	Armée secrète [Secret Army]
the Association	l'Association des Familles des Martyrs [the National Association of Martyrs' Families]
CGT	Confédération générale du travail [General Labor Confederation; a trade union connected to the Communist Party]
CNRS	Centre national de recherche scientifique [National Scientific Research Center]
DF	The SS Der Führer division
Einsatzgruppen	SS death squads [literally "inserted groups"]
EML	Etat-Major de liaison [liaison headquarters; French translation of the German *Verbindungsstab,* German military liaison with local Vichy authorities]
FFI	Forces françaises de l'intérieur [French Forces of the Interior]
FN	Front national [National Front; a Resistance group with Communist ties]
FTP	Franc-tireurs et partisans [Snipers (Irregulars) and Partisans; one of the most important Resistance groups, backed by the Communist Party]
GMR	Groupe mobile de réserve [Mobile Reserve Unit; a militarized uniformed police force in the service of the Vichy government]
GTE	Groupement de travailleurs étrangers [Foreign Workers Group]
Hiwis	Auxiliary troops of varied nationality in the German army
IHTP	Institut d'histoire du temps présent [Institute for Contemporary History; part of the CNRS]

Jedburghs Small teams of French-speaking SOE teams, who parachuted into France to carry arms and other supplies to the Resistance during WWII. They were code-named for a Scottish town known for its resistance to British dominion.

Légion Légion française des combattants et volontaires de la Révolution nationale [French Legion of Veterans and Volunteers for the National Revolution; an organization created by the Vichy government on August 29, 1940, to spread Pétainist ideology]

Maintien de l'ordre Maintaining Order; a Vichy security organization

MBF Militärbefehlshaber in Frankreich; German military command in France

Milice Militia; a French right-wing paramilitary police organization that helped the Nazis fight the Resistance

MLN Mouvement de libération national [National Liberation Movement; a Resistance group]

MRU Ministère de la reconstruction et de l'urbanisme [Ministry of Reconstruction and Urban Planning]

MUR Mouvements unis de la résistance [United Resistance Movements; a Resistance group]

NSDAP Nationalsozialistische deutsche Arbeiter Partei [National Socialist Workers (Nazi) Party]

Obergruppenführer Superior group leader; an SS rank

OKH Oberkommando des Heeres [the German army high command]

OKW Oberkommando der Wehrmacht [the Wehrmacht high command]

OSS Office of Strategic Services (U.S.)

OPJ Officier de police judiciaire [police officer from the Department of Criminal Investigation]

PCF Parti communiste français [French Communist Party]

PJ Police judiciaire [Department of Criminal Investigation]

Plantu A noted French political cartoonist

PS Parti socialiste [Socialist Party]

PZ Panzer [German for "tank"]

RG	Renseignements généraux [General Information; roughly equivalent to the American FBI]
RHMC	*Revue d'histoire du monde contemporain* [Review of Contemporary World History]
Ritterkreuz	A high German military decoration [literally "Knight's Cross"]
SA	Sturmabteilung [Storm Division; a Nazi political militia, succeeded by the SS following the "Night of the Long Knives," June 30, 1934]
Schupos	Schutzpolizei, or Security Police
SD	Sicherheitsdienst [Security Service; like the Gestapo a branch of the General SS]
SFIO	Section française de l'Internationale ouvrière [French Section of the Workers' International; the name of the French Socialist Party from 1905 to 1971]
SHAEF	Supreme Headquarters Allied Expeditionary Force; the Allied high command during the World War II European invasion
SHAPE	Supreme Headquarters Allied Powers Europe, command that succeeded SHAEF following the German defeat
SHAT	Service historique de l'Armée de terre [(French) Army Historical Service]; its records can be consulted in Paris, Château de Vincennes
SOE	Secret Operations Executive (Great Britain); equivalent to American OSS
Special Delegation	A consortium appointed by prefecture authorities and presided over by Paul Desourteaux that was made up of prominent citizens, craftsmen, and merchants, which replaced the town council of Oradour during the Occupation
SPW	German armored half-track
SRPJ	Service régional de la police judiciaire [Regional Service of the Criminal Investigation Division]
SS	Schutzstaffel [literally "defense squadron"; the Waffen SS were the "armored" SS]
STO	Service du travail obligatoire [obligatory labor service; established by Pierre Laval on February 16, 1943, to send Frenchmen for labor in Germany]

Totenkopf The SS Death's-head division

UGIF Union générale des Israélites de France [National Union of Jews of France; created by Vichy law on November 29, 1941, and overseen by the Police for Jewish Questions]

UREJ[F] Union de résistance et d'entraide des Juifs (de France) [Union of the Jews (of France) for Resistance and Mutual Aid; also known as l'Union juive de résistance et d'entraide (UJRE)]

Verfügungs-truppe The "reserve troops" of the SS

Wehrmacht Defense Force; the name of the regular German army between 1921 and 1945

Wiking The SS Viking division

Notes

Notes to Introduction

1. Sarah Farmer, *Martyred Village: Commemorating the 1944 Massacre at Oradour-sur-Glane* (Berkeley and Los Angeles: University of California Press, 1999).

2. Stéphane Audoin-Rouzeau and Annette Becker, *14–18, retrouver la guerre* (Paris: Gallimard, 2000) [see Bibliography for English edition.—Trans.]; George Mosse, *Fallen Soldiers: Reshaping the Memory of the World Wars* (New York: Oxford University Press, 1990); Stéphane Audoin-Rouzeau, *14–18, les combattants des tranchées* (Paris: A. Colin, 1986), *La guerre des enfants 1914–1918: essai d'histoire culturelle* (Paris: A. Colin, 1993), *Combattre* (Amiens: Centre Régional de Documentation Pédagogique, 1995), and *L'enfant de l'ennemi, 1914–1918* (Paris: Aubier, 1995).

3. Antoine Prost, "La guerre de 1914 n'est pas perdue," *Le Mouvement Social* 199 (April–June 2002): 95–102; John Horne and Alan Kramer, *German Atrocities, 1914: A History of Denial* (New Haven: Yale University Press, 2001); Frédéric Rousseau, *La guerre censurée: une histoire des combattants européens de 14–18* (Paris: Seuil, 1999).

4. Stéphane Audoin-Rouzeau, Annette Becker, Christian Ingrao, Henry Rousso, eds., *La violence de guerre, 1914–1945: approches comparées des deux conflits mondiaux* (Bruxelles: Complexe, 2002); Omer Bartov, *Crimes of War: Guilt and Denial in the Twentieth Century* (New York: New Press, 2002); Omer Bartov, *Mirrors of Destruction: War, Genocide, and Modern Identity* (Oxford: Oxford University Press, 2000).

5. Joanna Bourke, *An Intimate History of Killing: Face-to-face Killing in Twentieth-Century Warfare* (London: Granta, 1999).

6. For this concept, see Jay Winter, "Under Cover of War," in Jay Winter, ed., *America and the Armenian Genocide* (Cambridge, England: Cambridge University Press, 2003), 22–43. For an alternative view, see Roger Chickering and Stig Förster, eds., *Great War, Total War: Combat and Mobilization on the Western Front, 1914–1918* (Cambridge, England: Cambridge University Press, 2000).

7. Pierre Nora, *Les Lieux de mémoire* (Paris: Gallimard, 1984–1992).

Notes to Text

1—WHAT IS KNOWN ABOUT THE MASSACRE?

1. Among others, see Jorge Semprun: "There were survivors at Oradour-sur-Glane. From every quarter, throughout the centuries, women with tear-filled eyes blurred forever by visions of horror have survived massacres. They

would tell the story. Death, as if you were there: they were there." Jorge Semprun, *L'Ecriture ou la vie* (Paris: Gallimard, 1994), 60. [The name "Oradour" comes from a Limousin word denoting a chapel, derived from the Latin "oratorium"—Trans.]

2. [The Limousin is a former province of central France. The traditional capital is Limoges—Trans.]

3. "The story of Dr. Desourteaux's car is emblematic of the contradictions facing Oradour as a monument. As time goes by, the artificial will continue to encroach upon the real as long as conservation remains a priority. Conservation thus risks undermining the basic premise for preserving the ruins—for it was their authentic character that was supposed to give them meaning." Farmer, *Martyred Village,* 201. [We have consulted here and elsewhere the American edition of Sarah Farmer's book. The author refers to the French edition: Sarah Farmer, *Oradour: arrêt sur mémoire* (Paris: Calmann-Levy, 1994), 207; the title plays on the French cinematic term for "freeze frame"; see Bibliography for English-language edition.—Trans.]

4. AN Contemporary Section (Fontainebleau), MRU: 820.474.175. [The Bâtiments de France (Buildings of France) and Monuments historiques (Historical Monuments) are national agencies charged with questions of architecture and historical preservation.—Trans.]

5. Audoin-Rouzeau and Becker, *Retrouver la guerre,* 167–68. [The Rheims cathedral, partially destroyed by German bombing during World War I, was restored to its original state after that war.—Trans.]

6. [The Beaux-Arts (Fine Arts) is a rather vague term used to designate the French government's involvement in historical architectural matters. Specifically, the Beaux-Arts can refer either to the Académie des Beaux-Arts, an institution founded in the seventeenth century, or to the Ecole des Beaux-Arts, a national school founded in the nineteenth century to promote art and architecture.—Trans.]

7. Quoted from the "Report" of Maurice Finet, a deputy in the National Assembly, "Au nom de la Commission de l'Education nationale et des Beaux-Arts, de la jeunesse, des sports, et des loisirs"; 1041, National Assembly, 1946, appendix to the transcript of the Third Session, April 15, 1946, p. 3.

8. [Rocamadour, in the Lot département, is a well-known Catholic pilgrimage site.—Trans.]

9. ["Rural township" is an attempt to translate the French *canton.*—Trans.]

10. [The last brackets in text are Fouché's.—Trans.]

11. The concept of collective memory is from Maurice Halbwachs, *La Mémoire collective* (Paris: Presses Universitaires Françaises, 1950).

12. See Wolfgang Sofsky, *Traité de la violence* (Paris: Gallimard, 1998), 155–70, the chapter devoted to the massacre, translated from the German. [See Bibliography for German and English editions.—Trans.]

13. See André Desourteaux and Robert Hébras, *Oradour-sur-Glane. Notre village assassiné* (Montreuil-Bellay: Editions CMD, 1998). Sarah Farmer notes:

"In much that is written and said about Oradour, one notes a palpable tension between the desire to clarify the cause of what happened and an imperative that it remain unexplained." Farmer, *Martyred Village*, 56.

14. [In French, the word *négationniste* is used principally in reference to revisionist writings about the Holocaust and events under the Nazi occupation.—Trans.]

15. Jean-Noël Kapferer, *Rumeurs, le plus vieux média du monde* (Paris: Points-Seuil, 1987), 312. [See Bibliography for English edition.—Trans.]

16. [In French, "un incorporé de force" (a forced draftee) was a man who was made to serve by the Nazis when Hitler declared Alsace to be part of German national territory.—Trans.]

17. [Rochechouart is a town about fifty-five kilometers due west of Limoges; Saint-Junien is about thirty-five kilometers northwest of Limoges, not far from Oradour-sur-Glane.—Trans.]

18. [Guy Pauchou and Dr. Pierre Masfrand, *Oradour-sur-Glane. Vision d'épouvante: l'ouvrage officiel du Comité du souvenir et de l'Association nationale des families*. This is the document by Pauchou and Masfrand later referred to as *Vision d'épouvante*.—Trans.]

19. [In great part owing to pressure from Alsatian members of parliament, reflecting the feelings of their voters, French Alsatians who had been forcibly drafted into the German army were treated as victims, rather than perpetrators, of Nazi crimes. The "1953 trial" is the one that took place in Bordeaux: see Chapter 8.—Trans.]

20. A comic book written by Calvo in part under the Occupation and published in 1945 takes the form of a fairy tale: *La Deuxième Guerre mondiale chez les animaux* [The second world war among the animals] (republished Paris: Gallimard, 1995). The book evokes the massacres of Tulle and Oradour, each on a full page, which matches the period's image of itself and its prevailing representation.

21. Jacques Chardonne, *Le bonheur de Barbezieux* [Barbezieux's happiness] (Monaco: Editions du Rocher, 1947).

22. Negationists claim that an underground made up of Resistance fighters, foreigners, Jews, and Communists was the cause of the massacre, because of their presence in the village (see Chapter 8 below).

23. *Oradour* was a documentary in two parts—*Les Voix de la douleur* [Voices of grief] and *Aujourd'hui la mémoire* [Today the memory]—that was directed by Marc Wilmart and Michel Follin, a coproduction of France 3 and the General Council of the Haute-Vienne (copyright 1989; distribution INA: Institute national de l'Audiovisuel [National Audiovisual Institute]).

24. Ten cartons, numbered from 546 to 555.

25. [In French, *grille de lecture*.—Trans.]

26. [Louis Aragon (1897–1982), one of the founders of surrealism, was a noted writer. Frédéric Joliot-Curie (1900–1958) was Pierre and Marie Curie's son-in-law, a noted atomic physicist.—Trans.]

27. [In French, *Livre d'or* (golden book, or visitors' album)—Trans.]

28. *Livre d'or d'Oradour: l'engagement des intellectuels, un épisode en 1949* [The visitors' book of Oradour: The intellectuals' involvement, an episode in 1949], a catalogue, with the collaboration of Gilles Plazy (Limoges: Centre de la Mémoire d'Oradour–Conseil général de la Haute-Vienne, 1995), the full text of these records, with photographs by Willy Ronis, a newspaper account of the event, and the text of Joliot-Curie's speech.

29. The originals of the records of Liaison Headquarters 586 of Limoges, concerning Oradour, are in the departmental archives of Haute-Vienne.

30. The SHAEF records were given us by a family member of a survivor of the massacre. [SHAEF was established on February 13, 1944, under General Dwight D. Eisenhower and was disbanded on July 15, 1945, following the German surrender.—Trans.]

31. The original of the 16mm. film is in private hands. Its authenticity is confirmed by photographs, newspaper articles, and the victim's family.

32. [UJRE; in French, l'Union juive de résistance et d'entraide.—Trans.]

2—THE WAR CULTURE OF THE WAFFEN SS

1. Robert Musil, *Journaux* (Paris: Le Seuil, 1981), vol. 2. [See Bibliography for English edition.—Trans.]

2. Philippe Burrin, *Fascisme, nazisme, autoritarisme* (Paris: Points-Seuil, 2000), 143 ff.

3. [For a broad overall presentation, see Pierre Ayçoberry, *La Société allemande sous le IIIe Reich, 1933–1945* (Paris: Points-Seuil, 1998; see Bibliography for English edition), 25 ff. The SA was the Nazis' main political militia until on Hitler's orders its leader, Ernst Röhm, was assassinated in what has come to be known as the Night of the Long Knives, June 30, 1934.—Trans.]

4. Burrin, *Fascisme, nazisme, autoritarisme,* loc. cit.

5. Karl Jaspers, *La Culpabilité allemande* (Paris: Editions de Minuit, 1990), with preface by Pierre Vidal-Naquet. [See Bibliography for English edition.—Trans.]

6. Martin Broszat, *L'Etat hitlérien: l'origine et l'évolution des structures du IIIe Reich* (Paris: Fayard, 1985), 454. [See Bibliography for English edition.—Trans.]

7. The importance of this question for the rest of our study resides in the presence of Alsatians among the troops who committed the crime at Oradour. About twenty Frenchmen from Alsace, which had been annexed by Germany in 1940, participated in the massacre at Oradour. The Nazi authorities considered them Germans, but they were still French to the Allies and the Free French in London, who rejected the annexation of Alsace and the Moselle. For the most part they were "forcibly drafted" in February 1944, in accordance with draft board recruitment quotas. Volunteers (and there were some) enlisted in limited numbers earlier.

8. [Roughly five feet eight inches.—Trans.]

9. Bernd Wegner, *Hitlers politische Soldaten, die Waffen SS, 1933–1945* (Paderborn: Schöningh Verlag, 1997). [See Bibliography for English edition.—Trans.] The personnel of the Das Reich division and the troops present at Oradour in June 1944 would corroborate this.

10. The first four Waffen SS divisions to be established were called historic in Nazi hagiography: Leibstandarte SS Adolf Hitler [Hitler's Bodyguard SS], Das Reich [The Empire], SS Totenkopf [Death's-head SS], and SS Wiking [Viking SS].

11. For additional information and a comparison, see Christian Ingrao, "Culture de guerre, imaginaire nazi, violence génocide: le cas des cadres du SD," *RHMC,* 47-2: 265 ff.

12. We have decided not to use Weidinger's self-serving and mendacious publication, a classic of negationist history. It is a compendium of the euphemisms circulated by the Nazis. We do have at our disposal an archival document, *The Division Battle Order,* communicated to us by historian Hans Umbreit, of the Militärgeschichtliches Forschungsamt [Military History Research Office] in Potsdam. This document is a reconstruction executed under the direction of the French Occupation services in Berlin by former Wehrmacht employees in charge of statistics. We have consulted the archives of German units, the Das Reich division, and its chain of command, operating in France, in the form of American-origin microfilms produced by the Service historique de l'Armée de terre [Army Historical Service] in Vincennes. These archives were supplemented by works published in Germany: *Kriegstagebuch des Oberkommandos der Wehrmacht, 1940–1945* (Frankfurt: Percy Schramm, 1961); Georg Tessin, *Verbände und Truppen des deutschen Wehrmacht und Waffen SS im zweiten Weltkrieg, 1939–1945* (Osnabrück: Biblio Verlag, 1979); *Die Geheimen Tagesberichte der deutschen Wehrmachtführung im zweiten Weltkrieg* (Osnabrück: Biblio Verlag, 1985).

13. See Bernd Wegner, "The 'Aristocracy of National Socialism': The Role of the SS in National Socialist Germany," in *Aspects of the Third Reich* (London: Macmillan, 1985), 430 ff.

14. [A line separating the occupied zone of France in the North from unoccupied France in the South (with Vichy as its capital) following the Franco-German armistice of June 1940. The Germans occupied the southern zone on November 11, 1942, the anniversary of the World War I armistice.—Trans.]

15. [Brackets are Fouché's.—Trans.]

16. ["Pioneer" units were advance engineering or construction units.—Trans.]

17. See the catalogue of the exhibition, *Vernichtungskrieg: Verbrechen der Wehrmacht, 1941 bis 1944* (Hamburg: Hamburger Institut für Sozialforschung, 1998).

18. Orders permitting lax applications of punishment assured the troops of impunity. These are well known today, but it may be useful to recall their contents insofar as they also authorized in advance the Oradour

massacre. The orders were constantly being updated by different levels of the hierarchy. The first, dated May 13, 1941, was issued by the OKW: "Any resistance is punished, not by legal proceedings against the guilty parties, but by practicing a system of terror exercised by the Occupation forces and such as radically to suppress the slightest will to resist. . . . Commanding officers must find means to bring about order in the regions by applying appropriately stringent measures." *International Military Tribunal of Nuremberg,* 15:498. One of numerous repetitions, on July 28, 1941, specified that there were grounds for "spreading terror capable in itself of wiping out any will to resist among the population." *International Military Tribunal,* 22:309.

19. Jürgen Förster, "La Campagne de Russie et la radicalisation de la guerre: stratégie et assassinats de masse," in François Bédarida, ed., *La Politique nazie d'extermination* (Paris: Albin Michel, 1989), 177 ff.

20. See Raul Hilberg, *La Destruction des Juifs d'Europe* (Paris: Fayard, 1988), and Christopher Browning, *Des Hommes ordinaires: le 101e bataillon de réserve de la police allemande et la solution finale en Pologne* (Paris: Les Belles Lettres, 1994). [See Bibliography for English editions.—Trans.]

21. Förster, "La Campagne de Russie," 186.

22. [The Franco-Prussian War.—Trans.]

23. [The author adopts the Nazis' use of the term *bande,* which also has the meaning of "gang" and is associated with the word *bandit;* both these terms are important in his discussion of the Nazis' treatment of Resistance fighters and the inhabitants of the French towns near which they operated.—Trans.]

24. Quoted in Browning, *Des Hommes ordinaires,* 38.

25. Omer Bartov, *L'Armée d'Hitler. La Wehrmacht, les nazis et la guerre* (Paris: Hachette, 1999), 93 ff. [See Bibliography for English edition.—Trans.]

26. Ibid., 112, 111.

27. Walter Manoschek, *"Es gibt nur eines für das Judentum—Vernichtung": Das Judenbild in deutschen Soldatenbriefen 1939–1944* (Hamburg: Hamburger Edition, 1995), 59.

28. Out of a total of 5,700,000 Soviet war prisoners captured by German forces, about 3,300,000 died in captivity. See Omer Bartov, *The Eastern Front, 1941–1945: German Troops and the Barbarisation of Warfare* (London: Macmillan, 1985), 107. [Saint Martin's Press published an American edition in New York in 1986.—Trans.]

29. Taken from *Le Livre noir,* texts and eyewitness accounts collected by Ilya Ehrenburg and Vassili Grossman (Arles: Solin-Actes Sud, 1995). [See Bibliography for English edition.—Trans.]

30. Raul Hilberg, *La Destruction des Juifs,* 247. [*Sonderkommandos* means "special detachments"; "executive" means "having power to execute," that is, to kill.—Trans.].

31. Ibid., 260.

32. Ibid., 278.

33. Ibid., 281.

34. [That is, the hitherto unoccupied southern zone of France; on November 11, 1942.—Trans.]

35. See *Vernichtungskrieg,* exhibition catalogue.

36. [A city in south-central France, the scene of SS atrocities just prior to those at Oradour. See Chapter 4.—Trans.]

37. A Wehrmacht general named Mellenthin—testifying at the July 4, 1946, hearing of the Nuremberg tribunal—remembered that in 1943 Colonel Lammerding had demanded the execution of civilians captured in a raid directed against partisans in the region of Plotsk, in Byelorussia.

38. Himmler, *Discours secrets* (Paris: Gallimard, 1978), 190–91. [See Bibliography for German edition.—Trans.]

3—THE SS DAS REICH DIVISION IN FRANCE

1. [André Malraux, *La Politique, la culture: discours, articles, entretiens (1925–1975)* (Paris: Gallimard, 1996), 209. [Corrèze is a département on the southeast edge of Haute-Vienne. Its administrative seat is Tulle.—Trans.]

2. [That is, the Allies' Normandy landings on June 6, 1944.—Trans.]

3. Henri Cueco, *Le Volcan* (Paris: Balland, 1998), 16.

4. *Hitler. Directives de guerre, présentées par H. R. Trevor-Roper* (Paris: Arthaud, 1965), 181. [See Bibliography for English edition.—Trans.]

5. See Philippe Burrin, "L'appareil d'occupation," in *La France à l'heure allemande, 1940–1944* (Paris: Seuil, 1995), 92 ff. [See Bibliography for English edition.—Trans.]

6. [That is, southwestern and southeastern France respectively.—Trans.]

7. ["in-spite-of-ourselves."—Trans.]

8. [After Alsace and Lorraine were annexed by the Germans, following the armistice, they were administered as German territory. A Gauleiter was the Nazi administrator of a "Gau," or district.—Trans.]

9. This figure is given in *Saisons d'Alsace,* no. 117 (1992): "1942: L'incorporation de force."

10. [That is, the military tribune trials held in Bordeaux from January 12 to February 11, 1953; see the more extensive account of these important trials and their consequences in Chapter 8.—Trans.]

11. See Pierre Rigoulot, *La Tragédie des Malgré-nous* (Paris: Denoël, 1995).

12. Archives de la justice militaire (AJM) [Archives of Military Justice], Le-Blanc, file 13 of the Oradour proceedings.

13. Historical Service of the [French] Army (SHAT), microfilm no. 177 of the German units.

14. Ibid.

15. Excerpt from the Troop-movement Log of General von Brodowsky (the commander of main liaison headquarters 588, Clermont-Ferrand, June 1944), Published Appendixes of the Nuremberg Tribunal, serial number F 257, vol. 37 of the French edition.

16. [The Milice were armed French collaborator troops.—Trans.]

17. [The subhead "'Segregating' the Resistance" in French reads *la "discrimination" des résistants*.—Trans.]

18. We know about this operation through a military justice indictment dated March 12, 1951, drawn up by Commandant Guille in AJM with a copy included in the file of the Oradour proceedings.

19. See Serge Klarsfeld, *Le Calendrier de la persécution des Juifs de France, 1940–1944* (Paris: Beate Klarsfeld Foundation, 1993), 1028. [Drancy is a town in the Paris suburbs where Jews were assembled at a transit camp for shipment to Auschwitz and other concentration camps.—Trans.]

20. See Sofsky, *Traité,* 155 ff.

21. Jean Solchany, "Le Commandement militaire en France face au fait résistant," in *La Résistance et les Français* (Paris: Actes du Colloque CNRS-IHTP, 1995), 522.

22. Ibid., 523.

23. We refer the reader to Solchany, "Le Commandement militaire," as well as Umbreit's archival document, *The Division Battle Order.*

24. The source of this quotation is never given. It can be found in the troop-movement log of the fifty-eighth armored corps, SHAT microfilm no. 173, appendix.

25. See Nicole Loraux, *Façons tragiques de tuer une femme* (Paris: Hachette, 1985), 38 ff., and *Les Expériences de Tirésias* (Paris: Gallimard, 1989), 124 ff., [the chapter entitled] "Le corps étranglé" [The strangled body]. [See Bibliography for English editions.—Trans.]

26. [For example, Auguste Rodin's famous sculpture of this subject.—Trans.]

4—A HOT SPOT: THE MASSIF CENTRAL

1. Georges Guingouin, born in 1913, was a schoolteacher and militant Communist who joined the underground in 1940. He organized resistance in the rural area around Eymoutiers, Haute-Vienne. He became département head of the FTP [Francs-tireurs et partisans (Snipers and Partisans)] in June 1944, then a colonel in the FFI [Forces françaises de l'intérieur (French Forces of the Interior)] on August 3, 1944. He was a Compagnon de la Libération [Companion of the Liberation], and he was the Communist mayor of Limoges from 1945 to 1947.

2. [The large, sparsely settled mountainous and wooded area in central France.—Trans.]

3. *Kriegstagebuch,* 310. [Limoges is the administrative seat of Haute-Vienne, Oradour's département.—Trans.]

4. SHAT microfilm no. 177.

5. As of May 2, 1944, the total strength of the Das Reich division was 18,468 Waffen SS—that is, 460 officers, 3,010 noncoms, and 14,998 regular troops. *Die Geheimen Tagesbericht,* vol. 10.

6. [A distinction that no longer had any real significance by this time.—Trans.]

7. See Georges Guingouin, *Quatre Ans de lutte sur le sol limousin* (Paris: Hachette, 1974).

8. Monthly reports to the Vichy government, AD Haute-Vienne, 185 W 1-44.

9. [Towns in various sectors of the Dordogne département, whose administrative seat is Périgueux. The area is just south of Haute-Vienne.—Trans.]

10. [Two of the major Resistance movements in the former unoccupied zone.—Trans.]

11. Monthly reports to the Vichy government, AD Haute-Vienne, 185 W 1-44.

12. Ibid.

13. *Kriegstagebuch,* 309. [This was the very day of the Normandy landings.—Trans.]

14. [This is the date of the Oradour massacre itself.—Trans.]

15. From a document that is part of unpublished documentation of the Nuremberg tribunal, communicated by historian Hans Umbreit of the Militärgeschichtliches Forschungsamt (Military History Research Office). Taken prisoner, Blaskowitz committed suicide. (Italics in the text are Fouché's.)

16. AD Haute-Garonne.

17. Troop-movement log of the fifty-eighth armored corps, SHAT microfilm no. 173, appendix 6, *Measures against terrorists.*

18. Ibid., appendix 13.

19. This combat unit's movements were mapped out for the permanent exhibition at the Centre de la Mémoire d'Oradour; see the catalogue (Limoges: Centre de la Mémoire d'Oradour, 2000).

20. AD Haute-Vienne, 185 W 1-49. [A city of some 20,000 inhabitants, Tulle is the administrative seat of the Corrèze département. The préfet referred to was an official named by the Vichy government, the armed forces those of Germany.—Trans.]

21. From a copy of a poster signed "The General" announcing the hangings of the hostages in Tulle; it is in the Museum of the Resistance, Tulle.

22. Report of Préfet Trouillé of June 23, 1944, AD Haute-Vienne, 185 W 1-49. In the same report, the préfet thanks Laval for granting him the Légion of Honor for his actions during this period in June. He had his knight's cross given him discreetly by Vaugelas, the regional Milice chief. He was probably not aware of a letter of SS chief Knochen, Oberg's assistant in Paris, proposing to award him a "German decoration" as "an expression of German gratitude" because he had saved several wounded men in the garrison during the initial phase of combat. AN series AJ 40-545-17.

23. *Meldungen aus dem Reich, 1938–1945: die geheimen Lageberichte des Sicherheitsdienstes der SS,* edited by Heinz Boberach (Herrsching: Pawlak Verlag, 1984), 17:6599.

24. AN series AJ 40-969-2.

25. Eberhard Jäckel, *La France dans l'Europe de Hitler* (Paris: Fayard, 1968), 454. [See Bibliography for German edition.—Trans.]

26. 18th Armored Corps, appendix 20 of the KTB, SHAT, microfilm no. 173.

27. The archives of the Waffen SS division indicate both this confusion of orders misapplied or executed too late and information that failed to make its way up the chain of command: an SS division could experience any number of breakdowns. We have seen that it was understaffed with officers and being reformed.

28. An allusion to the sixty-sixth reserve corps, based in Clermont-Ferrand.

29. [The French State (l'Etat français) was the Vichy government, which had succeeded the Third French Republic during the Fall of France.—Trans.]

30. The quotations in this paragraph are from a note signed "Lammerding," dated June 10, 1944, in the troop-movement log of the fifty-eighth armored corps, SHAT microfilm no. 173, appendix 326. [The word *planned (planifiées)* evokes the perceived threat of Soviet Communist–style central economic planning.—Trans.]

31. "Division Agenda for June 10, 1944," troop-movement log of the second SS PZ DIV., SHAT microfilm no. 177. [The italics are Fouché's.—Trans.]

32. A "blank" Renseignements généraux report, AJM, carton 549, bundle 12. [A "blank" report is one not written on official paper; it can thus be considered top secret.—Trans.]

33. The internment camp at Nexon was created in 1939. It was the largest of the camps in Haute-Vienne used by the Vichy administration to intern foreigners, opponents of the regime, and Jews. In 1942 Nexon became a "center for rounding up and screening Israelites," and (like those in Gurs, Vernet, and other camps) it was a staging area for Drancy and deportation. [*Israélite* is generally considered a more polite term than *Juif* to designate Jews, in French.—Trans.]

34. Closing statement by Commander Guille, indictment dated March 12, 1951, AJM, carton 551, bundle 12. [Bourganeuf is about fifty kilometers northeast of Limoges.—Trans.]

35. Troop-movement log of the second SS PZ DIV., SHAT microfilm no. 177.

36. Correspondence from Georges Guingouin, September 30, 1995 (Centre de la Mémoire d'Oradour, 6 pages).

37. From a negationist publication by Weidinger.

38. Statements taken down by OPJ Pierre Arnet, AJM, carton 549, bundle 5.

39. The "Gerlach affair" fed local negationist rumors. See the declarations of two of the principal actors: Roger Chastaing, *J'étais FTP en Haute-Vienne* (La Veytizou, 1990) and the testimony of Marie-Thérèse Palan-Pradeaux, who was guiding the GMR men (Museum of the Resistance, Limoges).

40. Davoine transcript, taken down by Commissioner Pierre Arnet on December 9, 1944, AJM, carton 549, bundle 5, p. 88.

41. [The Nord is a northern département near the Belgian border, of which Lille is the administrative seat. Joseph Darnand (1897–1945) was a World War I hero who had joined the reactionary Action Française political movement in the late 1920s and led the Milice. As the Vichy government's Minister of State for Maintaining Order, he was in charge of the police. He was arrested by the Allies, tried, and executed in October 1945.—Trans.]

42. [In the eastern Moselle département; it had been the site of a well-known French defeat in the Franco-Prussian War in 1870.—Trans.]

43. Filliol was known as an agitator for the far right; a member of the groups that had made up La Cagoule [(literally, "the cowl"), a violent right-wing organization] during the 1930s; an attacker of Léon Blum [the Socialist leader]; in particular, the killer of two Italian anarchists, the Rosselli brothers, in 1937. A fervent Milice member, Filliol followed Darnand at the end of the period of collaboration and then disappeared. He was condemned to death in absentia by the court of Limoges. [Pierre Laval (1883–1945) started political life as a Socialist but left the party in 1911. After holding a variety of important government posts, including that of Prime Minister during the 1920s and 1930s, he was named Prime Minister in the Vichy government during the German occupation. He was tried for treason and executed in October 1945.—Trans.]

44. [Aloïs Brunner (1912–), an associate of Adolf Eichmann, was judged responsible for the deportation of 24,000 French Jews, as well as other actions against Jews of Germany and Greece. After World War II, he was condemned in absentia to life imprisonment for crimes against humanity, and to death for war crimes, but he was never captured.—Trans.]

45. A note of May 3, 1944, to the Limoges KDS [SS Police and Security Command], Centre de documentation juive contemporaine, Paris, XLVI-T.

46. We have found a report by a clandestine Mouvement de la Jeunesse sioniste [Young Zionists' Movement], Moreshet-Archives, Israel, D I 1058. Quoted by Renée Poznanski, *Les Juifs en France pendant la Seconde Guerre mondiale,* 524. The Mouvement de la Jeunesse sioniste was founded in Lyon in December 1941. Working with other Zionist organizations, it carried out clandestine activities (rescues, provision of false documents, and so on). In Poznanski, *Les Juifs en France,* 530, there is a report of the Limoges SRPJ concerning repressive measures against area Jews.

47. Davoine transcript; Patry transcript, AJM, carton 549, bundle 5.

48. [Fouché's brackets.—Trans.]

49. Patry transcript; Davoine transcript.

50. Paul G., transcript of hearing, September 8, 1945, taken down by Commissioner Pierre Arnet, AD Haute-Vienne, 186 W 1-130.

51. Patry transcript.

52. Louis Hamm, transcript of hearing, December 13, 1944, taken down by Commissioner Pierre Arnet, AJM, carton 549, bundle 5.

53. Ibid.

54. Bernard Vargaftig, *Lumière et présence,* catalogue of the exhibition *Autour de Fenosa* (Limoges: Centre de la mémoire d'Oradour, 1999). About the Foreign Workers' Group of Oradour, see the section on refugees in Chapter 5. [Aixe-sur-Vienne is twelve kilometers southwest of Limoges; Sereilhac, southwest of Aixe-sur-Vienne, is about twenty-two kilometers from Limoges.—Trans.]

55. The camp at Nexon had been used to intern foreign Jews, opponents of the Vichy regime, black market traffickers, and so on; the Oradour-sur-Glane Foreign Workers' Group had been transferred to Aixe-sur-Vienne in late 1942; Saillat's remained active up to the Liberation.

56. Patry transcript; Davoine transcript; Justin Darthout transcript, AJM, carton 549, bundle 5.

57. These photographs were taken after the massacre by members of the emergency rescue squads; some of them circulated in Limoges (see Chapter 7).

58. Files of the Limoges Court of Justice, AD Haute-Vienne.

59. Series of telegrams appended to the troop-movement log of the eighteenth armored corps, SHAT microfilm no. 173.

60. SHAT microfilm no. 171.

61. H. L., transcript of hearing, AJM, carton 546, bundle 1, p. 51.

62. Information on troop strength is drawn from several sources: (1) SHAT microfilm no. 177; (2) transcripts of Boos's hearings, in AJM, carton 552, bundle 13; (3) shorthand transcripts of hearings at the Bordeaux trial (National Association of Martyrs' Families of Oradour-sur-Glane and Centre de la Mémoire d'Oradour).

63. Barth's remark is quoted by several witnesses (Waffen SS soldiers) and is sometimes attributed to an SS sergeant named Staeger; AD Haute-Vienne, 180 W 1-130 and AJM (Le Blanc-Indre), carton 552, bundle 13. It was also quoted at the Bordeaux trial hearing in 1953.

5—WAS ORADOUR JUST AN ORDINARY VILLAGE?

1. See Albert Hivernaud, *Petite Histoire d'Oradour-sur-Glane de la préhistoire à nos jours* (Limoges: Imprimerie A. Bontemps, 1975).

2. [The subheading is the first line of a well-known sonnet by Arthur Rimbaud, "Le Dormeur du val" (The sleeper in the vale), which describes a peaceful rural spot but ends unexpectedly with the evocation of a soldier in the Franco-Prussian War who was slain by a bullet wound.—Trans.]

3. [Formerly, French grade-school pupils did not have class on Thursday afternoons.—Trans.]

4. [Camille Corot, *La Place du village* (The village square), graphite drawing, private collection, reproduction in *L'Occident romantique,* by E. de Keyser (Geneva: Skira, 1965), 140. [See Bibliography for English edition.—Trans.]

5. Quoted by Albert Béguin, *L'Ame romantique et le rêve* (Paris: José Corti, 1939), 331. [Etienne Pivert de Senancour (1770–1846) was a popular early Romantic French writer; his best-known work was *Oberman* (1804).—Trans.]

6. Alain Corbin, *Archaïsme et modernité en Limousin au XIXe siècle, 1845–1880* (Limoges: PULIM, 1999).

7. [*Occitanie* is a term used in France for the Midi (South), or *pays d'oc,* in whose dialects *oc* formerly expressed the affirmative, as opposed to the North, or *pays d'oïl,* where it was expressed by the word *oïl,* the ancestor of today's *oui;* southwestern France is still known today as Languedoc (language of "oc").—Trans.]

8. Gédéon Tallemant des Réaux, *Historiettes* [Little stories] (Paris: Gallimard, La Pléiade, 1960), vol. 1; for Madame des Loges, see pp. 606 ff., for the story of the kidnapping of a young woman by a certain Monsieur d'Oradour, see pp. 654 ff. [See Bibliography for English edition.—Trans.] [The Fronde was a revolt of the princes (1648–1652) against Cardinal Mazarin, the minister during King Louis XIV's minority before he ascended to the throne. Huguenots were Protestants, members of the Calvinist Reformed Church (that is, "non-comformists"), as opposed to the Catholic majority.—Trans.]

9. [Aquitaine, Poitou, and the Limousin are three provinces in southwest and south-central France. By the ancien régime is meant the monarchy. The Revolution is, of course, the French Revolution of 1789–1793.—Trans.]

10. Corbin, *Archaïsme et modernité,* stresses this feature; see also Emmanuel Todd, *L'Invention de l'Europe* (Paris: Seuil, 1990). [The French expression used by the author is *la famille souche.*—Trans.]

11. This expression [*l'entre-soi,* in French—Trans.] is borrowed from Gérard Monédières, who teaches at the University of Limoges.

12. Family archives in Oradour-sur-Glane. See Camille Mayran, *Larmes et lumières à Oradour,* preface by Gabriel Marcel (Paris: Plon, 1952), 112 ff.

13. [A reference to a patriotic song taught to French schoolchildren under the Vichy régime, "Maréchal, nous voilà!"—Trans.]

14. Denise Bardet did not quote writers who promoted a "positive culture" of war and violence (Junger, von Salomon), but rather the classics of German literature, reflecting the "absolute pacifism" of French schoolteachers.

15. [*Boche* was the familiar French derogatory term for the Germans, as *Kraut* was in English.—Trans.]

16. [Only after World War II, in 1945, were women in France granted voting rights and legal equality.—Trans.]

17. [The "deputy" was the representative to the national assembly.—Trans.]

18. [The Union sacrée was a cooperative agreement among opposing French political parties during World War I.—Trans.]

19. [The 1934 Front commun, uniting Socialists and Communists, prefigured the Front populaire (Popular Front), which brought the left to power in the 1936 elections under the leadership of Socialist Léon Blum, who was prime minister in 1936–1937 and again in 1938.—Trans.] Gaston Charlet, a Socialist lawyer, was elected in Limoges. He was deported, and then became a senator and deputy mayor of Limoges after the war. In the 1950s he would become the lawyer for the National Association of Martyrs' Families of Oradour.

20. [The Croix-de-feu [Cross of Fire], a veterans' organization headed by Colonel de La Rocque, was founded in 1927 and disbanded in 1936. It was a right-wing nationalist group and employed violent tactics against the left.—Trans.]

21. [In the political, historical context of France, conservative Republicans are partisans of a republic (as opposed to a monarchy or an empire), neither identical to nor entirely different from their counterparts in American politics; similarly, the "Radicals" were a center-right party in that geographical and historical context.—Trans.]

22. These postcards have documentary interest, and they reveal Joseph Beau's thinking about his political opponent. When he was mayor in 1908, Paul Desourteaux had given the name of his father, Emile, to the town's main street. Joseph Beau's postcards in the 1920s and 1930s mention a rue de la Gare or a rue Principale, but no rue Emile Desourteaux.

23. Although there was electricity, there was no municipal water system.

24. Could the monthly fair, set for the fifteenth of the month, take place on a Sunday if that was how the calendar turned out? An "irrevocable" decision of the municipal council in 1922 ended this debate, stating that the fair would not be shifted if the fifteenth of the month fell on a Sunday. Temporal power and business would not submit to the rules of the Church and its representative. (The measure was revoked in 1931.)

25. The war memorial in Gentioux (Creuse) is famous for its iconography: a child with its fist raised points to the words inscribed on the shaft of the monument: "Cursed be war."

26. "Will we go to war for the Sudeten people and for castles in Bohemia? . . . First of all, is France bound by its signature? For my part, I won't get tangled up in this legal problem. . . . No, the Sudeten people aren't worth the life of a single French soldier, a curse on politicians, who would involve the people of France for the defense of iniquity." Jean Le Bail, who wrote these lines in the *Petit Limousin* of September 19, 1937, was the new young federal secretary of the SFIO [Section française de l'Internationale ouvrière (French Section of the Workers' International)]. A philosophy agrégé who had come to Limoges a short time before, Jean Le Bail later had a career in parliament, representing Haute-Vienne until 1958.

27. [That is, the "appeasement" accords negotiated with Hitler by Neville Chamberlain and other major European leaders in 1938.—Trans.]

28. From an editorial in *Le Populaire,* September 21, 1937.

29. We have come across no archives concerning the activity of the Communist Party cell, apart from a Vichy police investigation of some of the former members of the party, which the Daladier government dissolved after the Russo-German pact of 1939. [Édouard Daladier, a veteran Radical-Socialist (later Radical) politician, was Prime Minister of France in 1938. One of the signatories of the Munich pact, he resigned his post in March 1940 after declaring war on Germany in 1939.—Trans.] In 1938 this cell participated

in the distribution of Jean Renoir's film *La Marseillaise,* financed by the CGT [Confédération générale du travail (General Labor Confederation)]. The militants of Oradour do not seem to have been notably active in the Resistance, but their influence had not completely vanished when, in the first municipal elections in May 1945, the secretary of the Communist cell, Aimé Faugeras, was elected mayor. Later, in 1947, he was reelected and was to remain mayor until 1953. One segment of the present electorate, which is proportionally stronger than the département's average, votes Communist in town, legislative, and European elections.

30. The Belgian administration turned up in Limoges. [The "strange defeat" was the surprisingly rapid collapse of the French and English armies, in June 1940, before the Germans' advance.—Trans.]

31. Pierre Poitevin, *Dans l'enfer d'Oradour: Le plus monstreaux crime de la guerre* (Limoges: Publication du Centre, 1944).

32. The June 18, 1940, appeal [Charles de Gaulle's radio address of June 18, 1940, calling on the French to resist the German occupation.—Trans.] seems not to have had any echo in the Limousin. The first major Resistance act was by Edmond Michelet in Brive, who had distributed a tract the previous day. It was during the summer of 1940 that the wounded Georges Guingouin escaped from a military hospital and immediately went under cover.

33. Léon Roche was the mayor and parliamentary representative of Oradour-sur-Vayres. According to Pierre Miquel, in *Les Quatre-vingts* (Paris: Fayard, 1995), 217, 252–53, Léon Roche, a member of the Socialist action committee, hid in the Indre département from 1942 onward. He was part of the Resistance with Thiébaut, from the département of the Meuse [a département in Lorraine, in northeastern France, in which Verdun is located—Trans.]. He died in 1945.

34. [Confolens is about thirty-five kilometers northwest of Oradour.—Trans.]

35. AD Haute-Vienne, Limoges.

36. AD Haute-Vienne, 1517 W 100.

37. AD Haute-Vienne, 4 M 260.

38. Dominique Veillon, *Vivre et survivre en France, 1939–1947* (Paris: Payot, 1995), 22. [Bas-Rhin is a département in northeastern France whose administrative seat is Strasbourg.—Trans.]

39. AD Haute-Vienne, 187 W 199.

40. [In the text, *le boche.*—Trans.]

41. [In the text, *Comité officiel du souvenir.*—Trans.]

42. See an article by Yolande Baldeweck dated August 29, 1999, in the Mulhouse daily *L'Alsace.*

43. [Lorraine is a region in northeastern France, bordering on Alsace, whose principal cities are Metz and Nancy.—Trans.]

44. [Charly is a small town in the Moselle département not far from Metz.—Trans.]

45. [That is, the fall of France in 1940.—Trans.]

46. AD Haute-Vienne, 185 W 1-49.

47. [Meurthe-et-Moselle is a département in Lorraine whose administrative seat is Nancy. Some of these Jews had come earlier from Germany or Alsace.—Trans.]

48. [Franche-Comté is a region of southeastern France whose principal city is Besançon.—Trans.] Sarah Farmer of the University of Iowa in the United States [currently associate professor of history at the University of California, Irvine—Trans.] undertook a census of the French and foreign Jews in the Oradour area. She notes the presence of a physician, a Dr. Stein, who came with his family from Jarnac (Charente). Forbidden to practice medicine, he nevertheless seems to have had an appreciative clientele who thought of him as "the maquis doctor." Dr. Stein enlisted in the army and took part in the siege of Royan. Returning to Jarnac, he committed suicide. His family subsequently emigrated to the United States. Another doctor, named Aron, from Strasbourg, lived in the hamlet of Lébourliat in the neighboring township of Veyrac. He also practiced medicine clandestinely.

49. [Bayonne is a city in the Pyrénées-Atlantiques (formerly Basses-Pyrénées) département on the Atlantic coast near the Spanish border.—Trans.]

50. Robert Pinède's correspondence is located in the microfilmed archives of the UGIF, in the Centre de Documentation Juive Contemporaine, Paris. [The French telephone system was part of the postal service.—Trans.]

51. We will see a consequence of this in September 1944, at a ceremony organized in the ruins by the UJRE.

52. Pierre Laborie, "Le statut des Juifs et l'opinion française," in *Le Monde juif* 142 (May–June 1991); see also Pierre Laborie, *Les Français trouble* (Paris: Desclée de Brouwer, 2001), 138.

53. See Desourteaux and Hébras, *Notre Village assassiné,* 82–83, which tells this story.

54. The results of municipal elections from 1919 to 1935 show unambiguously the rise of Joseph Beau's popularity and, conversely, the (all-male) voters' dissatisfaction with Paul Desourteaux. The latter received fewer than thirty votes in 1935 and Beau more than three hundred.

55. [*L'Humanité* was the Communist daily newspaper in France.—Trans.]

56. AD Haute-Vienne, 1517 W 54. [Martial Machefer survived the massacre.—Trans.]

57. AD Haute-Vienne, 985 W 454 (this reference was communicated to us by Pascal Plas, the département correspondent for Haute-Vienne of the IHTP). The GTEs succeeded the Compagnies de travailleurs étrangers [Foreign Workers Companies], created by the government of the Third Republic under the supervision of the Ministry of War. The Vichy regime kept them, under the supervision of the Ministry of the Interior, with a dual aim: economic output and police surveillance. The GTEs were part of a package of supervisory measures for the foreign Jewish population; see Renée Poznanski, *Le Juifs en France pendant la Seconde Guerre mondiale* (Paris: Hachette, 1997), 264 ff. [See Bibliography for English edition.—Trans.]

58. AD Haute-Vienne, 993 W 544.

59. A photograph, undated and of unknown origin, was shown by a member of the National Association of Martyrs' Families after the permanent exhibition of the Centre de la Mémoire d'Oradour had been set up (so it could not be exhibited). In the photograph one can identify the town fairgrounds before the fire, the pharmacy sign; thirty men or so in worn clothing are drawn up in lines facing a flagpole; "soldiers" in uniform are raising a flag; someone who seems to be the leader is off to one side, saluting the flag. [See illustrations—Trans.]

60. AD Haute-Vienne, 185 W 58.

61. Ibid., W 1-119. [Italics are Fouché's.—Trans.]

62. AD Haute-Vienne, 646 W 251, 252. The circulars and service notes concerning this sweep were published by Serge Klarsfeld in *Le calendrier de la persécution des Juifs en France* (Paris: Klarsfeld, 1993), 484 ff. This documentary material is to be found also in the Haute-Vienne département archives. There we were able to consult the lists of names, giving countries of origin, composition of families, professions, and addresses of foreign Jews incorporated into the GTEs of Haute-Vienne.

63. On the camp at Nexon and the other camps in Haute-Vienne, see Laurette Alexis-Monnet, *Les Miradors de Vichy,* preface by Pierre Vidal-Naquet (Paris: Editions de Paris, 1994).

64. Klarsfeld, *Le calendrier de la persécution,* mentions it.

65. [That is, Marshal Pétain's Vichy regime, which had succeeded the Third Republic under the German occupation.—Trans.]

66. "The recent police campaigns against stateless or foreign Jews have given rise in Catholic circles of the Haute-Vienne département to widespread protests stemming from the position taken by the Bishop of Limoges himself, Monsignor Rastouil, who condemns these measures, finding them barbaric, inhumane, and contrary to the doctrine of charity and mutual aid of the Catholic church. Before he became bishop, this prelate was a popular democrat [that is, a supporter of 'people's democracy'—Trans.]. On his arrival in Limoges, he found in Mgr. Ardant, the vicar-general of the bishopric whom he kept on in his office, a devoted associate, one who shared his ideas. Thus Mgr. Rastouil and Mgr. Ardant have gained great influence over the Limousin clergy, 80 percent of whom have sided with their directives. The result is that they are followed in their attitude toward the Jews by the priests of the diocese, who in private constantly protest against the 'inhumane' attitude of the French government toward these persecuted people. In this matter, Mgr. Rastouil sides with the position of the Archbishop of Toulouse and the Bishop of Montauban, whose opinions have been rather widely publicized, if we are to believe mail interceptions. . . . In addition, the bishop warmly welcomes Rabbi Deutsch of Limoges and often receives him in his palace. Moreover, I have been able to verify that the Bishop of Limoges has forbidden his clergy to be present at Légion rallies and to wear the Légion badge." A report by Préfet Lemoine, September 14, 1942, AD Haute-Vienne, 185 W 1/220.

67. In all, 725,000 Frenchmen were sent to Germany for STO service.

68. We have statistics only at district level, AD Haute-Vienne, 986 W 467, 993 W 207.

69. A report by the regional préfet on the state of public opinion for 1942, AD Haute-Vienne, 185 W 1-44.

70. The idea of adaptation has been developed by Philippe Burrin, *La France à l'heure allemande, 1940–1944,* (Paris: Le Seuil, 1995), 181 ff. [Traditionally, in France, butcher shops *(boucheries)* sold only cuts of meat; items such as sausages, pâtés, and prepared dishes were sold in separate shops known as *charcuteries* (here translated as "delicatessens"). In some cases, the two were combined. Similarly, *boulangeries* sold various kinds of bread, whereas pastry was sold in *pâtisseries*.—Trans.]

71. A report dated January 14, 1944, for the month of December 1943, AD Haute-Vienne, 185 W 1-44.

72. The regional préfet's monthly report, April 1944; AD Haute-Vienne, 185 W 1-44.

73. AD Haute-Vienne, 185 W 1-58. [Traditionally, French country people ate a darker, less refined bread *(le pain paysan)* than city dwellers were accustomed to.—Trans.]

74. Interview with Mme. Lavaud, the widow of M. Blanchon, on December 1, 1944, AJM, carton 549, bundle 5.

75. Report of Sûreté commissioner Pierre Arnet, AJM, carton 549, bundle 5.

76. Pierre Laborie's work has served as a methodological basis and a comparison check for what we have been able to learn about the state of public opinion in the Haute-Vienne département. See Pierre Laborie, *Résistants, Vichyssois et autres: l'évolution de l'opinion et des comportements dans le Lot de 1939 à 1944* (Paris: CNRS, 1980), and *L'Opinion française sous Vichy* (Paris: Seuil, 1990).

77. The sous-préfet of Rochechouart, September 1942, AD Haute-Vienne, 185 W 1-58.

78. Laborie, *L'Opinion française,* 285.

79. AD Haute-Vienne, 185 W 1-58.

80. Jean Hyvernaud, transcript of interview, November 15, 1944, AJM, carton 549 (quotation), confirmed by testimony signed by Lieutenant Colonel Georges Guingouin, Colonel Rousselier ("Rivier"), and Commandant Huart, AJM, carton 549, bundle 6.

81. In 1994, with the aid of the IHTP correspondent and the Resistance Museum of Limoges, the instructional services of the Haute-Vienne département archives mapped out the maquis bases as of 1944, indicating parachute-drop sites. The map did not indicate the presence of Allied missions, whose activity has been undervalued until now.

82. "Something had happened: a certain number of men had been there to see and know it, and they gave their lives for this irrefutable knowledge." Jean Cassou, *La Mémoire courte* (Paris: republished by Mille et Une Nuits, 2001), 65.

83. The history of the Resistance in the Limousin and of the Liberation has not as yet been a subject of academic historical research. The topic remains politically sensitive, and the historians' caution makes them avoid possible risks. Readers can consult the following specific and general publications: Marie Granet, *Ceux de la Résistance, 1940–1944* (Paris: Editions de Minuit, 1964), about Combat; Dominique Veillon, *Franc-Tireur. Un journal clandestin, un mouvement de Résistance, 1940–1944* (Paris: Flammarion, 1977); and Laurent Douzou, *La Désobéissance. Histoire du mouvement de Libération-Sud* (Paris: Odile Jacob, 1995).

84. Aimé Renaud, transcript of interview, November 3, 1944, AJM, carton 549, bundle 5.

85. Jeannine Renaud, transcript of interview, November 3, 1944, ibid.

86. See Michel Chantegros, *La Tragédie du 27 juin 1944 à Saint-Victurnien* (Saint-Junien: Les Rencontres de JADE, 1994).

87. Transcript of the interview on November 7, 1944, of a young woman born in Oradour and brought up in a Paris convent, who returned in June 1940. She was the mistress of the SS lieutenant colonel who was police commandant in Limoges; for this she was imprisoned at the Liberation.

88. The list of victims for the civil records (December 1944) allows us to identify these: AJM, carton 549, appendix for the PJ's investigation, the report of Commissioner Pierre Arnet; and Pauchou and Masfrand, *Vision d'épouvante.*

89. Compare Farmer, *Martyred Village,* 138; the corresponding passage in the English-language edition is slightly different.

90. Desourteaux and Hébras, *Notre Village assassiné,* 95 (quotation). The term "little people" comes from Pierre Sansot, *Les Gens de peu.*

6—ACCOUNT OF THE MASSACRE

1. We have given special emphasis to an investigation by the commissioner of the Limoges Sûreté, Pierre Arnet, which is preserved in the archives of military justice (AJM). This investigation was ordered by an evidence-gathering commission set up on September 20, 1944, by a prosecutory judge of the Limoges tribunal. It concluded with a report dated December 23, 1944. On November 25, 1944, the court handed the proceedings over to the military tribunal of Bordeaux. Undertaken more than three months after the events, the investigation did not allow all the witnesses of the massacre to be heard. Some had left the area, and the material means were insufficient at the time. However, the ninety-four interview transcripts constitute as a whole a body of the greatest importance. We have supplemented these interviews with other sources, such as additional information from the military prosecuting judge and from parallel investigations by SHAPE [Supreme Headquarters Allied

Powers Europe] and the Service des crimes de guerre ennemis en France [Service for Enemy War Crimes in France], AD Haute-Vienne.

2. Marcel Darthout, transcript of hearing, December 7, 1944, p. 83; Clément Broussaudier, transcript of hearing, November 9, 1944, p. 8; Robert Hébras, transcript of hearing, November 24, 1944, p. 51; Armand Senon, transcript of hearing, November 14, 1944, p. 26; Hubert Desourteaux, transcript of hearing, November 10, 1944; Mathieu Borie, transcript of hearing, November 9, p. 17; all in AJM, carton 549, bundle 5.

3. Yvonne Gaudy, transcript of hearing, August 24, 1949, AJM, carton 549, bundle 6; Sergeant Boos, transcript of hearing, July 4, 1947, AJM, carton 549, bundle 13, p. 49.

4. SS soldier Jean-Pierre E., transcript of hearing, September 24, 1945, AD Haute-Vienne, 185 W 1-130.

5. Paul G., transcript of hearing, September 8, 1945, AJM, carton 550, bundle 10, and AD Haute-Vienne 186 W 1-130.

6. Robert Hébras transcript.

7. Marcel Darthout transcript.

8. Hubert Desourteaux transcript.

9. Clément Broussaudier transcript.

10. Sergeant Boos, transcript of hearing, AJM, carton 549, bundle 13.

11. Yvonne Gaudy transcript. [Brackets are Fouché's.—Trans.]

12. Clément Broussaudier transcript.

13. Hubert Desourteaux transcript.

14. Marcel Darthout transcript.

15. Mathieu Borie transcript.

16. Martial Beaubreuil, transcript of hearing, AJM, carton 549, bundle 5, p. 77.

17. Martial Brissaud, report of the Limoges RG on July 4, 1944, AJM, carton 549, bundle 5, p. 102; Robert Besson and Jacques Garraud, ibid.

18. Armand Senon transcript.

19. Marguerite Rouffanche, transcript of hearing, November 16, 1944, AJM, carton 549, bundle 5, p. 30.

20. Roger Godfrin, transcript of hearing, December 1, 1944, AJM, carton 549, bundle 5, p. 67.

21. "Oradour-sur-Glane (Haute-Vienne) June 10, 1944: Photos and Documents Assembled by E. Munn, PWD SHAPE," a typewritten report in English, with dated original photographs; testimony gathered on September 3, 1944, accompanied by a dated photograph, private archive.

22. Marcel Darthout transcript.

23. Clément Broussaudier transcript.

24. A. L., transcript of hearing, June 28, 1946, AJM, carton 552, bundle 13, p. 9.

25. We estimate approximately between 130 and 150.

26. The Langs had taken refuge in Oradour. Madame Lang is quoted by Pauchou and Masfrand, *Vision d'épouvante,* 30: "Hiding behind a window

[the couple] witnessed the start of the tragedy. Madame Lang told us that 'the Krauts stormed into the open houses, guarding the exits, and drove people out.'" The Langs were not interviewed by the police and judges.

27. Marcel Darthout transcript.

28. Robert Hébras transcript.

29. Marguerite Rouffanche transcript.

30. Clément Broussaudier transcript.

31. Sofsky, *Traité*, 159.

32. Marcel Darthout transcript.

33. Marguerite Rouffanche transcript.

34. Marcel Darthout transcript.

35. Armand Senon transcript.

36. This sequence is screened in the permanent exhibit of the American Holocaust Museum in Washington, D.C.

37. Marcel Darthout transcript.

38. Sergeant Boos, transcript of hearing, July 4, 1947, AJM, carton 552, bundle 13, p. 49.

39. Marcel Darthout transcript.

40. Sergeant Boos, transcript of hearing, July 4, 1947.

41. Marcel Darthout transcript.

42. B., transcript of hearing, March 14, 1947, AJM, carton 552, bundle 13.

43. Jean-Pierre E. transcript.

44. Marcel Darthout transcript.

45. Doc. cit.

46. Jean-Pierre E. transcript.

47. Martial Beaubreuil, transcript of hearing, AJM, carton 549, bundle 5.

48. Armand Senon transcript.

49. Statement of the Ministry of the Army, October 3, 1946, archives of the Mirablon family. See also Laurent Douzou, *La Désobéïssance: histoire du mouvement de Libération-Sud* (Paris: Odile Jacob, 1995). Albert Mirablon is listed in the appendix of the movement's members.

50. SS soldier Paul G., transcript of hearing, September 8, 1945, AD Haute-Vienne, 186 W 1-130.

51. B. transcript, March 14, 1947; L., transcript of hearing, June 15, 1945, AJM, carton 549, bundle 6; Paul G., transcript of hearing of July 26, 1945, AJM, carton 549, bundle 6, p. 130.

52. Jean-Pierre E. transcript.

53. Martial Dauriat, an employee of the département railroad, transcript of hearing, November 4, 1947, AJM, carton 549, bundle 5.

54. Marguerite Rouffanche transcript.

55. L., transcript of hearing, June 28, 1946, AJM, carton 552, bundle 13, p. 9.

56. L., transcript of hearing, November 22, 1945, AJM, carton 552, bundle 13, p. 22.

57. Jean-Pierre E. transcript.

58. B., transcript of hearing, May 3, 1947, AJM, carton 552, bundle 13.

59. B., transcript, March 14, 1947.

60. Paul G., transcript of hearing of July 26, 1945, AJM, carton 549, bundle 6, p. 130.

61. Boos, from a voluntary statement in Great Britain on April 21, 1947, AJM, carton 552, bundle 13, p. 31.

62. Boos, from a hearing by the prosecuting military judge on May 3, 1947, AJM, carton 552, p. 49.

63. Boos, ibid.

64. Paul G., transcript of hearing of July 26, 1945, AJM, carton 549, bundle 6, p. 130.

65. Ibid.

66. Weidinger, as witness, transcript of hearing, AJM, carton 552, bundle 6; Werner, undated written statement, AJM, carton 552, bundle 6.

67. Robert Hébras transcript.

68. Mathieu Borie transcript.

69. Clément Broussaudier transcript.

70. Marcel Darthout transcript.

71. Armand Senon transcript; Marcel Darthout transcript.

72. Jean Pallier's text circulated anonymously under the title *Le témoignage d'un père de famille* [A father's story] and was published in two clandestine papers before the Liberation, in part in *Cahiers du témoignage chrétien* in July 1944, and in *Lettres françaises* in a special issue in August 1944 that was devoted entirely to Oradour and published the complete text of Jean Pallier's report, entitled *Sur les ruines de la morale* [On the ruins of morality]. A partial typescript was preserved in the files of military justice.

73. Marguerite Senon, transcript of hearing, December 6, 1944, AJM, carton 549, bundle 5, p. 49.

74. Jean Pallier text.

75. Paul G. transcript.

76. Boos, from a hearing by the prosecuting military judge on May 3, 1947, AJM, carton 552, p. 49.

77. Justin Darthout, transcript of hearing, December 8, 1944, AJM, carton 549, bundle 5. [Brackets are Fouché's.—Trans.]

78. Hubsh, transcript of hearing, AJM, carton 549, bundle 5, p. 90.

79. Marguerite Rouffanche transcript.

80. Armand Senon transcript.

81. Marcel Darthout transcript.

82. Hubert Desourteaux transcript.

83. Martial Beaubreuil transcript.

84. Jean Pallier text.

85. Report to the préfet dated June 14, 1944, AD Haute-Vienne, 185 W.

86. Sofsky, *Traité,* 168.

87. Boos, AJM, carton 552, bundle 13, p. 31.

88. B., transcript, March 14, 1947.

89. Testimony of Martial Machefer in a report to SHAPE.

90. Jean Hyvernaud, transcript of hearing, November 15, 1944, AJM, carton 549; René Hyvernaud, transcript of hearing, November 22, 1944, AJM, carton 549; Tarnaud, transcript of hearing, November 14, 1944, AJM, carton 549; Arthur Sénamaud, transcript of hearing, November 23, 1944, AJM, carton 549.

91. "A persistent moralistic vision of the crime under the ancien régime reinforced this silence by shrouding the victim in the shame of the act, transforming the mere fact that she experienced the condemned transgression through her senses and her actions into an act of infamy." Georges Vigarello, *Histoire du viol: XVIe-XXe siècles* (Paris: Seuil, 1998), 283. [See Bibliography for English edition.—Trans.]

92. Martial Machefer's statement was taken down by a "foreigner," which made it possible.

93. There is a display case dedicated in part to her in the Imperial War Museum in London.

94. The Ministry of Defense did not authorize consultation of Weidinger's files in the archives of military justice.

95. Mark C. Yerger, *SS-Obersturmbannführer Otto Weidinger* (London: A Schiffer Military History Book, 2000). This booklet, like numerous other publications vindicating the Waffen SS that are sometimes on sale at railroad station stands in France, is a good example of the accepted euphemistic treatment of Nazism.

96. Yerger, p. 81.

7—THE VICTIMS

1. Report to the Vichy government dated June 15, 1944, AD Haute-Vienne, 986 W 482 [Fouché's brackets]; see the statement of Louis Moreau, AJM, carton 549, bundle 5.

2. See the publication of these documents in our catalogue, *La Mémoire d'Oradour* (Limoges: Centre de la Mémoire d'Oradour, 1996).

3. AJM, carton 549. This report was published in June 1945 by the information services of the provisional government of the Republic; we used it in the 1996 catalogue.

4. See "Découvrir le Centre de la mémoire d'Oradour," Centre régional pédagogique du Limousin, Limoges, 2000, p. 91.

5. Pauchou and Masfrand, *Vision d'épouvante,* 103.

6. AJM, carton 549, bundle 5.

7. Report to the Commissioner of the Republic by Captain Charpentier on August 6, 1945, AD Haute-Vienne, 186 W 1-129.

8. See Marin Dacos, "La brutalité photographiée," *Sociétés et Représentations,* "Violences" issue (June 1998): 103. Photographs of the ruins and bodies appeared in all publications from 1944 to 1945. We have published some of these in cata-

logues of the exhibitions presented at Oradour-sur-Glane; not publishing them could have been taken as an attempt to hide the dead. But should we not question the justness of these pictures, which are anything but "just pictures"?

9. Louis Moreau, the town's Vichy-appointed mayor, transcript of hearing, November 23, 1944, AJM, carton 549.

10. Document from the Saint-Junien gendarmerie, AJM, carton 540, bundle 6, p. 84, undated.

11. Der Führer regiment's war diary, in file of Limoges EML [Etat Major de Liaison (liaison headquarters)] 586, concerning Oradour, AD Haute-Vienne.

12. Pauchou and Masfrand, *Vision d'épouvante,* 110.

13. Louis Moreau transcript.

14. The children's monument was later transferred to the new reconstructed town and placed in front of the school complex. It recalls the names of the children and the teachers.

15. Another, complementary method was used by André Desourteaux and Robert Hébras in *Notre Village assassiné;* it consisted of an alphabetical presentation by ten-year age groups.

16. Frank Delage, *Oradour Ville martyre* (Paris: Editions Mellotée, 1945), p. 40: "Every evening, after work was done, prayers were said over the graves in the cemetery."

17. Monsignor Rastouil cited in Poitevin, *Dans l'enfer d'Oradour,* pp. 131 ff., and Delage, *Oradour Ville martyre,* pp. 69 ff.

18. Rastouil cited in Poitevin, *Dans l'enfer d'Oradour.*

19. Ibid.

20. [The Reformed Church was founded by the disciples of Jean Calvin (1509–1564), who were known as Huguenots during the Renaissance and subsequent period. It has remained the principal Protestant denomination in France. With the Lutheran church, in Germany at first, and the Anglican church in England, it was one of three primary currents of original European Protestantism.—Trans.]

21. The pastor was using Louis Segund's translation, which is commonly used in the Reformed Church; the other text comes from the Bible of Port-Royal and Lemaitre de Sacy (Paris: Robert Laffont, coll. "Bouquins," 1990), 1011, and is perhaps closer to the original text. [This passage is rendered as follows in the King James and Douay versions of the Bible: "for fear was round about" (King James), and "terror was round about" (Douay).—Trans.]

22. Freund-Valade spent his career (as was normal in those days) in the prefectoral service: as sous-préfet of Erstein and then Aix-en-Provence, as secretary general of the Alpes-Maritimes police (1941), and as préfet of the Aude département (1942). His loyalty to the Vichy government and Marshal Pétain was never in doubt by the Occupation authorities, who looked on him as a difficult but honest opponent. Reports of June 10, 1944, by the German authorities on prefecture personnel, National Archives, AJ 40, 545-17.

23. Albert Chaudier's sermon was published by P. Poitevin and by F. Delage, op. cit. The text is preserved in the AD Haute-Vienne.

24. RG report dated June 22, 1944, AD Haute-Vienne, 986 W 481. Bishop Louis Rastouil had distanced himself from the Vichy regime prior to August 1942. He would underline his independence by refusing to take part in the funeral ceremony organized at the government's request after [Vichy Propaganda Minister Philippe] Henriot's execution [by the Resistance]. For this, he was arrested by the Milice and removed from his diocese. Albert Chaudier was named the chair of the département's Liberation Committee; he acted temporarily as préfet and commissioner of the Republic in Limoges. Marc Freund-Valade was dismissed from the prefectoral administration without any evidence being presented against him that he had been a collaborator. Later he would participate in adulatory writings about Laval published by the Hoover Foundation, and he referred to his speech at Oradour in that context: proof, for him, of his independence concerning the German occupying forces.

25. See Poitevin, *Dans l'enfer d'Oradour* (p. 175), Delage, *Oradour Ville martyre* (p. 92), and AD Haute-Vienne.

26. See Poitevin, *Dans l'enfer d'Oradour,* Delage, *Oradour Ville martyre,* and AD Haute-Vienne.

27. [In the French political system, the "head of state" was Marshal Pétain; the "government" would be Prime Minister Pierre Laval; both were condemned to death as collaborators after the Liberation, but Pétain's sentence was commuted to life imprisonment.—Trans.]

28. We should remember that innocence is the state of someone who is ignorant of evil. [The author's note to some extent contradicts the Anglo-Saxon notion that "ignorance of the law is no excuse." The French verb *engager* and the noun *engagement,* connoting both commitment and involvement, are not translatable by a single English term.—Trans.]

29. The Vichy government sent a protest to the German authorities through diplomatic channels via its representative on the Armistice Commission in Wiesbaden (see Chapter 8). Either Pétain or his cabinet supposedly attempted to get a courier through to the "Head of the Great German State." Hitler's representative in Vichy allegedly refused to see the courier, whose authenticity may be considered doubtful. This "dead letter" was put in the archives of the Secretary of State for Defense, SHAT.

30. "Honoring the French civilian victims as 'martyrs' ennobled an experience that had been, in many respects, humiliating, and in some cases dishonorable." Farmer, *Martyred Village,* 87.

31. In *La Nouvelle Republique du Centre-Ouest,* March 5, 1945, quoted in Farmer, *Martyred Village,* 83 (and 238n55). See also *Le Populaire du Centre,* Monday, March 5, 1945; AD, Limoges

32. See Farmer, *Martyred Village,* 78–80.

33. Farmer reconstructs "the visit of the old-timers" (ibid., 117–23), when she describes André Desourteaux, the former mayor's grandson, going through the ruins. The visit is filled out with anecdotes and enriched with genealogical research reconstructing a past that here was twice wiped out because it was destroyed.

34. For the three Resistance leaflets, see *La Mémoire d'Oradour*. [Katyn is a village west of Smolensk where the bodies of 4,500 Polish officers were found in 1943, a crime of the "Stalinist" Soviet Union that was officially acknowledged by Russia only in 1990. In 1944–1945, it would still have been thought (especially by Communists) to be an atrocity perpetrated by the Nazis.—Trans.]

35. Use of the "martyr" concept is not usual for a Protestant theologian. It recalls historical events: religious persecutions with no dogmatic consequences. The martyr is a witness to the faith, who sacrifices himself in order to sustain it.

36. Mouvement de Libération Nationale, *Les Huns à Oradour-sur-Glane-Haute-Vienne-France,* 1945.

37. "Large and small communities were defined as 'mystical bodies,' an expression simply designating any political institution. . . . Dying for the fatherland was (now) seen in a truly religious perspective, it was a sacrifice for the *corpus mysticum* of the State, which was no less real than the *corpus mysticum* of the Church." Ernst H. Kantorowicz, *Mourir pour la patrie* (Paris: PUF, 1984), 131, 133.

38. See Poitevin, *Dans l'enfer d'Oradour,* Delage, *Oradour Ville martyre,* and AD Haute-Vienne in notes 16, 17, and 23 of this chapter.

39. The Diamant and List-Pakin Archives in the Centre de Documentation Juive Contemporaine, Paris.

40. The word order is important here; reversing it would constitute an anachronism. Present-day historiography does not justify our reversing it. The Jewish militants of the French Communist Party at that time considered themselves Communists first.

41. Farmer, in *Martyred Village,* 124–27, has pointed out the importance of the town cemetery as a place for the expression of mourning by the victims' families. Audoin-Rouzeau and Becker, in the "Le deuil" chapter of *Retrouver la guerre* (pp. 199 ff.) have written ground-breaking pages on the subject of mourning by the families of World War I dead. Philippe Ariès, *Essais sur l'histoire de la mort en Occident* (Paris: Le Seuil, 1975), 193, notes "a taboo on mourning in the twentieth century." [See Bibliography for English edition—Trans.]

42. In the Limousin, processions are cyclical religious ceremonies recurring every seven years and consisting of a procession with the relics of local patron saints. They are organized by guilds whose representatives don symbolic emblems and supposedly traditional (as recollected by folklore) costumes for the occasion. The processions at Saint-Junien are among the most celebrated in the Limousin. A religious festival has become a tourist phenomenon.

43. The ceremonies at which a government member rekindles the flame at the Tomb of the Unknown Soldier, under the Arch of Triumph, are also silent.

44. François Mitterand's visit posed a problem: the Oradour community was welcoming one of the parliamentarians who had voted for amnesty for the condemned forced draftees in 1953. [See the next chapter for an account of trial and amnesty referred to—Trans.] The President of the Republic gave thanks for being invited to this commemoration; he acknowledged his personal political choice, which he justified by the context of the times;

then he spoke of the future of Europe and the peace that European union had already brought. He did not speak of reconciliation, as if the time for a gesture comparable to the one made at Verdun with German Chancellor Helmut Kohl had not yet come for Oradour.

45. Nicole Lapierre asked this question concerning the memory of the Jews of Plotsk, Poland, in *Le Silence de la mémoire, à la recherche des Juifs de Plock* (Paris: republished in Livre de Poche, Hachette, 2001), 38.

8—CONFLICTING ACCOUNTS

1. The term *instrumentalization,* which only recently entered the French lexicon (in 1946, according to the 1998 edition of *Le Robert*), has its origin in North American pragmatic philosophy. Instrumentalization is the use of a theory or an event in the service of political or other action. It refers here to a use that combines an appropriation with the possibility of determining a meaning that fits more closely with an ideology than to the event itself; it is a process that integrates itself into an ideology or a political intention. [See the section "The Instrumentalization of Oradour," below.—Trans.]

2. The theme of conflicting accounts was first dealt with in a colloquium held at Potsdam in January 1998 by the Marc Bloch Center (Berlin, CNRS) and the Einstein Forum (Potsdam), and published under the direction of Florent Brayard, as *Le Génocide des Juifs entre procès et histoire* [The genocide of the Jews, in trials and history] (Brussels: Editions Complexe, collection "Histoire du temps présent," 2001), 308 pp. Our paper was entitled "La Déception des témoins: le conflit des récits du massacre à Oradour-sur-Glane" [Witnesses deceived: The conflicting accounts of the massacre at Oradour-sur-Glane], pp. 189 ff; this text has been revised and expanded here.

3. According to a document published in facsimile by *L'Humanité* on February 4, 1953, during the [Bordeaux] trial hearings. It is not in the file that the newspaper put in the département archives.

4. Poitevin, *Dans l'enfer d'Oradour,* pp. 116 ff.

5. AJM, carton 549, bundle 6.

6. Report of the Limoges préfet to the Vichy government, dated June 16, 1944, AD Haute-Vienne, 986 W. On August 22, 1944, General Gleiniger negotiated the surrender of the German garrison in Limoges with a delegation of Allied officers through the intermediary of the Swiss consular delegate. The French Forces of the Interior, commanded by Georges Guingouin, surrounded the town. Taken away by elements who rejected the capitulation and were fleeing, notably SS men, Gleiniger died by either execution or suicide twenty or thirty kilometers out of Limoges.

7. Gleiniger reports dated June 12, 20, 1944, in File 586 of the EML, correspondence concerning Oradour, AD Haute-Vienne. This German "visit" is confirmed by a letter from the Vichy-appointed mayor to the préfet; it stirred up renewed fear among the people.

8. Nuremberg International Military Tribunal proceedings, hearing of August 6, 1946 (vol. 20, p. 245, of the French edition). Lidice was the place of a massacre in Czechoslovakia on June 10, 1942, in reprisal for the execution of SS "General" Heydrich by the Resistance. Heydrich, head of the Reich's Central Security Office (RSHA) and thus the highest SS police official, was the man who arranged the genocide of the Jews.

9. Concerning this "method"—called "hypercritical"—and how it differs from scientific criticism, see Henri-Irénée Marrou, *De la connaissance historique* (Paris: Seuil, collection "Points-Histoire," 1975).

10. Vincent Reynouard, *Le Massacre d'Oradour, un demi-siècle de mise en scène* [The Oradour massacre: half a century of stagecraft], published in Belgium in 1998. Its distribution in France was banned by order of the Ministry of the Interior. On Reynouard's activity as a militant, see Valérie Igounet, *Histoire du négationnisme en France* (Paris: Seuil, 2000), 561 ff.

11. Reynouard reproduced an archival document, which he claimed to have received from Faurisson: a mysterious source! [Faurisson was a well-known French negationist historian—Trans.] This was a report dated January 4, 1945, by a "judge" and SS commander named Okrent. This SS commander was the "legal consultant" of the SS Das Reich division from November 1943 to January 1945. The report had been requested by the Wehrmacht high command after a series of protests by the Vichy government to the Armistice Commission at Wiesbaden. The Vichy representative had submitted files concerning excesses committed by the Occupation troops at Frayssinet-le-Gelat, Marsoulas, Oradour-sur-Glane, Tulle. File concerning execution of civilians without trial by the German authorities in France (p. F-673 in the appendices of the Nuremberg International Military Tribunal, hearing p. RF-392, vol. 38, pp. 317 ff.). The high command—in a note dated March 5, 1945, signed by Keitel—requested that the Armistice Commission pursue "study of the affair with all necessary energy" in order to "refute all the blame incurred by the Wehrmacht and to counter enemy propaganda and immediately deny so-called German cruelty." This was read at the hearing of the Nuremberg International Military Tribunal on January 31, 1946, by prosecutor Dubost (ibid., vol. 6, pp. 422–23). This clearly shows something missing: the SS "judge," saying he lost his documentation, had not put forth a credible argument to the Nazi dignitaries. His situation as an SS "judge" made him an unusual jurist: he was not constrained by any written law to be applied but was expected to formulate an evaluation that met the requirements of his superiors. What did this "Okrent report" contain? The Oradour operation was presented as "a reprisal measure" following an attack on a "hospital convoy of about ten men of the Wehrmacht"; (a similar "scene" can be noted at Saint-Junien on June 8); the capture of a second lieutenant and his driver, "brutally manhandled by the populace, particularly the women" (this is the capture of Gerlach in Nieul—the women's role is a constant of the SS's phobic imagination). There is no mention of the capture of the commander of Battalion 3, which fueled other arguments. The SS troops

that arrived in Oradour "were met by rifle and automatic weapons fire." Finally there allegedly were "a considerable number of weapons" and ammunition reserves that led to explosions. Did these "facts" justify "ordering" a "judicial inquiry"? It has been lost. Presumably, a negationist is searching for it.

12. Thus the young Oradour woman who was the mistress of the SS police commander in Limoges reported that SS Meïr had told her: "Residents of Oradour killed some young SS men when they arrived in the town with their unit. Some women of Oradour then danced on their corpses. This unit was back from Russia, and when their comrades learned of the deaths of their fellow-soldiers killed in Oradour, they were disgusted [*sic*] and set the town on fire." The young woman added that she did not believe a word of it. (See chapter 5, note 87.) The SS account—which corresponds to what Nazi propaganda broadcast in the days following the massacre, although it is obviously ridiculous—nevertheless corresponds to what we have been able to learn about Nazi officers' imaginations.

13. The letter containing this information left Limoges on July 22, 1944, but did not arrive at the Paris offices of the ministry until December 27! The reply was quicker. On January 5, 1945, the office for urban planning wrote to its corresponding member in Limoges to confirm the minister's intent to appoint Monsieur Paquet. This letter stated: "The church will be preserved in the condition in which it was found after the fire and transformed into a 'temple of memory.'" AN. Contemporary Section (Fontainebleau), MRU: 820.474.175.

14. A letter from the Minister of National Education to the Minister of Reconstruction and Urban Planning dated December 28, 1944, AN 770, 695-41. In a second letter the same day (same page), Minister René Capitant, explained the plan: "The new town will be rebuilt a certain distance from the former village so as to leave this testimony to Nazi barbarity intact insofar as possible." He justified the choice of director: "Monsieur Paquet has shown the highest qualities as an artist and architect throughout his long career; he has never failed to exercise continuing cooperation with both the national committee for reconstruction and the national committee for city planning, on which he has represented the Beaux-Arts administration since 1940." The "Resistance Architects" in the Limoges district protested in vain against naming a high official who had served under the Vichy government.

15. A decision of the Council of Ministers on November 28, 1944, AN. Contemporary Section (Fontainebleau), MRU: 770, 695-41.

16. Among its "considerations" the order naming him specified: "The town of Oradour-sur-Glane constitutes a symbol of the acts of atrocity committed by the German army and its memory must be perpetuated for future generations . . .; there is good reason, both from a historical point of view and for public safety, to take steps to preserve it." Ibid.

17. Minutes of the Memorial Committee meeting on October 21, 1944, Justin Dupanier printers, Rochechouart, AD Haute-Vienne, and archives of the National Association of Martyrs' Families.

18. Ibid.

19. See Bertrand Tillier's article, "Le Monument aux martyrs d'Oradour-sur-Glane par Fenosa. L'histoire d'un 'non-lieu de mémoire' (1944–19..)," *Vingtième siècle* 55 (July–September 1997): 43–57, and the catalogue for the exhibition "Autour de Fenosa" (Limoges: Centre de la Mémoire d'Oradour, 1999).

20. Pauchou and Masfrand, *Vision d'épouvante.* Its writing is dated December 17, 1944, but it seems to have been revised during the first quarter of 1945, to judge by indications in the text; for example, there is an allusion to Aimé Faugeras, "the present mayor" (p. 67); in fact, he was elected mayor of Oradour-sur-Glane in the May 1945 elections. That he was a Communist is not pointed out in the text.

21. The Association's foreword to Pauchou and Masfrand, *Vision d'épouvante.*

22. On April 17, 1951, the president of the National Association of Martyrs' Families wrote to the president of the Council of Ministers, Henri Queuille, a deputy from the Corrèze, to complain and request that he put off the legislative elections set for the following June 10. The anniversary of the massacre "remains a sacred day, beyond all partisan conflict." [Henri Queuille (1884–1970) was the Prime Minister. Over a long political career, he occupied a number of major governmental posts—Trans.]

23. The law of September 15, 1948, established collective responsibility for war crimes, effective retroactively. It allowed that concurrent incapacities ("double incompetence") of civil and military justice to be disregarded, and both Germans and Frenchmen who had been accused to appear before military justice. This law, called for by the Oradour victims and voted for by the Alsatian members of parliament, brought forced draftees before the tribunal. It was an aberrant law for the French system, and it set off a polemic inspired by jurists—Donnadieu de Vabres, Ellul, and so on—who opposed what they saw as an abuse of constitutional law.

24. [Paul Ramadier (1888–1961) headed a number of ministries (Labor, Defense, Economic Affairs) during his political career before and after World War II, during which he was a member of the Resistance in the Rouergue region.—Trans.]

25. In August 1944, the clandestine *Lettres françaises* published a special issue devoted entirely to Oradour, with the complete text of Jean Pallier's report, entitled *Sur les ruines de la morale* [On the ruins of morality.—Trans.]

26. [The phrase "defense and illustration" is an allusion to Joachim Du Bellay's sixteenth-century poetic manifesto, familiar to French readers, *Défense et illustration de la langue française* (Defense and illustration of the French language).—Trans.] See Farmer, *Martyred Village,* 171–76, for the successive concurrent commemorations, and the catalogue of the exhibition devoted to the Livre d'or of June 10, 1949, in collaboration with Gilles Plazy (Limoges: Centre de la Mémoire d'Oradour, 1995). The catalogue reproduces in its entirety the material brought to Oradour by Louis Aragon, and the speech given that day by Frédéric Joliot-Curie.

27. [Paul Eluard (1895–1952), like Louis Aragon, was a founder of surrealism and a major Communist writer.—Trans.]

28. The text published in the Communist press, *L'Echo–La Marseillaise,* on September 24, 1949, AD Haute-Vienne, is presented as having been written by "the mothers of Oradour": "We, who can still see the flames issuing from our church, [bear] in our hearts the terrible memory of the massacre of our children, our husbands.... Our confidence in you is great, Marshal Stalin, because your daily struggle to safeguard Peace draws us every day into the action of all freedom- and peace-loving people for a future when there would be no more wars. The Fascists tried to destroy our village, but grass is growing once more in the ruins. The warmongers are yearning for still another massacre, but the mothers of Oradour, together with you, Marshal Stalin . . ." and so on.

29. We drew up a chronology of the legal proceedings (from 1944 to 1953) for the permanent exhibit in the Centre de la Mémoire d'Oradour: see pp. 118–21 of the catalogue (Limoges: Centre de la Mémoire d'Oradour, 2000).

30. AD Haute-Vienne, 186 W 1-130.

31. [In the French judicial system, the Garde des Sceaux occupies a role more or less equivalent to that of our Attorney General.—Trans.]

32. AN BB 18 35 75-2.

33. [Brackets are Fouché's.—Trans.]

34. AN BB 18 35 75-2. This file contains the letters of the Limoges district attorney to the attorney general from June 1944 onward.

35. See Farmer, *Martyred Village,* 135–70; Jean-Marc Théolleyre, *Procès d'après-guerre* (Paris: La Découverte, 1985), 102–73; Jean-Pierre Rioux, "Le Procès d'Oradour," *L'Histoire* 64 (February 1984): 6–17.

36. Press file, AN F 7-15 341; Archives of the INA [Institut National de l'audiovisuel (National Audiovisual Institute)] for radio broadcasts; Gaumont film library for the Eclair-Pathé newsreels.

37. *Le Parisien libéré,* January 13, 1953.

38. Lieutenant Colonel Gardon, who finished his career as a general and the head of military justice, played a role in the major issues of the 1950s and in the Algerian war. As a colonel he was assigned as legal counselor to General Salan's headquarters in Algiers. There he had to justify resorting to torture to get information in the fight against the "rebels" of the Front de libération nationale [National Liberation Front]. Pierre Vidal-Naquet, *La Raison d'Etat* (Paris: Editions de Minuit, 1962), and *La Torture dans la République* (Paris: Editions de Minuit, 1972). General Gardon was government commissioner during the so-called barricades trial in 1961, whose defendants were Algerian activists, members of the Organisation de l'armée secrète (OAS) [Secret Army Organization] who, as partisans of a French Algeria, opposed the Evian accords and an end to the war that gave Algeria its independence. [The Evian accords were signed on March 18, 1962, by France and the provisional government of the Algerian Republic—Trans.] See the indictment included in the typewritten shorthand record of the trial hearings; a copy from the Bordeaux military tribunal is at the Centre de la mémoire in Oradour.

39. See Pierre Baral, "L'affaire d'Oradour, affrontement de deux mémoires," in *Mémoire de la Seconde Guerre mondiale* (Metz: L'Université de Metz, 1984).

40. The reactions to the trial are from a file drawn up by the Renseignements généraux of the Haut-Rhin, along with information concerning the Communist Party's strategy in Alsace and its militants' discontent. The regional Communist Party leadership, which knew that numerous party members had been forcibly drafted and did not want to alienate them, had to yield to national directives that it disapproved of. A Communist lawyer who normally litigated for the CGT [a Communist labor union] was on the forced draftees' defense team. AN F 7 15. 341.

41. Ibid.

42. JO [Journal officiel (official journal), roughly equivalent to our Congressional Record] for the proceedings of February 19, 1953. [The brackets within the quotation are Fouché's.—Trans.]

43. *L'Aurore,* February 24, 1953, an article by Jean Lartéguy.

44. The German authorities were surprised at the differing treatment of French and German defendants. The death sentences were commuted to imprisonment. The effects of the sentencing process led to staggered departures from prison: the last men sentenced to prison terms were freed in 1962. The main defendant was SS Captain Kahn, the commander of the SS company, who died in Germany on April 14, 1977, according to information given to the French embassy in Germany by the Dortmund public prosecutor's office. AN Contemporary Section (Fontainebleau), MRU: 910.564.11.

45. AN (Paris): BB 18 3575/file 2: 1004 A 44.

46. *Oradour-sur-Glane, le village exterminé,* published by the Front national de lutte pour la liberté et l'indépendance de la France [National Front to Fight for the Freedom and Independence of France], was an anonymous publication, undated. The author was Marc Bernard (1900–1983), who won the 1942 Prix Goncourt [France's most prestigious literary award] for *Pareils à des enfants* [Like children] (Paris: Gallimard), a journalist for *L'Humanité.* See the 1944 text republished in the catalogue *La Mémoire d'Oradour* (Limoges: Centre de la Mémoire d'Oradour, 1996), 75–83.

47. Barrès, in *Les Déracinés,* wrote of a union of the dead with the living as the basis of a tradition in which the past of the dead necessarily exercised a decisive influence over the present of the living. Having roots in the soil was the source of the living's solidarity with the past. [Maurice Barrès (1862–1923) was an influential nationalistic writer whose novels—most notably, *Les Déracinés* (The uprooted) and *La Colline inspirée* (The inspired hill)—stressed the importance of French regional tradition.—Trans.]

48. [The following was communicated to us by J.-J. Fouché in explanation: "Robert Hébras, one of the five survivors, was president of the National Association of Martyrs' Families of Oradour in the early nineties. In 1993 he published a brochure entitled *Oradour-sur-Glane. Le drame heure par heure* (Oradour-sur-Glane: The tragedy hour by hour). The brochure gives his ac-

count, but [he] took advantage of his status as a witness to add his opinion about the trial, the forced draftees, and many other things for which he had no documentation. The crisis with the board arose not from errors contained in the brochure. Rather, he was accused of competing with the 'official book' of the Association . . . Hébras' brochure sold better than the Association's book and thus deprived it of some of its profits."—Trans.]

49. [See Chap. 4, note 17.—Trans.]

9—SOUVIENS-TOI—REMEMBER

1. ["Remember" is in English in the original text, as it is on signs throughout the ruins as well.—Trans.]

2. From Poe's "The Raven." See Edgar Allan Poe, *Le Corbeau; la genèse d'un poème: oeuvres en prose,* translation by Charles Baudelaire (Paris: La Pléiade, Gallimard, 1951), 979 ff.

3. [In its French edition, the title of Farmer's book is *Oradour: arrêt sur mémoire* (Oradour: Memory come to a stop).—Trans.]

4. See the chronology in Yves Bénot, *Massacres coloniaux, 1944–1950: la IVe République et la mise au pas des colonies françaises* (Paris: La Découverte, 1994), 178 ff.

AFTERWORD

1. [This Afterword was originally the Prologue to Jean-Jacques Fouché's book, but the translators believe it is more suitable, both chronologically and in terms of the narrative, in its present position.

[This opening ceremony was both an inauguration of the new Centre de la Mémoire d'Oradour and a commemoration of the terrible events that took place on June 10, 1944. The audience had first to be reminded of the butchery that left the village in ruins. There was need both for monuments and for an understanding of what they represented: in Fouché's words, the "specificity of the victims' misfortune and the recognition due them." Both the commemorative act and the ideas behind it, however, were predicated on people, and often people with opposing political sentiments. The Afterword suggests this, too: the roles played by Pétainists, Communists, Socialists, Gaullists, and local people of various persuasions in commemorations and in the preservation of the ruins, as well as in the elaboration of the "official" story of what happened. At the inaugural ceremony, this could be felt in the tension between French President Jacques Chirac, a Gaullist and the head of state, and absent Prime Minister Lionel Jospin, a Socialist and the head of government.

[The Afterword is the most personal part of Jean-Jacques Fouché's book and clearly illustrates the tension between objectivity and personal involvement so typical of what he achieved, not only here but in his work as founding director of the museum and visitors center at Oradour. For this reason, we felt it was important to keep it, although we feel it will be less confusing to non-French readers as an Afterword than as a Prologue to the account.—Trans.]

2. [The word *mémoire* has taken on a special meaning in French historiography, particularly in the wake of Pierre Nora's books on *les lieux de mémoire,* or "realms of memory" in the standard English translation.—Trans.]

3. [Verdun was the site of a bloody and lengthy siege in World War I.—Trans.]

4. See Pierre Nora, *Les Idées en France, 1945–1988* (Paris: Gallimard, collection "Folio-Histoire," 1989), 29.

5. The magazine *L'Express,* January 15, 1988, published a cartoon by Plantu concerning Algeria: on a map of the country the names of alleged massacre sites were replaced by Oradour-sur-Glane, repeated fifteen times over.

6. The concept of a "community" here designates a group of people that, feeling excluded from the "national community" at a critical time, organized itself with respect to its specific identity. The leaders of this community, the mayor and the president of the National Association of Martyrs' Families, exercise moral authority over the group and this "place of memory."

7. [In French, a *commune* is an administrative subdivision of a *canton* or (generally rural) township.—Trans.]

8. [The Elysée Palace, which is the official presidential residence, is often used, like "the White House," to represent the French presidency.—Trans.]

9. [TF-1 is one of three state-sponsored French television stations.—Trans.]

10. [See "Découvrir le Centre de la mémoire d'Oradour," Centre régional pédagogique du Limousin, Limoges, 2000, p. 103, for a partial text of this speech.—Trans.]

11. [Ibid.—Trans.] See François Julien, *Dialogue sur la morale* (Paris: Le Livre de Poche, Hachette, 1998), 8, which terms ethics "the evasion *du jour.*" Ethics is reduced to an evaluation of the moral norms being applied to concrete situations.

12. The National Association of Martyrs' Families and the municipality had excluded the possibility of an opening ceremony on June 10, the anniversary of the massacre, because that day was set aside for commemoration.

13. Eric Conan and Henry Rousso, *Vichy, un passé qui ne passe pas* (Paris: Fayard, 1994), 33. [See Bibliography for English edition.—Trans.] The chapter entitled "Le Vel' d'Hiv' ou la commémoration introuvable" [The Vel' d'Hiv' or the commemoration nowhere to be found] explains the origins of the February 3, 1993, decree establishing July 16 as a national day of commemoration. [The Vel' d'Hiv, or Vélodrome d'hiver (Winter bike-racing arena), was a staging-point in the roundup of Jews prior to their transfer to Drancy for shipment to the death camps.—Trans.]

14. [The Hebrew word for "Holocaust."—Trans.]

15. [The author has requested that his book end with these final two paragraphs. Originally they closed the last chapter, "Souviens-toi—Remember"—Trans.]

16. See Jean Bollack, *Pierre de coeur* (Périgueux: Pierre Fanlac Editions, 1991), 9.

17. See Peter Szondi, *Poésies et poétiques de la modernité,* edited by Mayotte Bollack (Lille: Presses Universitaires de Lille, 1981), which contains writings on Walter Benjamin, Bertolt Brecht, Paul Celan, and so on. [These are translations from the German into French of texts by Peter Szondi, drawn from a variety of sources. See Chap. 5 for Denise Bardet—Trans.]

Bibliography

Documentary Sources

ARCHIVE CENTERS

Archives nationales [AN], Section contemporaine: (Paris) Justice, Commandement militaire allemand en France; (Fontainebleau) ministère de la Reconstruction et de l'Urbanisme [National Archives, Contemporary Section (Paris) Justice, German Military Command in France; (Fontainebleau) Ministry of Reconstruction and Urban Planning]. P.M., *La Seconde Guerre mondiale: guide des sources conservées en France, 1939–1945* (Paris: AN et IHTP, 1994)

Archives de la justice militaire [AJM]

Archives départementales [AD] de la Haute-Vienne (AD 87), Limoges, Haute-Vienne: Marigeorges Allabert and Véronique Mercier, *Sources de l'histoire d'Oradour-sur-Glane conservées aux archives départementales de la Haute-Vienne* (Limoges, 1995, 63 pages, reprographie, avec une bibliographie des publications); non inclus les dossiers de la cour de justice de Limoges [repro copy, with a bibliography of publications; records of the Limoges Court of Justice not included]

Centre de la Mémoire d'Oradour (CMO) [Center for Memory at Oradour], Oradour-sur-Glane, Haute-Vienne: Copies de la documentation de l'Association nationale des familles des martyrs, et de la sténotypie du procès de Bordeaux avec des dossiers de presse [copies of documentation of the National Association of Martyrs' Families, and shorthand record of the Bordeaux trials with newspaper clippings]

Centre de documentation juive contemporaine (CDJC) [Center for Contemporary Jewish Documentation], Paris

Médiathèque du patrimoine [Media library for French heritage], Ministère de la Culture, Paris

Militärgeschichtliches Forschungsamt [Office of Military History Research], Potsdam

Service historique de l'Armée de terre (SHAT) [Army Historical Service], Vincennes

PUBLISHED SOURCES

Procès des grands criminels de guerre devant le Tribunal international de Nuremberg: 14 novembre 1945–1er October 1946. 41 volumes. 1949. [Published in English as *The Trial of German Major War Criminals: Proceedings of the*

International Military Tribunal Sitting at Nuremberg, Germany. London: H. M. Stationery Office, 1946– .]

Kriegstagebuch des Oberkommandos der Wehrmacht, 1940–1945 [Troop-movement log of the Wehrmacht high command]. Frankfurt: Percy Schramm [ex-secretary of the OKW], 1961.

Die Geheimen Tagesberichte des Deutschen Wehrmachtführung im zweiten Weltkrieg [The secret daily reports of the German army command in World War II]. Osnabrück: Biblio Verlag, 1985.

Books Consulted

[The publications devoted to the massacre that appeared from October 1944 through 1945, indicated in the Notes section, are not included here; nor are many books published subsequently that were not used. They could warrant a special study of the reception and renown of the Oradour "case." Review articles quoted and cited in the Notes are not listed here.—Trans.]

Alexis-Monet, Laurette. *Les Miradors de Vichy.* Preface by Pierre Vidal- Naquet. Paris: Les Editions de Paris, 1994.

Ariès, Philippe. *Essais sur l'histoire de la mort en Occident.* Paris: Le Seuil, 1975. [Published in English as *Western Attitudes toward Death: From the Middle Ages to the Present.* Translated by Patricia M. Ranum. Baltimore: Johns Hopkins University Press, 1974.]

Audoin-Rouzeau, Stéphane, and Annette Becker. *14–18, retrouver la guerre.* Paris: Gallimard, 2000. [Published in English as *1914–1918: Understanding the Great War.* Translated by Catherine Temerson. New York: Hill and Wang, 2002.]

Ayçoberry, Pierre. *La Société allemande sous le IIIe Reich.* Paris: Le Seuil, 1998. [Published in English as *Social History of the Third Reich, 1939–1945.* Translated by Janet Lloyd. New York: New Press, 1999.]

Azéma, Jean-Pierre, and François Bédarida, eds. *La France des années noires.* 2 vols. Vol. 1, *De la défaite à Vichy;* vol. 2, *De l'Occupation à la Libération.* Paris: Le Seuil, 1993.

Azéma, Jean-Pierre, François Bédarida, et al. *Les Années de tourmente, de Munich à Prague: dictionnaire critique.* Paris: Flammarion, 1995.

Bartov, Omer. *L'Armée d'Hitler. La Wehrmacht, les nazis et la guerre.* Paris: Hachette, 1999. [Published in English as *Hitler's Army: Soldiers, Nazis, and War in the Third Reich.* New York: Oxford University Press, 1991.]

———. *The Eastern Front, 1941–1945: German Troops and the Barbarisation of Warfare.* Oxford: Macmillan, 1985.

Bédarida, François, et al. *La Politique nazi d'extermination.* Paris: Albin Michel, 1989.

Béguin, Albert. *L'Ame romantique et le rêve.* Paris: José Corti, 1939.

Bénot, Yves. *Massacres coloniaux, 1944–1950: la IVe République et la mise au pas des colonies françaises.* Paris: La Découverte, 1994.

Bollack, Jean. *Pierre de coeur.* Périgueux: Pierre Fanlac, 1991.

Brayard, Florent, et al. *Le Génocide des Juifs entre procès et histoire.* Brussels: Editions Complexe, collection "Histoire du temps présent," 2001.

Broszat, Martin. *L'Etat hitlérien: l'origine et l'évolution des structures du IIIe Reich.* Paris: Fayard, 1985. [Published in English as *The Hitler State: The Foundation and Development of the Internal Structure of the Third Reich.* Translated by John W. Hiden. London and New York: Longman, 1981.]

Browning, Christopher. *Des Hommes ordinaires: le 101e bataillon de réserve de la police allemande et la solution finale en Pologne.* Paris: Les Belles Lettres, 1994. [Published in English as *Ordinary Men: Reserve Police Battalion 101 and the Final Solution in Poland.* New York: Harper Collins, 1992.]

Burrin, Philippe. *La France à l'heure allemande, 1940–1944.* Paris: Le Seuil, 1995. [Published in English as *France under the Germans: Collaboration and Compromise.* Translated by Janet Lloyd. New York: New Press, 1996.]

Canetti, Elias. *Masse et puissance.* Paris: Gallimard, 1966. [Published in English as *Crowds and Power.* Translated by Carol Stewart. New York: Viking Press, 1962.]

Cassou, Jean. *La Mémoire courte.* Paris: réédition Mille et Une Nuits, 2001.

Conan, Eric, and Henry Rousso. *Vichy, un passé qui ne passe pas.* Paris: Fayard, 1994. [Published in English as *Vichy: An Ever Present Past.* Translated by Nathan Bracher. Hanover, NH: University Press of New England, 1995.]

Corbin, Alain. *Archaïsme et modernité en Limousin au XIXe siècle, 1845–1880.* 2 vols. Limoges: PULIM, reprinted 1999.

———. *Le Temps, le désir, et l'horreur: essais sur le dix-neuvième siècle.* Paris: Aubier, 1991.

Delage, Frank. *Oradour ville martyre.* Paris: Editions Mellotée, 1945.

Desourteaux, André, and Robert Hébras. *Oradour-sur-Glane. Notre village assassiné.* Montreuil-Bellay: Editions CMD, 1998.

Douzou, Laurent. *La Désobéissance: histoire du mouvement de Libération Sud.* Paris: Odile Jacob, 1995.

Douzou, Laurent, Robert Frank, Denis Péschanski, Dominique Veillon, et al. *La Résistance et les Français: villes, centres et logique de décision.* Paris: CNRS-IHTP, 1995.

Ehrenburg, Ilya, and Vassili Grossman. *Le Livre noir.* Texts and eyewitness accounts collected by Ilya Ehrenburg and Vassili Grossman. Arles: Solin-Actes Sud, 1995. [Published in English as *The Black Book: The Ruthless Murder of Jews by German-Fascist Invaders throughout the Temporarily-Occupied Regions of the Soviet Union and in the Death Camps of Poland during the War of 1941–1945.* Prepared under the editorship of Ilya Ehrenburg and Vasily Grossman, translated from the Russian by John Glad and James S. Levine. New York: Holocaust Publications, distributed by Schocken Books, 1981.]

Farge, Arlette. *Des Lieux pour l'histoire.* Paris: Le Seuil, 1997.

Farmer, Sarah. *Oradour: arrêt sur mémoire.* Paris: Calmann-Lévy, 1994. [A modified version was published in English as *Martyred Village: Commemorating the 1944 Massacre at Oradour-sur-Glane.* Berkeley and Los Angeles: University of California Press, 1999.]

Förster, Jürgen. "La Campagne de Russie et la radicalisation de la guerre: stratégie et assassinats de masse." In *La Politique nazie d'extermination,* ed. François Bédarida. Paris: Albin Michel, 1989.

Girard, René. *La Violence et le sacré.* Paris: Grasset, 1972. [Published in English as *Violence and the Sacred.* Translated by Patrick Gregory. Baltimore: Johns Hopkins University Press, 1977.]

Granet, Marie. *Ceux de la Résistance, 1940–1944.* Paris: Editions de Minuit, 1964.

Grynberg, Anne. *Les Camps de la honte.* Paris: La Découverte, 1991.

Guillon, Jean-Marie, and Pierre Laborie. *Mémoire et histoire: la Résistance.* Toulouse: Privat, 1995.

Guingouin, Georges. *Quatre Ans de lutte sur le sol limousin.* Paris: Hachette, 1974.

Héritier, Françoise, et al. *De la violence: séminaire de Françoise Héritier.* Paris: Odile Jacob, 1996.

Hilberg, Raul. *La Destruction des Juifs d'Europe.* Paris: Fayard, 1988. [Published in English as *The Destruction of the European Jews.* New York: Octagon Books, 1978.]

———. *Exécuteurs, victimes, témoins: la catastrophe juive, 1933–1945.* Paris: Gallimard, 1994. [Published in English as *Perpetrators, Victims, Bystanders: The Jewish Catastrophe, 1933–1945.* New York: Aaron Asher Books, 1992.]

Himmler, Heinrich. *Discours secrets.* Paris: Gallimard, 1978. [Published in German as *Geheimreden 1933 bis 1945 und andere Ansprachen.* Hrsg. von Bradley F. Smith und Agnes F. Peterson; mit einer Einführung von Joachim C. Fest. Frankfurt-am-Main: Propyläen Verlag, 1974.]

Hitler, Adolf. *Hitler: Directives de guerre, présentées par H. R. Trevor-Roper.* Paris: Arthaud, 1965. [Published in English as *Hitler's War Directives, edited by H. R. Trevor-Roper, 1939–1945.* London: Sidgwick and Jackson, 1964.]

Hivernaud, Albert. *Petite Histoire d'Oradour-sur-Glane de la préhistoire à nos jours.* Limoges: Imprimerie A. Bontemps, 1975.

Igounet, Valérie. *Histoire du négationnisme en France.* Paris: Le Seuil, 2000.

Institut d'Histoire du Temps Présent [IHTP]. *Ecrire l'histoire du temps présent.* Paris: CNRS, 1993.

Jäckel, Eberhard. *La France dans l'Europe d'Hitler.* Paris: Fayard, 1968. [Published in German as *Frankreich in Hitlers Europa: Die deutsche Frankreichpolitik im Zweiten Weltkrieg.* Stuttgart: Deutsche Verlags-Anstalt, 1966.]

Jaspers, Karl. *La Culpabilité allemande.* Preface by Pierre Vidal-Naquet. Paris: Editions de Minuit, 1990. [Published in English as *The Question of German Guilt.* Translated by (pseud.) E. B. Ashton. New York: Dial, 1948.]

Julien, François. *Dialogue sur la morale*. Paris: Livre de Poche, Hachette, 1998.

Kantin, Georges, Gilles Manceron, et al. *Les Echos de la mémoire: tabous et enseignements de la Seconde Guerre mondiale*. Paris: Le Monde Editions, 1991.

Kantorowicz, Ernst H. *Mourir pour la patrie*. Paris: PUF, 1984.

Kapferer, Jean-Noël. *Rumeurs, le plus vieux média du monde,* Paris: Points-Seuil, 1987. [Published in English as *Rumors: Uses, Interpretations, and Images*. New Brunswick, NJ: Transaction Publishers, 1990.]

Kershaw, Ian. *Qu'est-ce que le nazisme? Problèmes et perspectives d'interprétation*. Paris: Gallimard, 1997. [Published in English as *The Nazi Dictatorship: Problems and Perspectives of Interpretation*. London and Baltimore: Edward Arnold, 1985.]

Keyser, Eugénie de. *L'Occident romantique*. Geneva: Skira, 1965. [Published in English as *The Romantic West, 1789–1850*. Geneva: Skira, 1965.]

Klarsfeld, Serge. *Le Calendrier de la persécution des Juifs en France*. New York: The Beate Klarsfeld Foundation, 1993.

Koch, H. W., ed. *Aspects of the Third Reich*. London: Macmillan, 1985.

Laborie, Pierre. *L'Opinion française sous Vichy*. Paris: Le Seuil, 1990.

———. *Résistants, Vichyssois et autres: l'évolution de l'opinion et des comportements dans le Lot de 1939 à 1944*. Paris: CNRS, 1980.

Lapierre, Nicole. *Le Silence de la mémoire: à la recherche des Juifs de Plock*. Paris: réédition du Livre de Poche, Hachette, 2001.

Loraux, Nicole. *Les Expériences de Tirésias*. Paris: Gallimard, 1989. [Published in English as *The Experiences of Tiresias: The Feminine and the Greek Man*. Princeton, NJ: Princeton University Press, 1995.]

———. *Façons tragiques de tuer une femme*. Paris: Hachette, 1985. [Published in English as *Tragic Ways of Killing a Woman*. Cambridge, MA: Harvard University Press, 1987.]

Ludewig, Joachim. *Der deutsche Rückzug aus Frankreich, 1944*. Freiburg: Rombach Verlag, 1995.

Malraux, André. *La Politique, la culture: discours, articles, entretiens, 1925–1975*. Paris: Gallimard, 1996.

Manoschek, Walter. *"Es gibt nur eines für das Judentum—Vernichtung": Das Judenbild in deutschen Soldatenbriefen 1939–1944*. Hamburg: Hamburger Edition, 1995.

Marrou, Henri-Irénée. *De la connaissance historique*. Paris: Le Seuil, collection "Points-Histoire," 1975.

Martres, Eugène. *Le Cantal de 1939 à 1945: les troupes allemandes à travers le Massif central*. Cournon d'Auvergne, France: De Borée, 1993.

Mayran, Camille. *Larmes et lumières à Oradour*. Preface by Gabriel Marcel. Paris: Plon, 1952.

Meldungen aus dem Reich, 1938–1945: die geheimen Lageberichte des Sicherheitsdienstes der SS. Edited by Heinz Boberach. Herrsching: Pawlak Verlag, 1984.

La Mémoire d'Oradour. Catalogue published by the Centre de la Mémoire d'Oradour. Limoges: Centre de la Mémoire d'Oradour, 1996.

Miquel, Pierre. *Les Quatre-vingts*. Paris: Fayard, 1995.

Mosse, George L. *De la Grande Guerre au totalitarisme: la brutalisation des sociétés européennes*. Paris: Hachette, 1999. [Published in English as *Fallen Soldiers: Reshaping the Memory of the World Wars*. New York: Oxford University Press, 1990.]

Musil, Robert. *Journaux*. Paris: Le Seuil, 1981. [Published in English as *Diaries, 1899–1942*. Selected, translated, annotated, and with a preface by Philip Payne, edited and with an introduction by Mark Mirsky. New York: Basic Books, 1998. Original German edition edited by Adolf Frisé.]

Nora, Pierre. *Les Idées en France, 1945–1988*. Paris: Gallimard, collection "Folio-Histoire," 1989.

Pauchou, Guy, and Dr. Pierre Masfrand. *Oradour-sur-Glane. Vision d'épouvante: l'ouvrage officiel du Comité du souvenir et de l'Association nationale des familles*. Limoges: Charles Lavauzelle, 1945. [The official publication of the National Association of Martyrs' Families—Trans.]

Paxton, Robert O. *La France de Vichy, 1940–1944*. Paris: Le Seuil, 1973. [Published in English as *Vichy France: Old Guard and New Order, 1940–1944*. New York: Columbia University Press, 1982.]

Péchanski, Denis. *Vichy 1940–1944, contrôle et exclusion*. Brussels: Editions Complexe, 1997.

Poe, Edgar Allan. *Le Corbeau: la genèse d'un poème: oeuvres en prose*. Traduction de Charles Baudelaire. Paris: Gallimard, La Pléiade, 1951.

Poitevin, Pierre. *Dans l'enfer d'Oradour: Le plus monstrueux crime de la guerre*. Limoges: Publication du Centre, 1944.

Poznanski, Renée. *Les Juifs en France pendant la Seconde Guerre mondiale*. Paris: Hachette, 1997. [Published in English as *Jews in France during World War II*. Translated by Nathan Bracher. Hanover, NH: University Press of New England, 2001.]

Reichel, Peter. *La Fascination du nazisme*. Paris: Odile Jacob, 1996. [Published in German as *Der schöne Schein des Dritten Reiches: Faszination und Gewalt des Faschismus*. Munich: Hanser, 1991.]

Reynouard, Vincent. *Le Massacre d'Oradour, un demi-siècle de mise en scène*. Coësmes, France: La Toison d'or, 1998.

Rigoulot, Pierre. *La Tragédie des Malgré-nous*. Paris: Denoël, 1995.

Rousso, Henry. *Le Syndrome de Vichy de 1944 à nos jours*. Paris: Le Seuil, 1990. [Published in English as *The Vichy Syndrome: History and Memory in France since 1944*. Translated by Arthur Goldhammer. Cambridge, MA: Harvard University Press, 1991.]

Sainclivier, Jacqueline, and Christian Bougeard. *La Résistance et les Français: enjeux stratégiques et environnement social*. Rennes: Presses Universitaires de Rennes, 1995.

Sansot, Pierre. *Les Gens de peu*. Paris: PUF, 1991.

Semprun, Jorge. *L'Ecriture ou la vie*. Paris: Gallimard, 1994.

Sociétes et Représentations. "Violences" issue. CREDHESS [Centre de recherches et d'études en droit, histoire, économie et sociologie du social], 1998.

Sofsky, Wolfgang. *Traité de la violence.* Paris: Gallimard, 1998. [Published in German as *Traktat über die Gewalt.* Frankfurt-am-Main: S. Fischer, 1996. Published in English as *Violence: Terrorism, Genocide, War.* Translated by Anthea Bell. London: Granta, 2003.]

Solchany, Jean. "Le Commandement militaire en France face au fait résistant." In *La Résistance et les Français.* Paris: Actes du Colloque CNRS-IHTP, 1995.

Szondi, Peter. *Poésies et poétiques de la modernité.* Edited by Mayotte Bollack. Lille: Presses Universitaires de Lille, 1981.

Tallemant des Réaux, Gédéon. *Historiettes.* Paris: Gallimard, La Pléiade, 1960. [Published in English as *Portraits and Anecdotes (Historiettes).* New York: Oxford University Press, 1965.]

Tessin, Georg. *Verbände und Truppen des deutschen Wehrmacht und Waffen SS im zweiten Weltkrieg, 1939–1945.* Osnabrück: Biblio Verlag, 1979.

Todd, Emmanuel. *L'Invention de l'Europe.* Paris: Le Seuil, 1990.

Topographie des Terrors: Gestapo, SS und Reichssicherheitshauptamt auf dem "Prinz-Albrecht-Gelände." Exhibition catalogue. Berlin, 1989.

Umbreit, Hans. *The Division Battle Order.* [Umbreit was a historian of the Militärgeschichtliches Forschungsamt (Military History Research Office) in Potsdam, who made available this archival document, a reconstruction executed under the direction of the French Occupation services in Berlin, by former Wehrmacht employees in charge of statistics.—Trans.]

Vargaftig, Bernard. *Lumière et présence.* Catalogue of the exhibition "Autour de Fenosa." Limoges: OCM, 1999.

Veillon, Dominique. *Franc-Tireur: un journal clandestin, un mouvement de Résistance, 1940–1944.* Paris: Flammarion, 1977.

———. *Vivre et survivre en France, 1939–1947.* Paris: Payot, 1995.

Vernichtungskrieg: Verbrechen der Wehrmacht, 1941 bis 1944. Exhibition catalogue. Hamburg: Hamburger Institut für Sozialforschung, 1998.

Vidal-Naquet, Pierre. *La Raison d'état.* Paris: Editions de Minuit, 1962.

———. *La Torture dans la République.* Paris: Editions de Minuit, 1972.

Vigarello, Georges. *Histoire du viol: XVIe–XXe siècles.* Paris: Seuil, 1998. [Published in English as *A History of Rape: Sexual Violence in France from the 16th to the 20th Century.* Translated by Jean Birrell. Malden, MA: Polity Press, 2001.]

Wegner, Bernd. *Hitlers politische Soldaten, die Waffen-SS, 1933–1945: Leitbild, Struktur und Funktion einer nationalsozialistischen Elite.* Paderborn: Schöningh Verlag, 1997. [Published in America as *The Waffen-SS: Organization, Ideology, and Function.* Translated by Ronald Webster. New York: Basil Blackwell, 1990.]

Wieviorka, Annette. *L'Ère du témoin.* Paris: Plon, 1998.

Index

Action française, 227
Agacinski, Sylvanie, 210
Aix-en-Provence, 240
Aixe-sur-Vienne, 62, 74, 86, 199, 228
Albussac, 47
Algeria, Algerian, Algiers, 10, 247, 250
Aliotti (Monsieur), 121
Alpes-Maritimes, 240
Alsace, Alsatian, 7, 8, 35, 36, 60, 65, 66, 78, 80, 81, 107, 120, 130, 138, 157, 172, 180, 189, 190, 191, 192, 194, 195, 196, 203, 208, 219, 220, 223, 231, 232, 246, 248
Alsace, L', 231
Ambazac, 86, 147
America, American. *See* United States of America
Amiens, 147
Anglican Church, 240
Aquitaine, 34, 70, 229
Aragon, Louis, 13, 14, 188, 219, 246, 247
Ardant (Monsignor), 233
Ardennes, 148
Arezzo, 119
Argenton-sur-Creuse, 47, 55
Ariège, 45
Armée secrète (Secret Army), 49, 54, 213
Arnet, Pierre, 227, 234, 235
Aron, Doctor, 232
Arras, 22, 147
Ashkenazi Jews, 83
Atlantic, 38, 232
Atlantic Wall, 94
Aude, 240
Aurillac, 46
Auriol, Vincent, 187, 194, 208
Aurore, L', 248
Auschwitz, 90, 210, 211, 224
Austria, 12, 21, 23, 76, 148
Avignon, 82
Avranches, 147
Avre (river), 22
B. (Alsatian SS soldier), 120, 126, 237, 238
Babi-Yar ravine, 25, 28
Bach-Zelewski, von dem (SS General), 24, 31
Bagnac, 38
Baïer (SS Sergeant), 122
Bail, Jean Le, 76, 230
Baldeweck, Yolande, 231
Balkans, 23, 40
Banat, 23
Barbarossa, Operation, 28
Bardet (Mayor of Saint-Victurnien), 83
Bardet, Camille, 71
Bardet, Denise, 70, 71, 168, 211ff., 229, 251
Barre-de-Veyrac, La, 63, 11, 137
Barrès, Maurice, 198, 248
Barrières, Les, 192
Barth (SS Lieutenant), 65, 66, 104, 118, 125, 126, 148, 191, 228
Bartov, Omer, 26, 217
Bas-Rhin, 80, 172, 231
Basses-Pyrénées. *See* Pyrénées-Atlantiques
Bayonne, 82, 212, 232
Beau, Joseph, 75, 84, 85, 86, 153, 161, 230, 232
Beaubreuil, Martial, 108, 124, 140, 236, 237, 238
Beaubreuil, Maurice, 108, 124
Beaux-Arts, 5, 218, 245
Belgium, 39, 227, 231
Bellac, 47, 57, 88, 184
Bellay, Joachim du, 246
Benjamin, Walter, 16, 251
Berezina (river), 28
Bergerac, 47
Bergmann, Joseph, 100, 138
Berlin, 42, 44, 50, 52, 148, 149
Bernard, Marc, 197
Besançon, 232
Besson, Robert, 109, 236
Betoulle, Léon, 98

Binet (Madame), 112
Bischheim, 172
Blanchon, 234
Blanquefort-de-Briolance, 39
Blars, 38
Blaskowitz (Wehrmacht General), 34, 45, 147, 225
Blond, Monts de (hills), 57, 97
Blum, Léon, 76, 227, 229
Bohemia, 22
Bolshevik, Bolshevism, Bolshevist, 23, 24, 27, 29, 39, 200
Bonheur de Barbezieux, Le, 11
Bonneaud, 97
Boos, Georg (SS Sergeant), 35, 65, 66, 103, 106, 118, 119, 120, 121, 122, 123, 126, 129, 130, 131, 132, 137, 144, 191, 193, 196, 228, 236, 237, 238
Bordeaux, 12, 14, 22, 35, 37, 66, 94, 180, 190, 191, 193, 194, 195, 223, 228, 235, 243, 247
Bordes, Les, 103, 107, 140, 141
Borie, Mathieu, 98, 103, 108, 121, 133, 236, 238
Börne, Karl Ludwig, 168
Bosnia, 209
Bouchoule (barn owner), 122, 134
Bourganeuf, 56, 226
Bourgeois (Alsatian deputy), 194
Boursicot, Pierre, 9
Brantôme, 44
Braunschweig, 18, 21
Brecht, Bertolt, 71, 168, 251
Bredel, Willi, 168
Brehmer (Wehrmacht General), 48
Bretenoux, 47
Brigueuil, 97
Brissaud, Martial, 109, 236
Brive-la-Gaillarde, 48, 50, 54, 82, 97, 231
Brodowsky, von (Wehrmacht General), 182, 223
Brouillaud, Jean, 9
Broussaudier, Clément, 102, 105, 107, 112, 114, 133, 236, 237, 238
Brunner, Aloïs, 59, 227
Buchenwald, 188
Büchner, Georg, 168
Buchovina, 211
Budapest, 100, 212
Burrin, Phillipe, 16
Bussière-Poitevine, La, 56, 135
Byelorussia, 25, 28, 31, 223

Cabrerets, 38
Cagoule, la, 227
Cahiers du témoignage chrétien, 10, 238
Cahors, 46, 47
Calais, 41
Calviac, 48
Calvin, Jean, 240
Calvo, 219
Canada, 149
Canou (Resistance Sergeant), 56
Capitant, René, 245
Cardailhac, 38
Carinthia, 12
Carlux, 47
Carsac, 47
Caudéran, 113
Caumont, 147
Celan, Paul, 211, 251
Center for Memory of Oradour (Centre de la mémoire d'Oradour), xiv, 9, 67, 204, 207, 209, 210, 211, 225, 228, 233, 247, 249
Centre libre, 171
Chaintron, Jean, 9, 60
Chalard, 112
Chaleix, Anna, 125
Chaleix, Maria, 125
Châlus, castle of, 69
Chamberlain, Neville, 230
Chamboran, de (Sous-préfet), 143
Chaptelat, 147
Chardonne, Jacques, 11
Charente, 3, 11, 47, 55, 61, 97, 185, 232
Charlet, Gaston, 229
Charly (-Oradour), 81, 231
Charpentier (Captain), 239
Chastaing, Roger, 226
Châteauneuf-la-Forêt, 53
Château-Thierry, 22
Chaudier, Albert (Pastor), 157, 158, 159, 171, 241
Cheissoux, 56
Chirac, Jacques, 207ff., 210, 249
Church, Reformed, 157, 193, 229, 240
Church, Roman Catholic, 75, 156, 160, 174, 185, 229, 233
Civitella della Chiana, 119

Clermont-Ferrand, 34, 35, 42, 46, 47, 53, 54, 182, 226
Cold War, 149, 176, 188, 189
Combat (Resistance movement), 97
Combeauvert, Poteau de, 56
Common Front. *See* Front commun
Communism, Communist, 5, 6, 9, 10, 13, 14, 15, 16, 17, 23, 24, 28, 29, 39, 40, 53, 54, 55, 58, 62, 72, 73, 74, 76, 77, 78, 79, 85, 86, 92, 95, 98, 99, 113, 114, 149, 160, 170, 172, 173, 176, 184, 187, 188, 189, 192, 194, 196, 200, 201, 202, 203, 210, 213, 214, 219, 224, 226, 229, 230, 231, 232, 242, 246, 247, 248, 249
Compagnies de travailleurs étrangers, 79, 232
Confédération générale du travail (CGT), 196, 213, 231, 248
Confolens, 47, 79, 97, 105, 185, 231
Corot, Camille, 67, 228
Corrèze, 33, 42, 43, 47, 48, 50, 97, 225, 246
Cressensac, 48
Creuse, 43, 47, 56, 97, 230
Creusot, Le, 22
Croix-de-Feux, 74, 77, 230
Croix de Guerre, 187, 195
Cueco, Henri, 33
Curie, Marie, 219
Curie, Pierre, 219
Cussac, 96
Czechoslovakia, 244

Dachau, 18, 20, 21, 35
Daladier, Édouard, 72, 230
Darnand, Joseph, 58, 59, 227
Darthout, Justin, 137, 238
Darthout, Marcel, 102, 105, 108, 111, 113, 116, 117, 119, 121, 133, 134, 139, 143, 236, 237, 238
Das Reich division, 6, 13, 16, 20, 23, 24, 28, 29, 31, 32, 33, 34, 35, 36, 40, 43, 46, 47, 57, 147, 149, 189, 192, 202, 221, 224, 244
Dauriat, Martial, 237
Davoine, Camille, 58, 59, 60, 61, 63, 227
Death's-Head division. *See* Totenkopf division
Demarcation Line, 22, 43, 86
Denis (storehouse owner), 122, 134
Der Führer (DF) division, 12, 14, 17, 20, 21, 22, 35, 36, 38, 39, 47, 50, 55, 56, 60, 132, 138, 148, 154, 180, 182, 213, 218, 230, 240
Desourteaux (Doctor), 4, 161
Desourteaux, André, 241
Desourteaux, Hubert, 103, 105, 108, 122, 124, 134, 140, 236, 238
Desourteaux, Paul, 75, 77, 84, 85, 114, 115, 116, 123, 201, 215, 218, 230, 232
Desourteaux family, 74, 75
Deutsch (Rabbi), 83, 172, 233
Deutschland regiment, 22, 45, 47, 56
Devillac, 39
Dictionnaire encyclopédique Quillet, 6
Diekmann (SS Major), 61, 64, 104, 118, 130, 132, 138, 147
Dieulidou, 111, 131
Dijon, 131
Dnieper (river), 28
Donnadieu de Vabres, 246
Dorat, Le, 53
Dordogne, 34, 43, 44, 48, 50, 211, 225
Dortmund, 248
Dournazac, 53
Drancy, 38, 59, 90, 207, 224, 250
Dresden, 148
Dubost, 244
Dugot (town clerk of Saint-Victurnien), 83
Dumas, Georges, 44, 97, 98
Dupic (cloth merchant), 137, 146
Dutreix, Armand, 97, 98, 125

E., Jean-Pierre (Alsatian SS soldier), 120, 123, 126, 129–30, 236, 237
Echo-La Marseillaise, L', 247
Ehrard (priest), 172
Eichmann, Adolf, 227
Ellul, 246
Eluard, Paul, 188, 247
Engiel, Raymond, 111
England, English, 69, 95, 149, 240
Erstein, 240
Espinasse (Father), 49
Europe, 21, 40, 45, 117, 125, 127, 144, 201, 203, 211, 243

Express, L', 250
Eymoutiers, 43, 57, 74, 200, 224

Fallingbostel, 30, 31
Farmer, Sarah, 10, 13, 205, 232
Faugeras, Aimé, 85, 195, 231, 246
Faure, Paul, 76
Faurisson, 244
Fauvette, La, 79, 141, 142
Fenosa, Apel. les, 186, 207
Feuchtwanger, Lion, 71, 168
Figeac, 38, 41, 46, 53, 54, 200
Filliol, Jean, 59, 227
First World War. *See* World War I
Flèche, La, 64
Fontenilles, 39
Forbach, 58
Forces françaises de l'intérieur (FFI), 97, 170, 202, 213, 224
Forces françaises libres (FFL), 65
Fougères, 64
Fougeron, André, 14
Foussat (miller), 124
frairie, 75, 76, 77
Franche-Comté, 82, 232
Franco, Francisco, 76, 78, 79
Franco-Prussian War, 24, 71, 222, 227, 228
Francs-tireurs et partisans (FTP), 10, 49, 96, 97, 100, 162, 170, 171, 172, 213, 224
Frayssinet-le-Gelat, 39, 244
"Fredo," Commander, 172
Free French, 220
Freemasons, 75, 82
French State, 164, 226
Freund-Valade, Marc, 157, 158, 240, 241
Fronde, 67, 229
Front commun, 74, 229
Front national (FN), 170, 172, 186, 208 (party of Le Pen), 213
Front populaire, 74, 229

G., Paul (SS soldier), 104, 125, 126, 131, 136, 227, 236, 237, 238
Gabaudet, 48
Gagnant, Jean, 97, 98
Gardon (French Lieutenant-Colonel, later General), 193, 247
Gargan, Mont, 176
Garonne (river, valley), 34, 35, 38
Garraud, Jacques, 109, 236
Gartempe (river), 67
Gatti, Armand, 192
Gaudy, Yvonne, 103, 107, 236
Gaulle, Charles de, 42, 53, 160, 169, 184, 194, 195, 208, 231
Gaullists, 9
Genari (SS Sergeant), 122, 132
Gentioux, 230
Gerlach (SS officer), 58, 60, 180, 226, 244
Germania regiment, 22
Germany, German, 3, 6, 10, 12, 13, 14, 16, 17, 18, 21, 22, 25, 26, 28, 29, 30, 35, 36, 37, 38, 39, 40, 42, 43, 44, 45, 47, 48, 49, 51, 53, 54, 56, 58, 61, 62, 70, 71, 76, 78, 80, 82, 90, 91, 92, 95, 97, 99, 100, 103, 105, 107, 108, 109, 110, 111, 113, 114, 116, 117, 118, 119, 120, 121, 123, 124, 125, 127, 128, 129, 130, 133, 134, 135, 136, 137, 139, 140, 143, 146, 147, 148, 149, 150, 151, 153, 154, 158, 159, 167, 168, 170, 171, 176, 180, 181, 182, 184, 187, 188, 189, 191, 193, 195, 202, 203, 210, 211, 212, 213, 214, 218, 219, 220, 223, 225, 227, 230, 231, 232, 234, 240, 246, 248
Gestapo, 33, 37, 39, 44, 60, 111, 116, 201, 215
Giroux, Pierre, 111
Glane (river), 67, 68, 69, 102, 103, 104, 108, 109, 110, 156, 207
Gleiniger (Wehrmacht General), 14, 181, 182, 243
Gnug (SS Adjutant), 66, 130, 131, 132
Godfrin, Roger, 110, 236
Gœbbels, Joseph, 180
Goldmann, Maria. *See* Kanzler family
Gorki, 28
Gourdon, 48, 54
Gramat, 38
Grand Dictionnaire encyclopédique Larousse, 6
Grand Robert des noms propres, 6
Graz, 21
Great Britain, 34, 66, 191
Great War. *See* World War I
Greece, 40, 227

Grenoble, 172
Grolejac, 48
Gromaire, Marcel, 14
Groupements de travailleurs étrangers (Foreign Workers' Groups), 61, 62, 79, 84, 86, 87, 88, 89, 90, 164, 213, 228, 232, 233
Guéret, 47, 50, 56, 57
Guernica, 203
Guille (Commandant), 224, 226
Guingouin, Georges, 42, 44, 48, 56, 57, 92, 97, 98, 224, 226, 231, 234, 243
Gurs, 226
Guyenne, 69

Halbwachs, Maurice, 218
Hamburg, 64, 148
Hauser (SS General), 22, 182
Haute-Garonne, 45
Haute-Vienne, 6, 12, 42, 43, 44, 47, 55, 58, 62, 68, 69, 70, 72, 73, 74, 76, 77, 78, 80, 88, 90, 91, 98, 157, 171, 176, 185, 208, 210, 223, 224, 225, 226, 230, 232, 233, 234
Haut-Rhin, 194, 248
Hébras, Robert, 102, 104, 113, 119, 133, 198, 236, 237, 238, 248, 249
Henriot, Philippe, 241
Herman Goering division, 119
Herzog, Roman, 203
Heydrich, Reinhard (SS General), 24, 244
Himmler, Heinrich, 19, 22, 31, 148
Hitler, Adolf ("Führer"), 12, 17, 19, 22, 23, 24, 25, 27, 183, 219, 220, 230, 241
Hiwis, 19, 213
Holocaust, 218, 237, 251
Hoover Foundation, 241
Huart (Commandant), 234
Hubsh (SS policeman), 138, 238
Huguenot, 69, 229, 240
Humanité, L', 14, 85, 232
Hungary, 23, 171
Hyvernaud, Jean, 145, 234, 239
Hyvernaud, René, 145, 239

Indochina, 143
Indre, 47, 50, 231
Iron Cross, 149
Israelite. *See* Jew, Jewish
Issoudun, 47
Italy, 119, 171

Jacob, Madeleine, 192
Jakobovicz, Aron, 100
Jakobovicz, David, 100, 166, 171, 172
Jakobovicz, Sarah, 100, 110, 111, 166, 171, 172, 173
Jakobovicz family, 100
Janaillat, 56
Jarnac, 232
Jaspers, Karl, 17
Jedburghs, 54, 214
Jelnja, 28
Jeremiah, 157
Jeune Combat, 172
Jew, Jewish, 14, 16, 21, 23, 24, 25, 26, 27, 28, 29, 37, 38, 39, 40, 43, 59, 62, 78, 80, 82, 83, 86, 87, 88, 89, 90, 111, 114, 118, 156, 164, 172, 173, 182, 200, 201, 202, 210, 211, 216, 219, 224, 226, 227, 228, 232, 233, 242, 243, 244
Joliot-Curie, Frédéric, 13, 219, 220, 246
"Joseph" (Alsatian refugee), 106, 107, 108
Jospin, Lionel, 210, 249

Kabbeck (SS Sergeant), 122
Kahn (SS Captain), 39, 61, 64, 103, 104, 118, 119, 120, 121, 129, 130, 131, 136, 144, 148, 191, 248
Kalisz (Poland), 100, 212
Kämpfe (SS Commander), 56, 57, 180
Kanzler, Dora, 100
Kanzler, Joseph, 100
Kanzler, Simone, 100
Kanzler family, 100
Katyn, 170, 242
Keitel, 244
Keskastel, 35
Kharkov, 30, 31, 32, 40
Kibuye, 209
Kiev, 25, 28
Kish, Egon Erwin, 168
Klagenfurt, 21
Klar (SS Lieutenant), 65
Kleist (SS Lieutenant, Gestapo official), 60, 138
Knochen (SS Colonel), 34, 225

Kohl, Helmut, 243
Kokern (Germany), 100, 212
Kosovo, 209
Krüger (Wehrmacht General), 64
Kursk, 30

L. (Alsatian SS soldier), 112, 126, 236, 237
Laborie, Pierre, 234
Lacapelle-Biron, 39
Lamaud family, 107
Lammerding (SS General), 24, 31, 40, 45, 51, 52, 58, 64, 148, 180, 191, 200, 223, 226
Lang family, 113, 236, 237
Lange (SS Lieutenant), 64, 66, 132, 137, 138
Languedoc, 229
Lartéguy, Jean, 248
Lauber (SS Sergeant), 120, 122, 123, 129, 136
Laudy (barn owner), 11, 117, 122, 133, 134, 139, 143
Laussou, 39
Lauzès, 38
Laval, 64
Laval, Pierre, 59, 90, 95, 143, 215, 225, 227, 241
Lavaud, Madame (widow of M. Blanchon), 234
Lebanon, 209
Lébourliat, 232
Leboutet, 86
Lecomte, 97
Léger, Fernand, 14
Légion française (des combattants et volontaires de la Révolution nationale), 84, 85, 87, 88, 89, 90, 92, 94, 95, 158, 170, 214, 233
Legion of Honor, 187, 188, 195, 225
Lemoine (Préfet), 233
Lenz (SS Adjutant), 122
Le Pen, Jean-Marie, 208
Lesparat, 98
Lestrange, Gisèle de, 211
Lettres françaises, 10, 13, 188, 238, 246
Lévy (Monsieur), 113
Libération, 192
Libération-Sud, 44, 97, 125
Lidice, 182, 244
Lille, 227
Limoges, 7, 8, 11, 12, 14, 16, 17, 34, 42, 43, 44, 46, 47, 49, 50, 51, 52, 53, 54, 55, 56, 57, 58, 59, 60, 63, 64, 67, 69, 71, 73, 74, 76, 77, 79, 80, 81, 82, 83, 84, 85, 86, 90, 97, 98, 99, 100, 108, 111, 112, 125, 130, 131, 132, 133, 135, 137, 138, 143, 147, 148, 150, 151, 152, 154, 156, 157, 158, 171, 172, 179, 180, 181, 189, 190, 191, 195, 200, 201, 202, 218, 219, 220, 224, 226, 227, 228, 229, 231, 233, 234, 235, 240, 241, 243, 245, 247
Limousin, 4, 13, 33, 36, 43, 50, 67, 69, 70, 71, 73, 75, 76, 80, 81, 95, 97, 134, 139, 147, 152, 157, 170, 171, 176, 191, 192, 195, 196, 201, 208, 210, 218, 229, 231, 233, 235, 242
Linz, 23
Lithuania, Lithuanian, 26
Loges, Madame des, 229
Loire, 34
London, 10, 42, 220, 239
Lonzac, 48
Lorraine, 78, 81, 110, 173, 223, 231, 232
Lot, 37, 38, 41, 48, 218
Lot-et-Garonne, 37
Louis XIV (King of France), 229
Louyat cemetery, 171
Lublin, 23
Ludwig, Emil, 168
Lutheran Church, 240
Lyon, 172, 227

Machefer, Martial, 85, 100, 110, 111, 232, 239
Maintien de l'ordre (Maintaining Order), 16, 58, 59, 150, 214
Malabre Quarries, 55
Malaise, La, 100, 111
Malmédy, 147
Malraux, André, 33
Mann, Heinrich, 17, 168
Mann, Klaus, 17
Mann, Thomas, 17, 71, 168
Mans, Le, 64
Marche, La, 69
Marsoulas, 45, 46, 147, 244
Masférat, Le, 141
Masfrand, Pierre, 11, 184

Masset, 136
Massiéra, 151
Massif Central, 33, 34, 42, 43, 46
Maurer (SS Sergeant), 65, 121, 130
Mauthausen, 148
Mayer, René, 195
Mazarin, Cardinal, 229
Mazouin, Roland, 5, 6
Mediterranean Sea, 38
Mein Kampf, 19
Meïr (SS Commander), 34, 245
Mellenthin (Wehrmacht General), 223
Mercier (grocery store owner), 108, 124
Metz, 231
Metzger. *See* Madame Pallier
Meurthe-et-Moselle, 82, 232
Meuse (département), 231
Meyer, 138
Mézières-sur-Issoire, 88
Michelet, Edmond, 97, 231
Milice, 16, 37, 38, 39, 44, 47, 50, 58, 59, 60, 61, 62, 63, 64, 99, 100, 111, 138, 139, 147, 150, 201, 202, 214, 224, 225, 227, 241
Milord (barn owner), 122, 134
Minsk, 25, 28
Mirablon, Albert, 125, 171, 201, 237
Mitterand, François, 176, 208, 210, 242
Monédières, Gérard, 229
Montauban, 34, 37, 39, 46, 47, 90, 233
Montbéliard, 193
Montflanquin, 39
Montluçon, 56
Montpellier, 82
Morcheval, château of, 147, 154
Moreau, Louis, 239, 240
Mortain, 147
Moscow, 29, 30
Moselle, 81, 220, 227, 231
Mouvements unis de la Résistance (MUR), 44, 97, 170, 214
Munich, 76, 230
Munn, E., 14, 236
Münster, 22
Musil, Robert, 16, 17, 168
Mussidan, 44

Nancy, 111, 231, 232
Nantiat, 86, 147
National Assembly, 6, 74, 195, 218, 229
National Association of Martyrs' Families, 8, 9, 10, 170, 173, 174, 175, 176, 188, 195, 196, 197, 198, 208, 209, 213, 228, 229, 233, 246, 248, 250
Nazi, xiv, 6, 12, 16, 17, 18, 19, 21, 23, 24, 27, 34, 35, 37, 40, 46, 50, 58, 62, 65, 70, 71, 76, 80, 81, 97, 100, 117, 144, 149, 151, 168, 173, 183, 187, 192, 193, 194, 200, 201, 202, 203, 207, 208, 210, 211, 214, 219, 220, 221, 222, 239, 242, 244, 245
Nell (SS noncom), 65
Netherlands, the, 22, 39
Neumeyer (Alsatian seminarian), 80
New Jersey, 125
Nexon, 56, 89, 90, 92, 200, 226, 228, 233
Nice, 59
Nieul, 57, 62, 63, 64, 65, 86, 137, 138, 139, 147, 199, 244
Nîmes, 34
Noailles, 48
Nora, Pierre, 208, 250
Nord, 58, 82, 227
Normandy, 42, 46, 51, 52, 97, 147, 202, 211, 223
North Atlantic Treaty Organization (NATO), 188, 189
Noyon, 22
Nuremberg, 182, 193, 223
Nussy Saint-Saëns (Bordeaux presiding judge), 192

Oberg (SS General), 34, 225
Oberman, 67, 228
Occitanie, 69, 229
Oignies, 39
Okrent (SS Commander), 244
OKW (Wehrmacht high command), 18, 19, 24, 30, 42, 44, 222
Oradour, Monsieur d', 229
Oradour-sur-Vayres, 8, 97, 200, 231
Oranienburg, 35
Orliac, 38

Pakowski (SS soldier), 126
Palan-Pradeaux, Marie-Thérèse, 226
Pallier, Jean, 82, 134, 135, 136, 137, 140, 141, 143, 150, 238, 246
Pallier, Madame (née Metzger), 82
Pancevo, 23

Paquet, Pierre, 184, 245
Paris, 39, 59, 82, 100, 172, 192, 211, 224, 225, 245
Parisien libéré, 192, 247
Paris Presse, 194
Pas-de-Calais, 30, 82
Patry (Milice member), 60, 61, 63, 138, 227
Pauchou, Guy, 9, 11, 185
Paulhac, 39
Périgueux, 44, 50, 51, 64, 147, 225
Perrin, François, 97, 98
Pétain, Philippe (Marshal), 71, 72, 75, 78, 83, 84, 89, 90, 95, 170, 183, 233, 240, 241
Petainist, 11
Petit Larousse, 6
Petit Limousin, Le, 230
Peyrilhac, 48, 57
Picasso, Pablo, 14
Picat, 152
Picha (SS Sergeant), 131
Pilsen, 22
Pinède, Robert, 82, 113, 232
Pinède children, 124
Plantu, 214, 250
Plas, Pascal, 232
Plotsk, 223, 243
Poe, Edgar Allan, 249
Poitevin, Pierre, 77, 138
Poitiers, 22, 138
Poitou, 70, 229
Poland, Polish, 21, 23, 76, 100, 171, 242
Populaire, Le, 76, 230
Popular Front. *See* Front populaire
Pottecher, Frédéric, 192
Poutaraud (garage owner), 122, 124, 134
Prague, 35
Protestant, 156, 157, 193, 229, 240, 242
Provence, 34
Puy-Gaillard, 107, 135, 143
Pyrénées, 35
Pyrénées-Atlantiques (formerly Basses-Pyrénées), 82, 232

Queuille, Henri, 246
Quezac, 38

Radical Party, 74, 75, 230
"Rainer." *See* Riffaud, Madeleine
Ramadier, Paul, 187, 246
Rastouil, Louis (Monsignor, Bishop of Limoges), 90, 156, 158, 233, 240, 241
Ravensbrück, 147
Red Cross, 151, 152
Reichenau, von (Marshal), 29
Reichstag, 16
Remarque, Erich Maria, 168
Renaud, Aimé, 98, 235
Renaud, Jeannine, 98, 235
Renn, Ludwig, 168
Rennert (SS Sergeant), 65, 66
Rennes, 30, 113
Renoir, Jean, 231
Renseignements généraux, 94, 151, 158, 195, 215, 226, 241, 248
Resistance, 4, 7, 8, 13, 23, 34, 35, 39, 42, 43, 47, 48, 49, 53, 54, 55, 56, 79, 92, 96, 97, 98, 99, 100, 133, 143, 144, 147, 149, 151, 158, 160, 162, 169, 170, 171, 172, 175, 176, 182, 183, 184, 185, 188, 189, 197, 200, 201, 202, 213, 214, 219, 222, 224, 231, 235, 241, 242, 244, 246
Reynouard, Vincent, 244
Rheims, 4, 218
Rhône, 34, 147
Ribérac, 44
Richard the Lion Hearted (King of England), 68
Riffaud, Madeleine ("Rainer"), 10
Rigout, Marcel, 6
Rimbaud, Arthur, 228
"Rivier." *See* Rousselier
Roby, Yvon, 133
Rocamadour, 5, 218
Roche, Léon, 78, 231
Rochechouart, 8, 9, 55, 87, 92, 95, 143, 144, 145, 151, 152, 184, 185, 199, 219, 234
Rodin, Auguste, 224
Röhm, Ernst, 220
Romania, Romanians, 211
Rommel, Erwin, 34
Roque, Colonel de la, 74, 230
Rosselli brothers, 227
Rouen, 147
Rouergue, 246
Rouffanche, Marguerite, 109, 113, 116, 126, 127, 139, 167, 236, 237, 238

Rouffignac, 48
Rousselier ("Rivier," Resistance Colonel), 8, 189, 234
Royan, 232
Russia, Russian (Soviet Union, USSR), 19, 23, 24, 25, 26, 27, 29, 40, 95, 125, 148, 188, 201, 202, 222, 226, 242, 245
Rwanda, 209

Sabra, 209
Sadon (Regional Préfet of Toulouse), 45
Saillat, 61, 62, 79, 87, 88, 138, 147, 199, 200, 228
Saint-Amand-Montrond, 47
Saint-Bonnet-de-Bellac, 147
Saint-Bressou, 38
Saint-Céré, 38, 48
Saint-Denis-des-Murs, 147
Sainte-Anne-Saint-Priest, 53
Saint-Flour, 43
Saint-Hilaire-Bessonies, 38
Saint-Jouvent, 147
Saint-Junien, 5, 8, 10, 43, 47, 55, 57, 58, 60, 61, 62, 66, 67, 73, 74, 82, 84, 86, 88, 91, 103, 111, 114, 125, 135, 137, 138, 141, 142, 143, 144, 151, 153, 174, 179, 199, 240, 242, 244
Saint-Léonard de Noblat, 90
Saint-Martin Terressus, 86
Saint-Martin-de-Villerval, 39
Saint-Maurice, 38
Saint-Paul d'Eyjaux, 59, 79
Saint-Priest-Taurion, 147
Saint-Sauveur-de-Bellac, 88
Saint-Victurnien, 83, 99, 100, 103, 150
Salan, General, 247
Salon-la-Tour, 147
Santrot (father), 85
Santrot (son), 85
Sauckel, 50
Saverne, 195
Schiltigheim, 80, 81, 106, 157
Schneider, 22
Schutzstaffel (SS), 7, 12, 15, 16, 17, 18, 19, 20, 21, 22, 23, 24, 26, 28, 30, 31, 33, 34, 35, 37, 38, 39, 41, 43, 44, 45, 46, 47, 49, 50, 51, 52, 53, 54, 57, 58, 59, 60, 61, 62, 64, 65, 90, 103, 106, 107, 109, 110, 112, 113, 117, 122, 123, 125, 126, 129, 130, 131, 132, 133, 136, 137, 138, 143, 144, 147, 148, 179, 180, 181, 182, 183, 189, 193, 199, 200, 201, 202, 213, 214, 215, 216, 223, 226, 228, 235, 243, 244, 245
Scotland, Scottish, 214
Secret Army. *See* Armée secrète
Section française de l'internationale ouvrière (SFIO), 86, 215, 230
Seghers, Anna, 71, 168
Segund, Louis, 240
Semprun, Jorge, 217, 218
Sénamaud, Arthur, 145, 146, 239
Senancour, Etienne Pivert de, 67, 228
Senon, Armand, 102, 109, 116, 124, 125, 134, 139, 236, 237, 238
Senon, Marguerite, 238
Sephardic Jews, 82, 83
Sereilhac, 62, 228
Service du travail obligatoire (STO), 91, 95, 96, 99, 100, 108, 113, 155, 215, 234
Service régional de la police judiciaire (SRPJ), 79
Shatilah, 209
Shoah, 210
Sicherheitsdienst (SD), 24, 37, 39, 44, 51, 138, 215
Simon (Milice member), 61, 238
Slutsk, 25
Smolensk, 28, 242
Smolevitch, 25
Social Democrat, 16
Socialist, 10, 17, 72, 73, 74, 75, 76, 77, 78, 79, 84, 85, 86, 91, 97, 99, 184, 187, 188, 196, 210, 214, 227, 229, 231, 249
Somme (river), 22
Souges, 35, 36
Souillac, 48
Souterraine, La, 47
Soviet Union. *See* Russia, Russian.
Spain, Spanish, 22, 62, 76, 78, 85, 86, 164, 171, 173, 182, 232
Speck, 50
Srebrenica, 209
Stadler (SS Colonel), 148, 191
Staeger (SS Sergeant), 112, 122, 228
Stalin, Joseph, 188, 247
Stalingrad, 95

Stein, Doctor, 232
Strasbourg, 35, 80, 81, 100, 157, 190, 194, 196, 231, 232
Stülpnagel, Otto von, 39
Sturmabteilung (SA), 17, 215, 220
Sudetenland, 21, 76, 230
Supreme Headquarters Allied Expeditionary Force (SHAEF), 14, 167, 215, 220
Supreme Headquarters Allied Powers Europe (SHAPE), 215, 235, 239
Sussac, 147
Switzerland, Swiss, 10, 243
Szabo, Violette, 147
Szondi, Peter, 211

Tallemant des Réaux, Gédéon, 69, 229
Tarnaud, 239
Terrasson, 44
Terrou, 38
Thiébaut, 231
Thouron, 86
Tixier, Adrien, 184
Todesfuge, 212
Todt Organization, 94
Töpfer (SS Sergeant), 65, 119, 131, 144
Totenkopf division, 31, 35, 216, 221
Toulouse, 33, 34, 38, 45, 64, 79, 90, 147, 191
Tours, 64
Trautmann, Catherine, 208
Traversat, 97
Trouillé (Préfet), 225
Troyes, 22
Tscheyge (SS Sergeant), 65, 122
Tulle, 30, 33, 42, 46, 47, 48, 49, 50, 51, 52, 64, 149, 151, 182, 200, 202, 219, 223, 225, 244

Ukraine, 23, 31
Union de résistance et d'entraide des Juifs [de France] (UREJ, UREJF, UJRE), 14, 15, 166, 171, 173, 216, 220, 232
Union générale des Israélites de France (UGIF), 59, 82, 83, 173, 216, 232
United States of America, 95, 125, 148, 171, 201, 214
Ussel, 47

Vardelle (Socialist député), 73
Vaugelas (Milice chief), 150, 225
Vel' d'Hiv (Vélodrôme d'hiver), 210, 250
Verdun, 207, 231, 243, 250
Vergt-de-Biron, 39
Vernet, 226
Vesoul, 22
Veyrac, 232
Vichy, 4, 11, 13, 16, 44, 49, 58, 59, 61, 62, 71, 72, 75, 78, 82, 83, 85, 87, 92, 94, 96, 115, 118, 143, 150, 151, 153, 158, 159, 164, 169, 170, 173, 183, 184, 185, 205, 208, 210, 213, 214, 221, 225, 226, 227, 228, 229, 230, 232, 233, 239, 240, 243, 244, 245
Vienna, 21, 212
Vienne (river), 55, 67
Villefranche, 46
Vincennes, 13
Vinnitsa, 31
Vosges, 194

Waffen SS, 7, 12, 15, 16, 17, 18, 19, 20, 21, 22, 26, 28, 29, 30, 31, 33, 35, 36, 38, 39, 41, 45, 46, 47, 48, 49, 50, 51, 52, 53, 55, 56, 57, 58, 60, 61, 62, 63, 64, 65, 66, 81, 88, 101, 103, 112, 114, 118, 123, 124, 126, 127, 129, 132, 135, 136, 138, 139, 144, 146, 147, 148, 154, 160, 179, 180, 181, 182, 183, 189, 190, 191, 199, 200, 201, 202, 207, 211, 214, 221, 224, 226, 228, 239
Wagner (Gauleiter of Strasbourg), 35
Wehrmacht, 14, 18, 24, 26, 42, 45, 55, 56, 126, 181, 202, 216, 221, 223, 244
Weidinger, Otto (SS Colonel), 17, 18, 20, 21, 23, 132, 148, 149, 180, 191, 221, 226, 238, 239
Weimar, 188
Werfel, Franz, 168
Werner (SS Captain), 57, 132, 238
Wiesbaden, 241, 244
Wiking division, 22, 216, 221
World War I, 23, 24, 71, 72, 73, 109, 221, 227, 229, 250
Würzburg, 17, 22, 149

Yugoslav, Yugoslavia, 23, 40

Zerman, Julien, 172

The Author

Jean-Jacques Fouché was born in the Charente département in 1940 and so is at least in part a native of the Charente-Limousin. After teaching philosophy until 1967, he abandoned his teaching career for work with a theatrical company and, then in 1968, won an internship at the Théâtre national de Strasbourg. From 1969 to 1972 he was on a Ministry of Cultural Affairs mission to Forbach, in the Moselle département, to set up a cultural center. From 1974 to 1983 he directed several cultural institutions, including the Maison de la culture in Châlon-sur-Saône. Until 1990 he was an inspector-general with the Ministry of Culture. He then entered the field of museum science, with the renovation program of the Museum of Air and Space under the Ministry of Defense. Applying in 1994 in answer to a job advertisement by the General Council of Haute-Vienne, he was made "head of project" of the Oradour Centre de la Mémoire d'Oradour, in charge of historical research and the curator of the permanent exhibition. As of 1999, he had set up five temporary exhibitions there, with their catalogues.

Since he finished *Oradour,* Jean-Jacques Fouché has gone on with his writings in the field of museum science, most particularly a comparative study of the museum collections at "realms of memory" in Germany and France. Recently he completed a book on Oradour and justice, concerning investigations, trials, and their aftermath in Alsace and the Limousin. Over the past three years he has also worked in radio and television production, in addition to his participation at colloquia and conferences.